MEDIA EDUCATION
GOES TO SCHOOL

CRITICAL ISSUES FOR LEARNING AND TEACHING

Shirley R. Steinberg and Pepi Leistyna
General Editors

Vol. 1

PETER LANG
New York • Washington, D.C./Baltimore • Bern
Frankfurt am Main • Berlin • Brussels • Vienna • Oxford

Allison Butler

MEDIA EDUCATION GOES TO SCHOOL

Young People Make Meaning of Media & Urban Education

PETER LANG
New York • Washington, D.C./Baltimore • Bern
Frankfurt am Main • Berlin • Brussels • Vienna • Oxford

Library of Congress Cataloging-in-Publication Data

Butler, Allison.
Media education goes to school: young people make meaning
of media and urban education / Allison Butler.
p. cm.
Includes bibliographical references and index.
1. Mass media—Study and teaching (Secondary)—United States.
2. Media literacy—Study and teaching (Secondary)—United States.
3. Education, Urban—United States. I. Title.
P91.5.U5.B88   302.23071'2—dc22   2009035450
ISBN 978-1-4331-0761-0 (hardcover)
ISBN 978-1-4331-0760-3 (paperback)
ISSN 2151-2949

Bibliographic information published by **Die Deutsche Nationalbibliothek**.
Die Deutsche Nationalbibliothek lists this publication in the "Deutsche
Nationalbibliografie"; detailed bibliographic data is available
on the Internet at http://dnb.d-nb.de/.

Cover design by Celena Orgel

© 2010 Peter Lang Publishing, Inc., New York
29 Broadway, 18th floor, New York, NY 10006
www.peterlang.com

All rights reserved.
Reprint or reproduction, even partially, in all forms such as microfilm,
xerography, microfiche, microcard, and offset strictly prohibited.

For two infinitely influential individuals:
Jasmin, just because
Mom, just because she taught me everything

Table of Contents

Acknowledgments xi

Introduction
Media education goes to school: Gathering together the threads 1
Intersecting frames of knowledge production 4
Knowledge production made tangible 10
Layout of the book 16
Why this book matters 19
Notes 21

1 From protective to critical:
The trajectory of media education in the United States 23
Epistemological positions on media studies: Protection to celebration 24
Defining media education 30
In/formal media education: Corporate versus classroom 38
Absence of media education in American classrooms 42
Beyond fascination with technology 45
Conclusion 47
Notes 49

2 To whom does school belong?
Urban public education in neoliberalism 51
Development and decline of the urban school system 54
NYC points of transition 56
Urban concerns: How to education poor students of color? 64
School reform 66
Conclusion 76
Notes 78

3 Knowing participants:
Ethical questions of feminist, qualitative research 79
Framing the research: Methods and organization 83
Conceptual methodological frames: Cultural studies and feminism 85
Trust, truth and knowing participants 89
Authority versus friendship: Shallow cover 96
Conclusion 98
Notes 100

4 "I mean, in what high school *don't* they use media?"
Questioning media integration at LSHS 101
Media studies at LSHS 102
Defining media education 109
Video production 115
Integration across the curriculum 116
Conclusion 121
Notes 123

5 "It all depends on the person":
The value of small, theme-based,
education for underserved, inner-city youth 125
Definition and value of small schools 126
Definition and value of theme-based schools 130
Integration of theme 133
Understandings of labels: Underserved and inner city 135
Concerns within school: Interpersonal and architectural relationships 142
Conclusion 148
Notes 150

6 "That's what they want and a lot of kids follow it":
Representations and understandings of adolescence and education 151
Being a teenager: Media representations and personal experiences 153
Personal experiences: Education 168
Reflections from the first graduating class 170
Conclusion 173
Notes 175

7 Integrating media education:
What is missing, what is needed 177
Radical change needed 178
Necessary paradigm shifts 180
Notes on paradigm shifts in classrooms 184
Expanding meanings of "literacy" 191
Teacher training 197
Skills assessment and research 198
Conclusion 200

8 Conclusion:
Looking outside to understand the inside 203
The need to integrate media education 204
What change is needed 206
What students deserve 207
Community awareness: The "ghetto Rodeo Drive" 208
Conclusion..214

Works Cited 217

Index..227

Acknowledgments

The act of writing (and editing) is a task often undertaken by a single physical body. However, all the bodies, brains and especially hearts named here contributed selflessly and invaluably to the work–it could not have been written without them.

First and foremost: Thanks to my participants, the foundation of this text. Without them, there would be no book, no words, no frame for my thoughts and curiosities. In addition, they provided both life and research inspiration beyond the boundaries of these pages. I think of them daily and am honored and humbled by their trust. They are the truest of teachers and the brightest of stars. The faculty, staff and associates of LSHS, especially TC, PW and BP, supported the process and encouraged my inquiries. LB recognized the struggles like no other and is a vital ally. MS was simultaneously an insufferable boor and wildly humorous, an altogether strange and wonderful combination. During the process, EA and BP provided multiple levels of support, including reading drafts, sharing conversations and being strong in so many ways during very dark moments. BP is a shining example of unending patience, good humor and profound insight.

For the initial inspiration and opportunity to begin writing, I am indebted to Kathleen Tyner whose strength of scholarship and personality, not to mention boundless energy and attention to detail, are monumentally appreciated. For continued conversation, support and the additional four-legged distractions who make it all worthwhile, I thank Robert Wosnitzer. Thanks to Emilie Zaslow for supportive conversations and wise observations. Radha Hegde went out of her way to provide clear advice and practical guidance from the outset; I am wholly grateful. Robert Jensen's keen eye for organization and language is immensely appreciated. Sharon Mazzarella selflessly answered questions and pointed me in a most beneficial direction. There are not enough accolades to adequately express the support, tireless labor and encouragement provided by Wendy Chen. She was an early and continuous champion of the subject who paid critical attention, possesses an amazing spirit and an eye for detail. Wendy's assistance was a gift throughout for which I am forever grateful.

At my academic home, Western Connecticut State University, I am blessed to be a part of a collegial, friendly and irreverently funny department. I extend great gratitude to Hugh McCarney, a welcoming, encouraging, informative and an all-around good person. Thanks to the students in my spring 2009 Media Literacy course who were unwitting and willing test subjects for many ideas and thoughts that now appear on these pages. Special thanks to my colleague and friend DL Stephenson for brilliance and support in regular discussions and debates and to Truman Keys for keeping me alert. I also thank my part-time academic home, NYU, specifically the Media, Culture and Communication Department and most importantly, Ted Magder, who provided support and opportunities for teaching and advancing many of these ideas. From Peter Lang, I thank Sophie Appel, Bernadette Shade and Chris Myers, all of whom consistently alleviated my anxiety and were regularly encouraging and supportive; it has been a pleasure to work with them.

Numerous nontraditional teachers entered and altered my life at pivotal moments and always taught me what I needed to know. Richard consistently opens his house (which made the writing possible *and* pleasurable) and Peter keeps a regular eye on us and for that I am quite grateful. J, Shannah, Anne Margaret and especially Laura kept me aligned. Julio reminded me of what I missed so much that, when present, makes life so much clearer. Stephen and Elizabeth provide constant peace of mind.

I live every day in wonder at my family of origin and family of choice and cannot possibly express that wonderment enough. I am blessed with a family whose strength of character, fortitude and grace are inspirational. Cousin Anne, my lifelong champion, put up with me for the last few days of writing *and* bought lobsters! My sisters Stephanie and Jennifer are beautiful and dedicated women. The Ohio crew, especially Jacob, Sarah and Eva, are stellar individuals and, collectively, an impenetrable force of joy. Thanks to Christopher and Jennifer for their support and encouragement and Charlotte, because she sang to me and made me laugh. Andrew, Peggy and Jasmin: you deserve exponential thanks. You provided shelter, sustenance, support and so much more during the writing of this text. You never indicated I outwore my welcome, so you are still and forever stuck with me. Extra-extra special thanks to my shadow, Jasmin: stay curious and inquisitive (and, if I may be so selfish: nearby). There is no adequate way to acknowledge my parents, Elie and Jack. Where does one begin when one has parents who taught five children to think, to appreciate, to critique, to stay focused, to be responsible, to be civilized, to be practical, to do the right thing, and to follow through on our tasks? You are wonderful parents and rock-solid human beings. Thanks to Isia, Ted, Aviva and Zale for extending the concept and comforts of family. Thanks to Jake for the laughs, over and over and over again. Brian is my savior and friend, consistent in his inconsistency, and always available for (or predicting the need for) rescue. Thanks to my fierce and fantastic, ambitious and brilliant spiritual sisters and best friends, Chris, Sherry, Lisa, Celena and Aviva. Friendship is personified through these powerful women. Special thanks to Celena, who blesses me with both friendship and art. Extra special canine thanks to the most important, most consistent, non-traditional non-person, Sancho: my four-legged boon companion, my constant reminder, my home wherever we roam.

Introduction

Media Education Goes to School: Gathering Together the Threads

In July 2008 I received the following text message: "I went to freshmen orientation & loved every second of it. It's such a solid fit for me, I feel like I totally made the right decision. I'm so excited for fall!" Popcorn[1], a young man of mixed African heritage sent me this message as he prepared for college and while it is difficult to ascertain emotion from a text message, I felt that this was a genuine expression of positive feelings with an underlying subtext of bravery. For the first time in his life, Popcorn would leave home, depart the protective confines of familiar New York City and intimate friends. For the first time since the 9th grade, he would enter classrooms in an unfamiliar environment, would know none of his teachers or his fellow classmates. As a young black man who grew up with great economic difficulty in an urban environment, it is statistically unlikely that Popcorn will succeed in college. If he does, he is statistically likely to succeed in legitimate employment beyond his peers who dropped out of high school or graduated with no plans to attend college (Allen 1996; Eckholm 1996; Steele 1999; Western 2006). On this July weekend, neither Popcorn nor I were thinking about statistics, but rather about the joy he was feeling about his upcoming university adventure.

Popcorn is a member of the first graduating class of Lincoln Square High School (LSHS), a public school in New York City, part of new school reform and designed, in part, to ensure that students such as Popcorn – known more for his statistical and demographic position than for his bright and complex identity – do not grow invisible within the largest public school system in the nation. A strategy of new school reform is to reach out to young people prior to them becoming lost in the system and provide a rigorous pedagogical environment that works to move them beyond their negative environments and help foster their commitment to school. The current wave of new school reform, jumpstarted in 2002 with Mayor Bloomberg's takeover of the public school system, dismantled many of the large, failing comprehensive high schools and increased the quantity of small, theme-based non-academically selective schools that drew underprivileged youth from throughout New York City to intimate settings with approximately 100 students per grade and administration-controlled discretionary budget.

A major tenet of the movement to increase the development of small schools is the inclusion of a specific theme to provide a consistent, continuous thread of organization to students' experience of their education. The opportunity to include a theme alternative to the standard core curriculum opens doors to innovative learning experiences. LSHS's theme is media and it was the initial intent of the school to use analysis and production of the media to foster community awareness and activism.

Including media studies in secondary school in more than one-off or tangential projects provides space for radical and socially important curricular developments. Generally speaking, it is not until university that American students have the opportunity to begin any formal, critical study of the media, yet they are audience and consumers of media for the majority of their lives. As pecuniary and ideological consumers, young people in underserved environments consume the messages of the media, which, most often, construct them as negative, criminal or otherwise subservient bodies in the larger landscape. An individual like Popcorn–dark skinned, from Harlem, living with a single mother and extended family members–is most easily categorized/labeled as a drug dealer, rap star, athletic hopeful, or some such position that emphasizes the physicality of his body and the labor done to extricate himself from his negative social environment. At age 18, that Popcorn has not decided what he wants to do with his life–but knows he wants to complete college, take as many exciting courses as possible and pursue his art/photography/writing/filmmaking dreams in some capacity–is perfectly 'normal,' but does not fit the media or social image of who or what Popcorn is to become.

The inclusion of alternative curricula, such as media studies, in the secondary school system can act as an intervention, bridging the gaps between the messages and stories young people receive as audiences, their critical understanding of the media and the ways in which young people make meaning of their educations as a training ground for their entry into adult society. Media education[2] cannot solve the myriad problems of a struggling urban environment, but implementation of the concepts of media education into secondary schools can provide young people with the skills of critical inquiry and critical analysis and thereby develop multi-dimensional education experiences where young people are interpellated into an active learning environment, including increased awareness about their roles as audiences, scholars and participants in the culture industries. Media education can be a catalyst for change within the urban school system. The inclusion of media studies in secondary schools can be a radical, innovative break from traditional pedagogy, especially standardized testing, that further subjugates young people in underserved environments. This book locates its foundation within critical media and urban education studies and is opposed to the increased reliance on neoliberal orthodoxies that promote the individual, private enterprise and the free market above the betterment of the community, as a way to explore actual work done to include media education principles in a New York City public school. The *actuality* of media studies inclusion is fraught with struggle and difficulty, which this book will cover in detail.

In the official, public language of the Department of Education, small, theme-based schools read as nearly flawless. In actuality, it is a deeply problematic initiative based largely on political rhetoric that ultimately does not thoroughly serve the needs of underserved youth. While a few select schools may succeed in the face of systemic adversity, most do not. This book looks at one particular school that had the opportunity to include a rigorous media education across its curriculum, but failed at that inclusion. The media theme was diluted at best and served to replicate the students' already negative social and political positions. To explore this, I draw from my two years working at LSHS and, more importantly, from the understanding and meaning making of Popcorn and his peers. I intend this book as a place where media scholars pause, reflect and examine what is learned when media education principles are envisioned for–but not rigorously incorporated into–urban education.

Young people are positioned in a conflicted space in both media and education. They are sophisticated audiences, readers and–in an age of increasing user-generated content–producers and distributors of media, yet are not formally invited to think critically about their media experiences. Furthermore, it is students who experience most directly the changes made in schools, but who are often the least informed or taught about the changes in their education. To work within this space of multiple conflicts, I privilege the stories told by students about how they understand and make meaning of media and media education in a small-school setting.

The primary data in this text are drawn from interviews with students from LSHS who are participants in the project of theme-based education within new school reform. Overall, their stories reveal that the study of the media is not included in their school, they do not possess the tools to either speak critically about the elements that constitute media education or speak authoritatively about the organization and intent of their school as part of new school reform. Ideas of activism and radical pedagogy are mobilized in the present as cultural and social moments that fail students and serve to replicate their already disenfranchised positions. Professionally and personally, I am an advocate of media studies inclusion in secondary education. Using the culture industries as a foundation, media education rejects no pedagogical avenue as invalid for inquiry and neither punishes nor celebrates young people's choices but rather works to critically inquire the influences and implications of those choices within a tightly structured ideological and capitalist culture. Media education is neither value free nor politically void of influence and the integration of it into a highly bureaucratic system is grounds for conflict. However, if not cautiously integrated, media education will fail both the school and the students and ultimately work to reinforce oppressive pedagogical aims.

This book explores how media education is uncomfortably enfolded into one start-up school and how adolescent identity development, in connection to school and learning, is revealed through participants' awareness of school reform. Media studies and media education theories are mapped alongside theories on urban school reform, specifically the changes made in the New York City public school system, to examine the diluted success of theme-based education in one specific public school. This book represents a unique contribution to the field of media learning because it originates in the classroom and tackles knowledge and impact of school reform from those most closely involved: the students themselves.

Intersecting Frames of Knowledge Production

Media Education

Media education asks students to critically analyze and produce media texts as a way to learn about both the broad landscape of the culture industries. Critical media education draws from young people's knowledge of and role as regular audiences and readers of media and without punishing or diminishing their pleasures, works to develop more thicker and greater nuanced awareness and understanding. In the United States, 'media education' means many, often disparate, things. The National Leadership Conference on Media Literacy provided the foundational American definition of a media literate individual as one who "can decode, evaluate, analyze and produce both print and electronic media" (Aufderheide 1993, p. 1). The fundamental objective of media literacy is to foster "critical autonomy in relationships to all media" (p. 1). There is no singular thread of media education development in the United States. Today, most scholars agree on two things: all students deserve some form of media education in their primary and secondary schooling and any media education curriculum should include elements of analysis and production. These agreements manifest in multiple ways and often through disaggregate epistemologies. As we grow into the 21st century and digital and new media increase rapidly, especially the popularity of social networking sites and increased user generated content, media education scholars work to expand and refine the definitions and implementation of media education. Increasingly, young people are directed to explore their own production (including original work and alterations of existing work) and distribution of media. This is pointedly discussed in Jenkins (with Puroshotma, Clinton, Wiegel & Robison 2006) white paper on media education, the most recent comprehensive research on American media education. Closer examination of young people's production and distribution role deserves greater attention within media education.

Media literacy education occupies contested space in American pedagogy. Although the United States exports a great deal of electronic media across the globe, it does not make formal space to educate its own populace (Tyner 1998). Indeed, a major reason why other countries, with less indigenous media, educates its youth is precisely *because of* the massive American influx of media (Buckingham 2003). The major tenets of media education in the United States, traced more thoroughly in Chapter One, alternate between protecting young people from the dangers of the media and celebrating their use and manipulation of the media. Within this spectrum, media education works "to develop students' literacy and critical thinking skills so they will become lifelong autonomous learners" (Goodman 2003, p. 48). Media education makes students into more formally informed media producers which bolsters "the 'passive' knowledge that is developed through critical analysis" with the "'active' knowledge that derives from production" (Buckingham, Grahame & Sefton-Green 1995, p. 12). The literature of media education is well-organized and neatly presented; its intentions and suggestions are clear and easy to understand. However, the reality is much less organized: My goal is to look at media education in the reality of the school day and all its messy, unclear parameters.

Cultural Studies and Critical Pedagogy

A fusion of cultural studies and critical pedagogy, with their shared inquiry into the everyday experiences of subjugated bodies and respect for multiple understandings of texts and possible fields of study, inform the organization of this text. Postwar Britain witnessed the fusion of youth and media cultures, forming a scaffold for cultural studies. The media, according to Hall and Whannell (1965) "provide youth with the information and ideas about the society into which they are maturing" (p. 20). Early cultural studies scholars did not see the media as imparting their will on youth cultures, but rather inquired into *how* young people choose *what* media and what they *do with* their media of choice. Rather than resigning themselves to the belief that young people engage 'too much' with electronic media–a quantity and quality of time that is never unequivocally defined–cultural studies scholars instead explore young people's choices and the pleasure they garner from their choices (Buckingham 1993a). Cultural studies examines identity development and social awareness within cultures deeply and regularly influenced by, and influent upon, the media industries. Foundational work in cultural studies that examined youth cultures focused on how young people self-identified and grew into their identities within the broad, intersecting social, political and media cultures in which they lived (Corrigan & Frith 1976; Hall & Jefferson 1976; McRobbie 1976; Hebdige 1979; Willis 1977). Young people actively participate in their own project of identity development, and do so as part of the larger environment in which they live and grow. Therefore, cultural studies focused on young people's process of 'becoming,' seeing it as a continuously developing, multidimensional project. Hall (1996) argues that identities are not "'who we are' or 'where we came from,' so much as what we might become, how we have been represented and how that bears on how we might represent ourselves" (p. 4). Selves cultivate within the project of identity development, which is a political endeavor that shifts with changes in environment, technology, education, and many other social categories.

A particular concern within this project is the intersection of ethnicity, gender and social class as sensitive bits of identity development, especially when situated within the experience of school, which young people are told is the way to improve their social and cultural capital, yet is often the place where they are regularly reminded of what they lack. Much research on young people of color defines them as deficient, not meeting the qualities of privilege associated with white, middle class status and media representations reinforce this belief (Leistyna 1999; Lipsitz 1998). Urban youth of color negotiate both their own identity and intellectual development concurrent with the knowledge that they are subjugated by the larger society that externally labels them as deficient based on their skin color or geographic location. Urban youth of color are compared against an unachievable middle class white standard. The cultural norms of urban families, in contrast to, and punished by, the middle class white standard, include single-parent households, extended family relations, early entry into the labor force, non-dominant literacy expertise and less time in lower quality schools. Young people growing up in this environment who contend with these conflicting messages must learn to negotiate an identity path not supported by the larger, dominant society.

    A major institution of dominant society within which young people regularly engage is school. The institution of school divides youth of privilege from underprivileged youth early in age and perpetuates those divisions throughout the tenure of schooling. Critical pedagogy works to make explicit those boundaries and to explore alternate ways to construct education. Critical pedagogy works to undo adherence to a traditional, test-based pedagogy that favors students whose social and cultural capital readies them for a test-taking environment. The foundational voice of critical pedagogy, Freire (1970/2000) argues the oppressed are divided bodies, discouraged to work for their freedom, or with each other in community and encouraged to accept their oppression, which, over generations, settle into an uncomfortable, but expected and accepted status quo. In large part, the oppressors and oppressed internalize expected behaviors, therefore, as Freire writes, "as long as the oppressed remain unaware of the causes of their condition, they fatalistically 'accept' their exploitation" (p. 64). Individual oppressors might not be aware of their role in the process of dismantling the self-authority of the oppressed, reducing them to things, labels and stereotypes. Freire warns, "the oppressed have been destroyed precisely because their situation has reduced them to things. In order to regain their humanity they must cease to be things and fight as men and women" (p. 68). The system of oppression needs to be undone in order to enable individuals to make change; critical pedagogues work within the educational environment to foster such change.

    Critical pedagogy works diligently to undo bodies and release minds from the tangle of things. Inspired largely by Freire (1970/2000) and intersecting avenues of cultural studies and critical theory, critical pedagogy works to complicate the educational terrain as a site for social change. Duncan-Andrade and Morrell (2007) write that critical pedagogy is an approach to education "rooted in the experiences of marginalized peoples; that is centered in a critique of structural, economic and racial oppression; that is focused on dialogue instead of a one-way transmission of knowledge; and that is structured to empower individuals and collectives as agents of social change" (p. 183). In his exploration of the ritual culture of schooling, McLaren (1999) discusses culture as informed and organized by "rituals and ritual systems" which are imprinted in schools; school culture is "informed by class-specific, ideological and structural determinant of the wider society" (p. 5). Critical pedagogy exposes and works with the inequalities within schools, schooling, the students within and critiques the deficient educations received by poor urban students of color.

Critical pedagogy itself runs the risk of becoming formulaic, of resting too securely on the divisions it made explicit. Kincheloe (2007) writes the debate between "a democratic, inclusive, socially sensitive objective concerned with multiple sources of knowledge and socioeconomic mobility for diverse students from marginalized backgrounds" and the "standardized, exclusive, socially regulatory agenda that serves the interest of the dominant power and those students most closely aligned with the social and cultural markers associated with such power" must serve as a caution against complacency (p. 12). Both too easy and too tempting is continued pointing at the same problems rather than working through them or working to see emergent problems. To advance critical pedagogy beyond rehashing a debate is to point to the latest site for oppression, the adherence to neoliberal philosophies that create a greater gulf between the points of debate.

Neoliberalism

An ideology commonly understood among the larger American population is the belief in freedom. Freedom is generally understood to be a good thing, especially if its opposite is understood to be captivity. No American would willingly agree to captivity and modern-day post-industrial power structures do not explicitly, willfully engage in practices of captivity. Yet, rarely is 'freedom' clearly defined and when it is, the actuality and pervasiveness of ideological 'captivity' becomes that much clearer. Freedom is the strongest illusion of neoliberalism, paving the way to a seamless consent to hegemony.

Within neoliberalism, freedom is a specific thing, the pointed possession of increasingly fewer economic barons. Klein's (2007) detailed exploration of 'disaster capitalism,' what she defines as "orchestrated raids on the public sphere in the wake of catastrophic events, combined with the treatment of disasters as exciting market opportunities," serves 'freedom' in its new context (p. 6). Freedom is understood to be for and in the service of a particular slice of the population. More layers need to be undone in order to see both the definition of freedom and a clear distinction from its antonym, captivity. Disaster capitalism serves the interests of neoliberalism, encouraging those in positions of power to maintain their power through increased subjugation of the oppressed.

In the age of neoliberalism, freedom is the purview of private enterprise, connected to the free market and values the role of the individual. David Harvey's (2005) in-depth dissection of neoliberalism discusses the incomplete, uneven spread of 'freedom.' He writes, "the assumptions that individual freedoms are guaranteed by freedom of the market and of trade is a cardinal feature of neoliberal thinking, and it has long dominated the US stance towards the rest of the world" (p. 7). Essentially an economic position that values free market enterprise, the deregulation of institutions and the dismantling of social services, neoliberalism serves the economic elites, reflecting the "interests of private property owners, businesses, multinational corporations, and financial capital" (Harvey p. 7). Neoliberalism sparks a physically subtle, but ideologically strong, captivity, one that publicly embraces average individuals while privately destroying the structural foundations and social services on which they rely. Harvey writes that neoliberalism "makes it all too clear why those of wealth and power so avidly support certain conceptions of rights and freedoms while seeking to persuade us of their universality and goodness" (p. 38). The support by those in wealth and power is clear because a small capitalist class have unadulterated power in institutions necessary for the maintenance and well-being of industrialized and post-industrialized society. Freedom, therefore, is marked by an increase in capital and control by the few, and captivity can be understood as an invisible bind felt by an increasing number of people who are bifurcated from each other in the absence of community and their own decrease in capital and control.

What Harvey (2005) and Klein (2007) do not explicitly discuss in their dissection of neoliberalism is the impact on youth cultures or education. Grossberg (2001) writes about "trends and practices" that hurt young people, such as cuts in social services, decreased federal dollars for education, increased fears of failures of education, increased belief that incarceration of youth is a proper course of action and decreased respect for the civil liberties of young people, all directly related to the spread of neoliberalism (p. 117). Because these cuts focus specifically on young people, they are forced into compliance by their absence of control or contribution. Neoliberalism treats all bodies as docile, demur to the control of the economic power barons, and therefore chips away at active, productive ideas of citizenship. Grossberg (2001) argues the actions of neoliberalism speak and act the language of hatred of, and discontent toward, youth in its devaluation of labor, community, education and absence of social support for youth development.

Neoliberalism washes over the nation in the form of decreased social services and increased interests in private enterprise; caught in the space where increase meets decrease resides public schooling. Private enterprise, in the guise of increased monies spent on testing and surveillance, meets public enterprise, whose legend involves teaching all young people under the belief that education is the most surefire route out of poverty and toward a better, more fulfilling active citizenship. Giroux (2008) argues neoliberalism has unabashedly changed the face and intent of public schools, turning them into prison-like environments that contain and train children as regimented members of an increasingly militaristic society. He writes, "schools were once viewed as democratic public spheres that would teach students how to resist the militarization of democratic life ... now they serve as recruiting stations for students" (p. 44). Poor students in urban schools are 'recruited' into a regimented life through a regular reminder that they are less worthy than their more economically privileged peers. Neoliberalism operates most powerfully in its invisibility (Giroux 2008; Klein 2007). The task for those opposed to the influx of neoliberalism is to make it visible.

Knowledge Production Made Tangible

Understanding the Environment: Lincoln Square High School

The New York City Public School system has over 1500 schools serving just over 1 million young people (New York City Department of Education, *About us*). New York City is the largest public school system in the United States, serving a diverse collection of young people, the majority of whom are of African and Latino heritage, from lower working class and impoverished economic backgrounds. Despite the lofty rhetoric of radical pedagogy, the structures of the school system carry more weight than individual schools. LSHS is part of new school reform which includes a collection of newly formed, small schools designed to reach out to underprivileged youth and whose curricula is focused around a primary theme. The goal of small, theme-based high schools is to ensure that no student is forgotten or allowed to be invisible and that all students will have a competitive chance at their college and career of choice. The overarching theme of small, theme-based education is to encourage students to work their way out of their socially and economically negative circumstances through education.

This rhetoric, however, does not translate to the reality of these schools, or to LSHS in particular. The demographic makeup, geographic environment of the school, and the actual space in which the school is housed, are constant reminders that, despite changes in language and organization, LSHS students are primed to replicate, not break out of, social and political inequalities. The majority of LSHS students are African- or Latino-American; there are a small number of white and Asian-American students. Many are from immigrant families and are the primary English speakers in their families. Many students will be the first to graduate high school and the first to contemplate, let alone attend, college. The majority of LSHS students live at or below the poverty line and the school is eligible for Title 1 funding, which entitles students to free or reduced lunches and free breakfasts. Most students travel from the South Bronx, Washington Heights, Harlem or Inwood to the Midtown school. Many live in public housing projects and a small, but significant, number have been in and out of the shelter, foster care and Child Services systems. A significant number of students enter the 9th grade at Level 1, meaning they are functionally illiterate, operating below grade level.

With a population just under 400 students, LSHS exceeds national standards in negative areas of public health and well being. Currently, one in 100 American men, primarily African-American and Latino, are in prison (Liptak 2008; Western 2006). In the 2007-2008 school year, at least six male students were permanently or temporarily discharged from school while they were imprisoned. Three young men faced significant sentences for armed robbery and weapons possession. For the first time since 1991, teen pregnancy is on the rise (Altman 2008; Harris 2007). During the 2007-2008 school year, five girls were pregnant or gave birth and several more girls were suspected of handling unwanted or unplanned pregnancies on their own, without school help. The New York City Department of Education expects a 90% daily school attendance rate (New York City Department of Education, *Empowerment Schools*). In the 2007-2008 school year, LSHS had abysmally low attendance, with an average of 74%; in unofficial estimates, 30% of students come to school late. Official attendance is only taken one time a day, so students who show up late are marked present, irrespective of arrival time and there are no accurate estimates on lateness.

LSHS is located in a geographic area typical of New York City: as extreme wealth moves in, it pushes the extremely poor further to the edges. The school is located in a literal and figurative intersection between art, commerce and urban blight. It is settled uncomfortably between Lincoln Center, a series of housing projects, the West Side Highway and Columbus Circle. Students traveling by subway, bus or on foot jostle for space with wealthy Upper West Side residents, gourmet markets and boutique shops, and with performers, laborers and students of Julliard, the Metropolitan Opera, the New York Philharmonic, and the New York City Ballet. Given the amount of development on the West Side, they also regularly dodge construction laborers erecting high-rise apartments buildings. Because of the construction and a slight valley in the road, even on the sunniest days, the school building rests in permanent shadow.

LSHS is one of seven schools housed in a concrete building. Many schools, but not LSHS, have uniforms that range from color requirements to specific school-monogrammed shirts. In a building with seven schools, a uniform develops school unity as much as it serves to separate and categorize students from different schools. The building used to house one large school but because of a variety of problems, it was shut down and phased out year by year while small schools were phased in each new school year. The building is a severe concrete and glass square, partially surrounded by an equally unforgiving outdoor plaza. Part of the plaza is enclosed by a wire mesh fence; the front of the plaza that skirts the main entrance has a series of once brightly painted, box-like structures that serve as makeshift seats and tables. Four floors are above street level and there are two levels of basement classrooms. Each of the seven schools occupies a floor or series of hallways in the building. The students in each school are not allowed in any other school's space, though roughly 3000 students enter and exit through the same doors at staggered start and end times to the school day and all students share the cafeteria, gym and auditorium spaces. All students must enter through scanning, where their bags are examined through X-rays, they must remove belts and any metal objects, their bodies are randomly scanned and their belongings may be searched. Per New York City rules, no students are allowed to bring in any electronic devices, including cell phones and iPods.

LSHS occupies one basement level in the building; there is no natural light and the cement walls have a vertical wale, reminiscent of prison bars. The basement often leaks or floods, there are mice, and because of its location under and next to the building's ventilation system, one classroom may be insufferably hot while the one next door might be frigid. To combat the prison-like environment, classrooms are painted bright colors, however, with the neon lighting and lack of natural sunlight, these rooms appear more garish than welcoming. No student has anything positive to say about the physical surroundings.

At LSHS, in theory, study of the media is employed in specific media courses and across the school's curriculum. In actuality, this is not the case. For two years, I worked to develop the media education curriculum in both specific media classes and across the core courses. I am confident that, due to forces largely beyond my control, I failed wholeheartedly at this effort in part because the standards of success were inflexible and did not embrace alternative or critical pedagogies. I entered LSHS with the naïve belief that I could develop the media education curriculum despite systematic restraints. This book and its organization grew out of inspiration from that failure.

Media education could not be thoroughly integrated at LSHS for internal reasons, including a top-down, disjointed, disorganized management with high teacher turnover as well as systemic reasons, including an absence of teacher training in media education that left teachers–and ultimately students–unprepared. There was never a clear trajectory of media classes at LSHS. In its first four years, there was a smattering of disorganized, piecemeal classes under a 'media' umbrella, which will be discussed in Chapter Four. Many of the classes did not last for an entire school year due to multiple teacher turnover within the school year. The individuals hired to teach these classes were not licensed teachers, but rather professionals and artists in their fields. In part because there is no licensure in media education, hiring professionals in the field initially appears like an innovative idea, a way to connect schools with communities. However, the media professionals lacked pedagogical training and the school system lacked formal space for legitimate hiring of non-licensed classroom based individuals. What resulted was little consistency within 'media' courses, no formal development of the curricula and no scaffolding of knowledge. The inconsistent inclusion of media studies at LSHS dually mirrors the inconsistency in the students' lives and their inability to clearly articulate the qualities behind what are promoted as the unique aspects of the project of new school reform.

The core subject teachers had no formal media education training and if they included media studies into their courses, it was predicated on their own colloquial knowledge or creative thinking. Teachers were also not trained in how to expand their subjects to enfold the theme, so even teachers interested in expanding their curricula often did so in a disjointed manner. This is no fault of theirs: there is no formal professional development within the Department of Education on theme integration and there is no formal, streamlined media education training. Indeed, what I learned when I first began organizing the threads of this research was that a major gap in the students' experience was their teachers' lack of media knowledge. Chapter Seven discusses this gap further and suggests ways to remedy it in future research.

Media education integration could also not succeed for systemic reasons beyond the walls of LSHS. Mayoral control of the school system and subsequent new school reform happened quickly without corresponding attention paid to the enacted changes, leaving schools unprepared to follow through with the attention to detail needed to make actual changes successful. Control of the school system by a mayor with a corporate business background means that changes occur through the lens of neoliberalism. New school reform occurs within a neoliberal ethos and small, theme-based schools with alternative pedagogy uncomfortably intersect with increased pressure of high-stakes standardized testing and regimented school environments. Despite attempts at radical change in the school system, conservative values still take precedence, which translates to continued systematic failure of economically underserved and socially disenfranchised youth. In a neoliberal political environment that defends itself on personal choice rather than community responsibility, small, theme-based schools are destined to fail. Given the rigid strictures of the public school system and the pressures marked by an increasingly competitive local, national and global marketplace, the intellectual desires of students are often neglected in favor of testing, statistics and citywide performance numbers. If a school must adhere to the broad expectations of city and state standards, a theme that does not "fit" the standards cannot be fully integrated.

Despite the changes made to the New York City public school system that rhetorically made more room for alternative curricula, the actual unfolding of new school reform revealed schools not so different from their pre-reform iteration. Admittedly, schools grew smaller and teaching staffs grew larger, but there is no causal evidence that smaller schools and smaller classes are automatically better. In times of economic, social and political upheaval, schools and school systems cling to traditional tropes of success, such as standardized test scores. Standardized test scores, however, reveal little about the daily reality of particular schools and generally reveal a school's ability to train students how to takes tests, rather than what they have learned as students. The bulk of this book focuses on how young people make sense of their own school and how that may speak to understandings of the system of schooling and how it impacts struggling urban youth.

Understanding the Methods: Qualitative Data Gathering

The inspiration for this book grew from my two years at LSHS. I felt consistently and continuously hobbled by the system and despite my academic training in media education, felt at a loss when trying to integrate media education curricula. However, my feelings of frustration paled in comparison to the frustration and ultimate apathy experienced by many students. On too many occasions to count, I watched students resign themselves to the bureaucracy of the system and heard them say, with defeat, "Oh, you know how it is at *this* school." Yes, I did, but not from the perspective they lived through. They had learned to anticipate and accept their school would let them down. I could certainly see and often empathized with their frustration, but I did not know *how* or *what* they knew about their school and the larger institution of school. Ultimately, at the end of the day, end of the school year and the end of my tenure at LSHS, I was able to return to the safety of the academy and my relatively privileged existence. For the most part, I live a life where I am rarely insurmountably subjugated and where I am often given the opportunity and space to respond to my critics. While there were days that I felt like a victim of the system within the walls of LSHS, with perspective, I very much was not. The young people within the school and especially those who participated in this research articulated their thoughts, understandings and meaning making on media, media education and their experiences with education. Though their answers were often unsophisticated, misguided and absent critical autonomy, they were articulate, clear and revealed their frustrations and anxieties. For the most part, however, they sourced their frustrations and anxieties to themselves rather than to the system or any authoritative space. How do young people do this? Because I argue that new school reform manifests as rhetoric rather than action, I look closely at those words used to describe young people and explore how young people understand and make meaning from this language.

To better understand what young people knew about the media and media education within their school and how it fit into the larger puzzle of new school reform, I engaged in semi-formal interviews to illuminate the students' understanding of the media and their experiences with media education and engaged in participant-observation of the development of the school to contextualize the participants' words. As a researcher/scholar within the school, I was able to explore the students' lives from a multi-dimensional, interdisciplinary perspective, which Chapter Three discusses in detail. Qualitative research does not claim to answer questions about how schools are the way they are or why public education has taken the paths it has taken. What these data do is paint a picture of how certain students feel and make meaning of their educations, particularly their experiences with alternative curricula in new school reform and how this experience may prepare them for the future, at a moment in time.

Layout of the Book

In order to best understand how these threads have come together, I look at them inside the LSHS classroom and trace from this space and where they might travel beyond the school's walls. Chapters One and Two frame the media education trajectory within United States' secondary schools and map out particular moments in the history of urban schooling, specifically the monumental changes in the New York City public school system. How has media education been conceptualized as part of the education system? Why is media education not in more schools across the country? There are multiple ways to approach the study of the media and Chapter One focuses on key definitions of media education and attempts to include media education into secondary schools in the United States. Special attention is paid to the different epistemological approaches to the study of young people and media in the United States.

There is a vast literature on the history of American schools and I do not profess the audacity to trace the history of American urban education in one chapter; instead, I look at key moments in time that illuminate how a school like LSHS came into being, beginning with hobbling of the urban school model by the success of the post-WWII suburban school; the 1968-1969 Ocean Hill-Brownsville strikes that restructured New York City public schools; and Mayor Bloomberg's 2002 takeover of the school system that re-centralized the system and made space for new school reform in its current incarnation. Along the way, key snags in urban education are explored as intimately connected to neoliberal orthodoxies that pervade the school system and the young people educated within its walls.

To apply the literature to the real lives of students who live beyond the pages of a book, Chapter Three discusses in detail the methodological approach taken in this study. Because I worked in the school for two years, I was offered a unique view of the development of the school, including all those bits of life that have little if anything to do with pedagogy. I was also familiar with the majority of my participants prior to conducting formal research with them and argue that it was precisely because of our familiarity that they trusted me with their stories. What are the ethical and methodological implications of familiarity with participants? Had I been an 'outsider' entering the field, I would not have been afforded such an intimate glimpse into their lives.

A premise of qualitative methodology, particularly data gathered from interviews and in a quasi-ethnographic style, is that data deserves to speak for itself. The job of the scholar is to provide space to illuminate salient details. Therefore, the bulk of this text is made up of the stories told by the participants about their experiences in school. Much research has been done on the treatment of youth of color living in disadvantaged environments. I believe, however, that it is important to continue telling these stories, especially as the social and political climate continues to change in ways that further subjugate these young people. How do individuals, negatively labeled by the larger society as somehow degenerate, understand themselves?

Irrespective of the attraction of a theme, New York City Schools still must adhere to larger city, state and national standards that measure school and student success. This limits the time and intensity that can be devoted to the theme, especially a theme that moves beyond the traditional core course curriculum. Chapter Four discusses how, if at all, the study of the media is integrated into LSHS. While 'the media' are an intimate and regular part of most Americans' everyday lives, rarely is formal space made for the study of the media in a secondary school environment. Yet, the intention was to weave media education thoroughly throughout the school. Chapter Four shares the media studies course trajectory in the first four years of LSHS and shares the participants words how they understood the inclusion of media in their school.

How does the study of the media fit into the larger frame of new school reform? Chapter Five discusses the value of small, theme-based schools and how the participants understand theme-based education. For those students who experience small, theme based schools, how do they understand these schools? Schools have long been a way to measure the nation's success: if schools and students are doing well, it follows then that the nation must be doing well. I also explore how the young people understand the labels 'underserved' and 'inner city' that are applied to them. Young people know negative labels are applied to them and when their schools replicate these labels, they are provided with few options to break out of their negative circumstances. In subtle and explicit ways, they learn they are less important and less valuable to society than their socially and politically advantaged peers. The subjugation students experience outside of school is replicated, not eradicated, inside the walls of their school. For the most part, the participants do not see themselves as underserved, inner city bodies and are not able to critically define these terms. Lastly, this chapter explores how the participants critique their school, specifically the interpersonal relations formed with faculty and administration and their overwhelming frustration with the surveillance and 'safety' mechanisms employed in their school building.

Both 'adolescence' and 'schools' are not separate from the environments in which they are found and are not immune to media representations. Chapter Six explores how the participants make meaning of adolescence and education from both the media's representations of these social categories as well as their own experiences as adolescents attending an urban school. In a school that is supposed to teach media education, the participants further reveal the absence of critical media knowledge in their acceptance or rejection of media messages about school, urban environments and teenagers. This chapter also shares the reflections of the 12th grade participants, the first graduates, on the breadth of their experiences with new school reform.

LSHS fails at media education integration. As Chapter Four shows, the integration of the media was piecemeal at best and with little cohesion or scaffolding of skills. This need not be the case. Despite the seemingly insurmountable barriers facing schools, teachers and students, media studies can be implemented in schools. Chapter Seven explores what needs to be done in order to integrate media education into school and revisits understandings of critical media literacy and multiliteracies to frame both short-term shifts in the current classroom incarnation as well as creates a foundation for necessary radical paradigm shifts in urban education. This chapter is not meant as a panacea, but rather as a space to begin to imagine real change and its possibilities as envisioned through alternative pedagogy.

This introduction and the majority of this text paint a grim picture. We are living in globally grim times and, when examining the broad landscape, it is difficult to make the argument that reorganizing the urban school system is an acute need. The temptation to brush aside the struggles of a school year, even a school day, to examine broad-scale global concerns is one that is resisted in this text. I believe the face of global struggle represents an opportune moment to study the urban school system. Productive change occurs when we are fully aware of the environment in which we are working. Therefore, Chapter Eight exits Lincoln Square High School to examine how the school fits into its larger community as a way to mark avenues for change. This book is not intended to solve the problems of the American urban public school system, but rather to make the portrait of the current environment explicitly clear so that a foundation for change can be made.

Why this Book Matters

First and foremost this book matters because the urban youth who attend school today enter the workforce or academy woefully under-prepared. We are not living in a time where the under-prepared have the luxury of being fixed later and neoliberalism is making the strictures of entry to labor and university that much more restricted. Young people who are not provided the invisible social cues that bolster success, those who do not inherit any degree of influential social or cultural capital, are primed for and will replicate failure.

Alternative curricula, such as media education, invite students to enter into potentially unfamiliar topics and material with a degree of expertise. In part because young people are versed in a variety of media and possess a great deal of colloquial expertise on their media of choice, they can speak about the media with a great deal of authority. This authority can be both transformative and translated across the curricula and provide a foundation for transparent learning. Providing students with a place to exercise their authority–where they may know more than their teacher–teaches lessons about responsibility and power. Media education does not belong 'only' in media literacy and production courses; a powerful media education curriculum weaves its way through the entire curricula. The media are not discrete pieces, mutually exclusive from other aspects of our life, therefore education of them should be inclusive and across the core curriculum.

Students may be experts in the media, but they are not pedagogical experts. The job of the teacher is to provide a proper foundation and execution of material. However, there is no space in American teacher education for media education licensure. This needs to change. This book illustrates what happens when an innovative idea is enacted without proper foundation. No teacher at LSHS was trained in media education or knew the basic fundamentals of integrating media studies into their course plans. There are materials available for teachers, however, if it is not deemed important to make time and space for these materials, they will gather dust and do no one–teacher or student–any good.

The integration of media studies across the curriculum demands radical change in the seats occupied by the students, in the front of the classroom, in the principal's office and in the offices of those who determine the development and deign what is important in the curriculum presented to those students in their seats. This book works to introduce the current environment, to articulate places where specific change is needed and to develop the beginning of a conversation on change.

Notes

[1] All institutional, proper names and some identifying information have been changed in order to protect participants' confidentiality. Youth participants chose their own cover names.

[2] In Great Britain, where the formal study of the media has a lineage clearer than in the United States, the preferred terminology is 'media education.' In the United States, the preferred terminology has been 'media literacy,' but there is no singular definition of what is meant by either 'media' or 'literacy,' nor clarity of where, how or to what extent this term should be learned. Through the exploration of the literature, I defer to the authors' terminology, however I prefer the more inclusive and active 'media education' and use that term when discussing my own work.

Chapter 1

From Protective to Critical:

The Trajectory of Media Education in the United States

Much of the conversation about childhood and adolescence in America today is a conversation about media. And yet, following decades' old patterns, there has been little sustained attention on the place of media education in the standard curriculum of America's schools. Media use among young people is a constant focus of social concern with little corresponding social change. As a culture, we spend a significant amount of time with popular media; however, we rarely pause to study them closely. Young people are sophisticated audiences–and increasingly, producers and distributors–of media long before they are critical scholars. Young people are often caught in a maelstrom of concern *about* them without their own contribution to that concern. They are identified, often derisively, by their position in time and space with little to none of their own input.

When a new technology is introduced into society, it is accompanied by simultaneous fear and fascination, especially by adults regarding the impact on young people. Young people are a perpetual focal point for adult fears about changes in technology and their impact on society. In today's global media environment, where data is created and disseminated almost instantaneously, current fears include how and in what capacity young people are impacted by global transmissions, especially the ease and availability of accessing the globe in the privacy of one's home through social networking and user-generated content. To stave off reactionary responses, one must pause to ask if these changes are a passing trend, a collection of fears that will fade away once the inevitable next technology comes along, or a new way of understanding the world that young people must learn to navigate.

These concerns are valid, but must be explored in context. What is experienced now will inevitably shift and certain fascinating bits will become pieces of nostalgia, while others will become ingrained into and an integral part of society. Some shifts–including the increased private and personal use of advanced technologies for local and global transmission of data–will probably sustain. Today's young people and young people of future generations will know the world as instantaneously accessible with constant, streaming updates. Despite the familiarity–indeed, because of the familiarity–young people deserve to be educated about their experiences with global media.

The scholarly conversation about media education in the United States has occurred in fits and starts for at least 20 years, but has never ventured on a clear, uninterrupted path. This chapter traces the epistemological spectrum of media studies, situates the United States' position and explores the foundational definitions of media literacy/education and their metamorphoses through the past 20 years. I explore why media education is absent in most American classrooms, examine the role of informal 'corporate' media education and explore the cultural fascination with technology.

In the United States, students are consistently and well trained in the media from their own vast access, exposure, and experience with media and technology. But does this 'count' as education? For the commercial media industries, it likely does, as private capitalist enterprises look for quantity and quality of audience. If the media industries' job is to 'teach' young people to be good and regular media consumers, they have done their job well. In this way, the American experience of with media education intersects with larger neoliberal concerns. Gandy (2002) writes, "Neoliberal political philosophy has found a comfortable berth ... that denies the possibility of an institutionalized representation of common or collective interests" (p. 449). The American implementation of media education is highly individualistic, private, and aspires to betterment through the middle class value system. Rarely is the private, capitalist intent of our media industries questioned; they are accepted as somehow 'natural.' Much media studies works to understand content and interpret representation rather than challenge structural foundations. Drawing from the narrow orthodoxy of neoliberalism discussed in the introduction, this chapter works to show how media education, inherently cross-disciplinary, can challenge that orthodoxy.

Epistemological Positions on Media Studies:

Protection to Celebration

There have been waves of concern over young people's role as audiences through most of the history of electronic media in the United States. A late-20th-century concern was the negative impact of increased popular media–especially television–geared toward young people and the negative effect on their development as successful members of society (Postman 1994, 1985;

Winn 1977). An early 21st-century wave of concern includes young people actively involved as producers and distributors of media texts, especially via social networking, through user-generated content sites and mobile media. The formation of this concern vacillates from a protective, conservative epistemology that reinforces young people's youth and vulnerability to a celebratory epistemology that admonishes adults' lack of comprehension of young people's natural knowledge and expertise.

The most common incarnation of media education in the United States is the inoculative, or protectionist, approach where adult-authority figures impose their knowledge and expertise as a way of warding children from the supposed evils of mass media (Barker & Petley 2001; Bragg 2001; Brown 1998; Buckingham 2001, 1991; Domaille & Buckingham 2001; Halloran & Jones 1992; Hobbs 1998; Kellner 2002; Kellner & Share, 2007; Scharrer 2002). The grounding assumption of protectionism is that once young people learn the evils of the electronic media, they will choose to turn them off and make wiser leisure and entertainment choices. Protectionism is a defensive position, both in its philosophy and in its intention to develop armor against media influence.

The protectionist stance acknowledges only narrow, limited options for media use, wherein all electronic, popular media are bad for young people, who, because of their youth, are incapable of anything beyond simple acceptance of presented messages. This value-laden approach ignores young people's pleasure with electronic media as an activity choice and distrusts their ability to participate actively and critically in their media choices. The protectionist position reinforces the adult-child hierarchy, positioning adults as above influence, critically aware and authoritative over media messages. Furthermore, certain children are believed more susceptible than others. Negative media effects happen to children absent cultural and social capital, whose intellectual armor is down and who have few other (perceived or real) social options (Buckingham 2001). This is a circuitous way to say that the children of the poor, whose domestic and academic environments do not meet middle-class standards, are inevitably more harmed by the media than the children of the middle or upper classes, bolstered by their social and cultural capital.

While the idea of 'direct effects' has lost sway in intellectual and academic circles, it still holds a subtle presence in popular studies on young people and identity development (Pipher 1994; Pollack 1998; Postman 1994, 1985; Winn 1977). Indeed, even otherwise politically and socially liberal scholars find it easy to blame the media for society's ills (*cf* Alonso, Anderson, Su & Theoharis 2009; Aronowitz 2004; Delpit 2002; Greene 1988; Hong 1996; McCarthy, Rodriguez, Meecham, *et al.* 2005). There is no empirical evidence that media are the direct cause of socially inappropriate behavior, however, they remain an alluring enticement and convenient scapegoat. When the media are blamed for social ills, more complex and self-reflective questions need not be tackled.

Often, the use of the term 'effect' and the need to protect children is written or spoken about so casually its use is rarely challenged. 'Media effects' is accepted terminology and the need to protect young people is taken-for-granted as right and noble behavior. No one will explicitly claim they do *not* care about the welfare of children, however, claiming the desire to protect them is a vague, context-void approach. When media education is employed as a way to protect children, a great deal of responsibility for a wide variety of social scenarios is foisted onto one source. Scharrer (2002) inquires how a media literacy curriculum can be expected to end or reverse media effects. She observes, "Just as exposure to media is but one (important but not individually operating) factor shaping our ideas, views, and actions, participation in a media-literacy curriculum is only one factor to weigh against a multitude of others in determining a persona's susceptibility to media effects at any given point in time" (p. 356). Epistemological belief in the singularity of media effects oversimplifies the multiple, complex, daily social encounters we experience that influence our worldviews.

At the other end of the spectrum is a celebratory position that values and encourages youth participation in media as audiences and producers. While this position is initially refreshing because there is little blame and young people are acknowledged as active participants in their choices, it also assumes that any media choice is an inherently good choice and critical inquiry is not necessary (Buckingham 2000b). In Buckingham's (2000b) critique of the celebratory position he writes, "children are seen to possess a natural, spontaneous creativity, which is somehow (perhaps paradoxically) released by the machine" (p. 45).

The celebratory position ignores various social and economic divisions: not all young people have the same access to the wide variety of media and celebration of youth media use further privileges young people already in a position of privilege. As digital, mobile and advanced technologies increase for private users, Buckingham (2008) observes "advocates of the new 'digital generation' regard technology as a force of liberation for young people…"

(p. 13). However, he cautions, this belief in liberation is generally focused on young people who possess the ways and means to access advanced technology, the 'early adopters,' "who, as I have suggested, are also likely to be privileged in other areas of their lives" (p. 18). Jenkins *et al.* (2006) counter this when they write that "Contrary to popular stereotypes [private media] activities are not restricted to white suburban males" (p. 6) and they share several vignettes of students of low socioeconomic status who nevertheless meet with digital success on their own. The celebratory position supports neoliberal ethos by supporting individual relationships with the media, denying the question of access, and reframing it as a question of interest and ability.

Very few people adhere firmly to either end of the spectrum; more often, there is movement along the spectrum. Buckingham and Sefton-Green (2003), in their analysis of the multiple texts connected to *Pokemon*, challenge adherence to any dogmatic position. Drawing from the sociological debate between structure and agency, Buckingham and Sefton-Green posit pedagogy as a third way to explore the complexities of media use. They write, "we want to suggest that the frequent *opposition* between structure and agency is mistaken; and we want to propose a rather different formulation of the relationship, based around the notion of *pedagogy*" (p. 380, italics in original). Pedagogy examines how and what is learned in a variety of social contexts and works within the structure and agency debate. Young people who collect and play with *Pokemon* cards, or watch the show, engage in a social activity and act out the characters and their skills. They do not exclusively exercise agency because the framework for the game is set, nor are they exclusively acted upon because they develop the game and its incarnations through their play. Buckingham and Sefton-Green (2003) argue too many binary structure/agency, either/or, good/bad debates do not examine the multiple levels of interaction in which young people engage. While *Pokemon* may ultimately be seen through the lens of history as a passing trend, the multiple ways with which it was engaged defy binary dichotomies. A theory of pedagogy, Buckingham and Sefton-Green (2003) write, "is ultimately a theory of activity–or at least of *process*. It requires an attention to the dynamic relationship between 'teaching' and 'learning'–or between texts and their reading and use–that does not simply invest power in one at the expense of the other" (pp. 396-397, italics in original).

Examining young people's use of media through a pedagogical frame explicates multiple points along the spectrum of protection to celebration.

More nuanced ways to approach the study of the media are themselves fraught with tension. Kellner and Share (2007) discuss media arts and media literacy as moments within the broader scope of media studies. Media arts teaches students "to value the aesthetic qualities of media and the arts while using their creativity for self-expression through creating art and media" (p. 7). The media arts position focuses on creation and production of texts and aesthetic pieces and is found inside schools as stand-alone classes or outside the classroom in afterschool or community-based programs. In Kellner and Share's estimation, the media arts position "favors individualistic self-expression over socially conscious analysis and alternative media production" (p. 7). This approach celebrates individual creation and accomplishment over political challenge, activism or promotion of social justice. As it teaches young people about 'aesthetic value,' media arts posits a defensive position, teaching quality, 'correct' choices, developing 'taste' and furthering elitist attitudes about high/low cultures.

Kellner and Share's (2007) critique of media literacy views it as a familiar, but ultimately vacuous phrase without clear discussion of intent and purpose. The media literacy ethos that has entered American classrooms via individual teachers and national membership associations is, according to Kellner and Share, linked to a "conservative base that does not engage the political dimensions of education and especially literacy" (p. 8). American media literacy remains closely connected to its protective, defensive roots and treats media texts as independent of their larger context. Much American media literacy projects remove media from their larger sociopolitical, institutional contexts and aim to teach young people how to deconstruct individual media texts and messages. Young people learn, for example, to deconstruct messages within advertisements, but not necessarily that advertisements are part of a larger private, commercial enterprise. Work done in the name of media literacy are often one-off, discrete projects that 'fit in' but do not connect to the large curriculum and are created, ready to use, by individuals other than the classroom teacher (Bragg 2001; Goodman 2003). They are created with the intent of making work easier for the classroom teacher, however, in so doing, they become a tangible reminder that *someone else* knows more about the subject than both the students and the classroom teacher and will disseminate that knowledge as necessary. This firmly situates media literacy within neoliberalism where information is distributed on a need-to-know basis with experts acting on individuals' opportunities for data gathering from an invisible space. Within the frame of neoliberalism, the less young people know about the operations of the media industries the better.

A more complex point along the spectrum is critical media literacy. 'Critical media literacy,' the current phrase in use by media education scholars, highlights the complex relationship we have with the media and emphasizes its political and social connections. Critical media literacy is inquiry-based and engages in critiques of ideology, including close examination and analysis of representations of gender, race, class and sexuality (Kellner & Share 2007). Critical media literacy counters hegemony as it encourages students to challenge commonsense assumptions of the meanings of media texts. According to Kellner and Share, critical media literacy should be taught through production to make "analyses more meaningful and empowering as students gain tools for responding and taking action on the social conditions and texts they are critiquing" (p. 9).

While it is a more complex and context-rich approach to the study of the media, critical media literacy nevertheless reveals the motivations and concerns of its definers. The language of Kellner and Share's (2007) definition of critical media literacy reveals a belief that the media are manipulative and young people are easily swayed victims. They write critical media literacy "not only teaches students to learn from media, to resist media manipulation and to use media materials in constructive ways, but it is also concerned with developing skills that will help create good citizens and that will make individuals more motivated and competent participants in social life" (p. 16). Left unclear is what a 'constructive' use of media is, how 'good citizens' are defined and what it means to be 'motivated' and 'competent.' This position encourages activism and respects personal choice and pleasure; however, the underlying assumption is that with increased activism, personal choice and pleasure will shift to 'better' choices. While this very well might be a natural process on the route of critical inquiry, I am left with two concerns. One, there is an assumed 'correct' way to be a good citizen, which, left undefined, may not include of the multiple incarnations of family and citizenship in a multi-ethnic, multi-class, multi-geographical nation. This could, then, unintentionally punish or segregate young people from one another who do not or cannot follow this route to good citizenship and subtly train young people to aspire to a white, middle-class ideology they cannot achieve. Two, while this definition of critical media literacy believes in the active involvement of young people in their audience and production choices, the dissemination of knowledge reinforces adult-youth hierarchies. While much critical media literacy talks against adherence to teacher-student hierarchies, there is a reinforcement of the hierarchy in the language used in the definition.

Defining Media Education

No responsible discussion of media education can occur without inclusion of the British model of media studies, which serves as a foundation for global understanding and framing of critical media literacy studies. Great Britain (especially England, specifically, London) has formalized the study of the media in their primary and secondary school system[1]. Media education is part of the Language Arts curriculum through primary and secondary schooling. Upper-level students can sit for exams in media studies. The inclusion of digital media in texts and lessons lags behind their development and inclusion in the broader culture[2].

The inclusion of media education must be understood in context and the history of media studies in British primary and secondary schools draws deeply from its social and political history. The intersection of increased technological developments, increased youth population and increased production and import of popular culture, especially music, in postwar Britain helped develop the avenue of Cultural Studies focused on youth and popular culture. Hall and Whannell (1965) saw a connection between technological developments and a growth in the youth population that culminated in a "fairly direct connection ... between the younger generation and the media" (p. 20). This connection was deemed worthy of study rather than dismissal. The direct connection between 'the younger generation and the media' grew stronger throughout generations. Popular media are easily dismissed by a society that continues to value 'great' literature, but today, increased access to advanced digital technologies, especially social networking sites and user-generated content on the Internet, which can be accessed from the privacy of one's home, has made 'dismissal' increasingly difficult.

Great Britain: Concepts of Media Education

Young people spend a great deal of time with the media, that time is often social and contributed to identity development (Buckingham 1993b). A continuous theme throughout Buckingham's writings, and one that has served the British definition and implementation of media education, is the idea that an essentialist perspective on both youth and media remains popular because it positions adults in a position of power over young people. Adults generally create texts either for other adults or for young people, rarely consulting any young people in the process (Buckingham 2000a). Implementing critical media education works, in part, to consult young people on their learning.

Drawing from a deep history in Marxist theory, critical theory and Cultural Studies, the British media studies approach tackles questions of structural power, production value, popular culture appreciation, pleasure and learning; it articulates an integral combination of analysis and production to make learning multidimensional. The foundational texts in this area of study grow from Bazalgette's (1992) work in cinema studies with the British Film Institute, Buckingham's (2000a, 2000b, 1993b, 1991) and Buckingham and Sefton-Green's (1994) work inside middle and secondary school classrooms, analysis of media industries and questions of young people's social development and Grahame's (1991) work in production.

The media studies approach to media education is grounded in classroom and community work and acknowledges and draws from student experience and expertise. It uses students' familiarity and pleasure as entrypoints to critical analysis of the media and student production as practical application to the understanding of media industries. This approach to media education draws from students' personal and colloquial knowledge and builds on that knowledge, teaching nuanced and intricate understanding of media industries and how these industries are interconnected with their lives. The British approach to media education must contend with politics, budgets and systemic racism, its own progression within the spectrum from protection to celebration, and absent teacher training and assessment. Media teachers are not specialists in media studies, per se, but most often literature teachers confident in textual deconstruction who 'insert' media inquiry into their literature classes. However, because it is a conversation of pedagogy within the national school system, it is more formally recognized as part of the educational culture than any patchwork inclusion in American schools.

The media studies model of media education developed six key aspects, refined into four key concepts that provide the basis for inquiry and study. Bazalgette's (1992) *Key aspects of media education* discuss agency, category, technology, language, audience and representation, with questions supporting each aspect[3]. Buckingham (2003) advanced these into four key concepts: production, language, representation and audience[4] with discussions, questions and activities that highlight the intersections and application of the concepts. Both Bazalgette and Buckingham (2003) caution against subdividing the aspects/concepts into discrete activities because the tasks of analysis, critical inquiry and production are applied across a variety of media texts and study of the media are interconnected and should be treated holistically. The concepts focus the formal study of the media in secondary and primary schooling on a fusion of analysis and production; they serve to complicate and categorize the critical approach to the study of the media; and they work to engage students actively in their learning about the media without punishing their pleasure or enjoyment of the media, and are exploratory, rather than defensive or protective[5].

America: Media Literacy

Media literacy in the United States has many definitions and is found in many disparate locations. When media studies are found in organized curricula and pedagogy inside classrooms, this is the exception rather than the accepted lesson plan. Work in media literacy is often found in and/or funded by community, private, corporate, commercial or religious organizations (Goodman 2003; Thoman & Jolls 2003; Tyner 1998). Though inclusion of media studies in classrooms has shifted from an overtly protectionist position, it is still piecemeal and mostly defensive in tone. Individual courses in media studies or application of the media to other courses often reveal an ideology of discomfort. For example, when media literacy is part of a health class, the media are equated with viruses or diseases (Bragg 2001). There are multiple Internet locations where interested teachers can download ready-made media literacy activities, but these tend to be 'one-off' activities to be 'added on' to already complete curricula[6]. Teachers who develop media literacy curricula generally do so on their own, with little administrative support, scant professional development and no formal teacher training (Domaille & Buckingham 2001; Furness 2007; Goodman 2003; Kellner 2002; McLaren & Hammer 2007; Moore 2008; Scharrer 2002; Tornero 2008; Torres & Mercado 2007; Tyner 1998).

Despite the vast quantity of electronic media produced in the United States and the significant amount of time citizens spend with the media, it is not something that has been formally introduced as a topic of study in secondary schools. Since the 1970s, media education has jump-started in a variety of pedagogical areas, but has not laid claim to one particular trajectory and is not defined as a field (Tyner 1998). Much of what has been done in the United States in the name of media education is a defensive attempt to simultaneously blame the media for society's ills and teach children the evils of the media with the goal being that they will choose to 'turn off' harmful media. Clearly, much of what has been done in the United States clings to the protectionist end of the epistemological spectrum.

Many scholars–both those directly involved in media education and those tangential to it–have worked to define media literacy. In the United States, the use of 'media literacy' can mean many things, not necessarily connected directly to classroom learning, but rather reflect an adherence to anti-intellectual, simplified, catchphrase-oriented problem-solution dichotomies. Silverstone's (1999) thoughtful, lyrical manifesto on the importance of studying the media provides what appears an offhand definition of media literacy, but one whose elements are found in much of the more earnest, classroom-based, developmental literature on the subject. He writes media literacy:

> requires not more and no less than other forms of literacy: a capacity to decipher, appreciate, criticize and compose. It also requires, at least in my perception of it, an understanding of the proper location of the textual claim, historically, sociologically, anthropologically. It requires an appreciation both of mystery and of mystification (p. 37).

What Silverstone captures, that many American scholars working to integrate study of the media into primary and secondary school classrooms struggle with, is clarity within complexity. The early work of media literacy in the United States falls neatly in place with larger neoliberal concerns, emphasizing individuality, bowing to the power of private enterprise and diluting complicated conversations into short, sharp–though ultimately empty–turns of phrase.

Foundational American Definition: The Aspen Institute

American definitions of, and attempts to include, media literacy into the classroom stem from the Aspen Institute's (1992) National Leadership Conference on Media Literacy. The Aspen Institute defines media literacy as "hands-on and experiential, democratic (the teacher is researcher and facilitator) and process-driven. Stressing as it does critical thinking, it is inquiry-based. Touching as it does on the welter of issues and experiences of daily life, it is interdisciplinary and cross-curricular" (Aufderheide 1993, p. 2). While this definition is concise and embraces democratic principles, it is a simple, uncomplicated definition that does not encapsulate the complexities involved in studying the media or the reality of media education in the United States. In just under 20 years since this definition, media studies in the United States has not gown significantly in complexity.

Compare the detail of the British concepts against the American definition and it is easy to see why there are so many disjointed 'understandings' of media literacy in the United States and why so much disparate work can be done in its name. Some of the confusion associated with media literacy can possibly be located at the moment when American scholars decided a simple definition was preferred to a more complex, thorough exploration. What has resulted, with the benefit of hindsight, is a sloppy inclusion of many ideas, philosophies and epistemological beliefs.

Shifting Definition: Expanding the Inquiry

In 1998, *The Journal of Communication* ran a special issue that asked scholars to discuss their conceptualizations of media literacy. The questions posed and discussed in the *Journal* asked where media literacy should occur, how it should be assessed, how it should be defined, why young people should study the media, the epistemological positions on studying the media, why media literacy is not successful in the United States, multiple ways of understanding the media, and the role of activism and production in media studies (Brown; Christ & Potter; Hobbs; Kubey; Lewis & Jhally; Meyrowitz). The *Journal* drew primarily from Western scholars with access to the most advanced media at the time. While they worked to complicate the subject matter and advance the definitions and confusions surrounding the inquiries of media literacy, for the most part, it was a simplified, relatively conservative, conversation.

The language used to organize media literacy in the *Journal* reveals the larger motivations and concerns of the authors. Brown (1998) defines media literacy as the:

> ability to analyze and appreciate respected works of literature and, by extension, to communicate effectively by writing well. In the past half-century it has come to include the ability to analyze competently and to utilize skillfully print journalism, cinematic productions, radio and television programming and even computer-mediated information and exchange (p. 44).

That Brown begins with 'respected' works of literature and the ability to write well belies a protective, traditional belief; of secondary concern is analysis of all other media. With his focus on 'respected works of literature,' Brown situates himself in the traditional space where the teacher-authority simultaneously guides students to the 'correct' media and *away* from 'other' media.

Lewis and Jhally (1998) argue in favor of an activist media literacy that focuses on production. An activist media literacy helps "people become sophisticated citizens rather than sophisticated consumers" (p. 109). They concede that while media education "should certainly teach students to engage media texts," its more important task is to teach students "to engage and challenge media institutions" (p. 109). Revealed through this language is the elitist position that sophisticated citizens choose not to consume media, yet are still capable of critical analysis. This position runs the risk of rejection by young people who do not want to be told what not to like and it shrugs off active engagement with media, arming students against media consumption.

Much has changed–but just as much remains the same–in American media literacy since 1998. Most pertinently, the *need* for media education is no longer a question; it is generally agreed upon that young people deserve education about the media in some capacity and at some point in their schooling. While Hobbs's (1998) 'seven great debates' seem blissfully outdated at this juncture in the conversation, many of the concerns posed in 1998 remain and many more have developed. There is still an absence of clear methods of assessment, little to no teacher training and a strong presence of the protectionist, defensive position remains.

What has changed since the Aspen Institute's meeting and since the *Journal of Communication*'s issue on media literacy is the rapid advancement of digital media, computer mediated communication and increased social networking via high-speed Internet connections. Indeed, when Brown (1998) writes that media competence includes "even computer-mediated information and exchange" (p. 44), we can see how far digital media technologies have advanced in the decade since this definition. Discussions of media literacy today almost certainly emphasize, if not *begin with*, competence in 'digital and computer mediated information and exchange.' Whereas once institutions outside the home possessed the most advanced technologies, today they are found as often within the home, contributing both to young people's early and consistent experiences with media and the need to provide formal education on such technologies. This early and consistent use of media re-ignites both protectionist and celebratory epistemologies: scholars, parents and pundits alternately fear the new digital media for invading young people's homes and private spaces or embrace it for its supposed democratizing impact.

21ˢᵗ-Century: Critical Media Literacy

Current discussions of media literacy emphasize attention to the critical and a focus on the social and political environment of a variety of media. Scholars working within critical media literacy see the study of the media as a necessary part of every young person's education. Critical media literacy is understood as a pedagogy that teaches young people to see and analyze media texts as "products of social production and struggle" (Kellner 2002, p. 93). Students of critical media literacy are challenged to see the impact of their role as audiences and consumers of media (Steinberg & Kincheloe 2004a). Critical media literacy works against complacency or passive acceptance of media messages, "teaching students to be critical of media representations and discourses" (Kellner 2002, p. 93). Critical media literacy is lashed to participatory democracy and active inquiry into the construction and foundation of local culture and how it fits into a national and global environment. Teachers of critical media literacy work against imposing their own value systems or adult authority and foster respect for young people's developing critical skills and articulation of choice (Steinberg & Kincheloe 2004a). The foundational approach taken in critical media literacy is a "collaborative approach between teachers and students" to both challenge the teacher-student hierarchy and respect young people's investment in and knowledge of media culture (Kellner & Share 2007, p. 94). Students and teachers must approach material critically, be willing to engage each other and challenge their own assumptions (Furness 2007). The traditional teacher-student hierarchy is undone through acknowledgment of the important role that young people play in taking ownership of their learning and knowledge production. Young people *know* a great deal, though it is undoubtedly colloquial and critically uninformed; however, if they learn that inquiry into developing their knowledge is supported, they begin the route to autonomous learning.

Critical media literacy is a foundation for maneuvering change in classroom practice and organization and works to dismantle the corporate takeover of schooling and young people's culture, endemic to neoliberal orthodoxy. Critical media literacy makes explicit how the media informs young people's worldview. Critical media literacy draws from the personal and places it within a larger social context wherein young people make connections to larger sociological concerns (McLaren & Hammer 2007). Inclusion of critical media literacy rejects corporate organization of schools and emphasizes "that young people do not exist to fulfill the needs of corporations, and schools are not the testing grounds for corporations" (Mashburn & Weaver 2007, pp. 565-566). In its radical approach to the organization of learning, critical media literacy protects schools from corporate interests, thereby undoing the unsupported neoliberal belief that private enterprise improves schools.

Critical media literacy, however, is not unified in definition or expression. Like most American efforts at media education, critical media literacy has developed from many disparate locations with a variety of motivations. Generally speaking, it represents individual efforts at change, without a guiding canon or institutional support. The struggle in this is that scholars work alone and changes made remain individual; the excitement is that there is room for great change and influence. Individual changes may be powerful, but if the individual changes remain in isolation, they are restricted from collaborative growth. Because media education is a global concern, there are those who are concerned with the global understanding and awareness of media education.

Global Understanding of Media Education: UNESCO

Media education is a global concern, however there is no singular global approach to the teaching and learning of media studies. Respecting the variety of global interests, approaches and concerns, UNESCO has convened conferences that explore the needs and interests of those interested in implementing media education into schools and community settings. The UNESCO conferences on media education work to define and formalize understandings of media education (2001) and develop teaching training and curriculum development (2008).

To better understand the global concerns with media education, Domaille and Buckingham (2001) distributed surveys to 72 media education experts in 52 countries that asked about experiences and concerns with introducing media education into schools. Their report draws from and analyzes the respondents' answers about their country's application of the study of the media. Overall, they found that the spectrum of concern ranged from developing countries' need to provide basic print literacy to countries with established media education curricula where "there are clear signs of weariness among its most prominent advocates" (p. 10). There is an epistemological shift from protection to empowerment while there remains an overarching concern that the study of the media in the primary or secondary schools is not taken seriously by governments or funding organizations. The debate continues over whether media literacy should be established as its own series of courses or established within and across core curricula.

The United States poses a unique conundrum, which Domaille and Buckingham (2001) detail. The United States is the "world's leading media producer" where "one might expect to find a substantial and coherent curriculum in media education" (p. 75). However, this is not the case in part because of tensions revealed when trying to implement media education in an environment with "diverse conceptualizations of media, technology, education and schooling" (p. 75). According to their report, media literacy in the United States continued to reflect protectionist views, which, by 2001, were "relatively rare elsewhere in the world" (p. 76).

The 2008 conference focused more broadly on curriculum development, teacher training and the continued need to understand and make connections across the globe. The conference brought together 18 global experts from Africa, Asia-Pacific, Europe, North America, Latin America, the Arab States and representatives from the UNESCO education sector. The formal reports were focused on teacher education and curriculum development. The expert participants at the 2008 conference were concerned with the exponential increase in media texts, global telecommunication proliferation, institutional power differentials and the impact of all of this on society and on young people specifically. The UNESCO expert group employ the term 'media and information literacy' which is centered on five core competencies, "comprehension, critical thinking, creativity, cross-cultural awareness, and citizenship" (Moore 2008, p. 6).

In/formal Media Education: Corporate Versus Classroom

American youth are incredibly well educated in the media and often come to school knowing more than their teachers about a range of popular culture subjects. Generally speaking, this knowledge is not privileged in the classroom and young people are adept at suppressing their personal interests when crossing the classroom threshold. The power of the mass media cannot be fully dismissed as irrelevant *just because* young people have consistent experience and great familiarity with the media. The mass media do have a great deal of power *and* young people do have a great deal of knowledge and skills; there is a continuous tension between the two. Young people's knowledge and skill is colloquial, personal and, as often as not, focused on the pleasures of entertainment or the joys of personal media production. The media's power is not, as some fear, rooted in content or commercialization, but rather in finance. The mass media industries have more financial power than any individual and thus can be more adept at changes that serve their best capitalist interest and creating a hermetically sealed process: greater financial control serves to bolster the process of hegemony by providing more 'options,' thereby smoothing the process of consent via exposure to content and representation. For this smoothing to be successful, greater finance is accessed. The process repeats itself fluidly and appears 'natural' and 'normal.'

Advances in media literacy education are often triggered by tragic events that make parents, public intellectuals and educators concerned that young people are somehow harmed. In this respect, advances in media literacy match Klein's (2007) definition of 'shock doctrine' where public policies are advanced or restructured in the face of tragedy, often for the profit and betterment of private interest rather than public good. The current 'crisis' advancing the formal study of the media is fears about increased digital technologies and social networking. Buckingham (2007) tweaks the accepted usage of 'digital divide'–one that separates the digital 'haves' from the digital 'have nots'–to a division between private and formal use of media. He writes there is "a new and widening gap between young people's out-of-school experiences of technology and their experiences in the classroom" (p. 112). Students are often more adept than their teachers with digital technologies and personal electronic communications, which jostles accepted traditional classroom hierarchies and transmissions of knowledge. Furthermore, some young people have greater access to advanced technologies in their homes, perpetuating the division between classroom and home learning.

The current fear is not about preparing students for a digital future, but reigning in their expertise. Jenkins *et al.* (2006) are not opposed to the informal education inherent in personal media use. They situate it as part of participatory culture where there are "relatively low barriers to artistic expression and civic engagement, strong support for creating and sharing one's creation and some type of informal mentorship whereby what is known by the most experienced is passed along to novices" (p. 3). Jenkins *et al.* (2006) believe that the more time young people spend with their own personal media use and creation, the more comfortable and adept they will be in the anonymous and multilayered social interactions that characterize digital, online communication. This will, in turn make them better at anonymous digital navigation and they "will be better able to multitask and make rapid decisions about the quality of information they are receiving and will be able to collaborate better with people from diverse cultural backgrounds" (p. 10). Young people may in fact be better prepared for a digital future than generations past, however, they still deserve structured learning opportunities; their colloquial knowledge could serve as a space to radically restructure models of education to include their skills and abilities.

Concerns about the power of the mass media reflect the relatively broad curriculum provided by electronic mass media, whose 'classroom' is beyond school walls. Corporate culture aimed at children has replaced schools as their primary educator (Kalantzis & Cope 2000; Morrell 2008; Steinberg & Kincheloe 2004a). Morrell (2008) writes, "…it is difficult to argue against the reality that media are, for today's youth, their primary cultural influence, surpassing the family and the school" (p. 156). I believe it *is* possible to argue this point; the media are a significant cultural influence, but do not operate independently of family, school and peer influences. The media industries, however, do have more financial power than traditional cultural influences and can therefore create more quantity of material, thereby possibly exaggerating the range of their influence. The 'commercial educators' 'teach' for pecuniary accumulation, audience hold, individual gain and, in so doing, Steinberg and Kincheloe (2004a) write, "produce educational forms that are wildly successful when judged on the basis of their capitalist intent" (p. 16). Mass media in the United States are commercial, profit-oriented businesses *not* in the service of the public good but in the service of private enterprise and profit margins. Audiences are expected to consume consistently and if they happen to be pleased by the content, this is an added bonus. The media industries have never been coy about their motivations, and by providing material that is entertaining and enjoyable, audiences may easily be lulled into believing institutional benevolence. As audiences, we consent to the form and content we are offered and, in so doing, grow to believe we are given what we desire, not what the industry desires for us. Our complacency feeds institutional success.

The media are incredibly successful at teaching young people how to interact with them in a way that is both enjoyable and continuous. There is little to no mark of 'schooling' on media texts and yet they are highly successful at educating young people to continuous, progressive usage. There is an increased quantity of available media and technological outlets since the mass media first began marking products and marketing to young people (Steinberg & Kincheloe 2004a). What results is that traditional boundaries of authority and understandings of childhood are eroded, helped along in large part by the mass media who make themselves consistently and continuously available for usage and learning. This is not a new argument (Meyrowitz 1986; Postman 1985); however it is an argument that, once again, appears increasingly sensitive and particularly pertinent. Because of quantity and rapidity of growth and access, it feels increasingly sensitive; because corporate media are now explicitly reaching into classrooms–in the form of textbook development, test preparation, providing technology, school support and lesson planning–as new ways to reach young people, it feels particularly pertinent (Giroux 2007; Mashburn & Weaver 2007; Steinberg & Kincheloe 2004a; Torres & Mercado 2007). Torres and Mercado (2007) write that in the service of government policy and corporate interest, the mass media "are taking over education and impacting teacher education, teachers, and children" more than educators are aware of or able to admit (p. 547). Changes appear to both happen faster and with less awareness by those formerly in authoritative positions.

That liminal space between formal and informal education appears at a critical point at this time in history, given that many (but not all) young people have vast access to a variety of media. Moore (2008) observes it is tempting to think that because young people are adept at appropriating the media for their own personal use, they do not need media education. However, young people's personal use of media does not suffice for critical, formal inquiry; the personal and the critical deserve formal attention. Formal media education focuses on intentional learning and focused, critical engagement within a variety of media forms. Contemporary concerns might need relocation from the fear of eroded boundaries between adult and youth to inquiry into the division–and possible fusion–of informal and formal education. Formal education need not be punitive or belittle young people's pleasure, informal knowledge or out of classroom production experience, but rather formalize that learning in an intentional, critical space. Writing on developing critical literacy skills of urban youth, Morrell (2008) argues, "Even young people who possess 'critical instincts' will need to learn those essential literacy skills that enable them to powerfully navigate socially sanctioned language systems" (p. 7). Irrespective of topic, students deserve formal, intentional learning. In a further elaboration of the space between informal/corporate media education and formal/classroom learning and the need for learning, Tornero (2008) writes that absent intentional, critical education, "economic, cognitive and cultural gaps arise that can be extremely difficult to overcome ... what may be on the surface considered as progress and modernization becomes a renewed form of submissiveness to technological determinism" (p. 6). Young people deserve to be formally educated–even about subjects which they already know a great deal–in order to be competent, participatory citizens in their communities.

There is a bridge between informal and formal media education, one on which the adept teacher and school system can capitalize. Jenkins *et al.* (2006) write that some children are acquiring the new skills of media literacy "through their participation in the informal learning communities that surround popular culture" and teachers can incorporate these skills into the classroom (p. 56). This dramatically reorganizes the structure of the classroom: the teacher learns from the student; students' interests, expertise and competencies are validated; and the classroom becomes a more active space. Jenkins *et al.* do not blindly celebrate informal media learning or believe that it has successfully entered the classroom, noting, "the integration of these important skills and cultural competencies remains haphazard at best" (p. 56). Acknowledgment of the problem and interest in solving it are a start, but soon encounter seemingly insurmountable pedagogical obstacles endemic to the American school system.

Absence of Media Education in American Classrooms

The United States of America is the largest producer and exporter of electronic media, without corresponding import of media from other countries. Despite the quantity of media produced in the United States, there is a conspicuous absence of formal study of the media. There is great lamentation over the media's influence on young people, which is often the full-stop of the conversation. To lament the absence of quality media is, in some ways, a safe space to languish: time spent lamenting means time *not* spent tackling more complex issues and working to make change. Several scholars have commented on the apparent contradiction between the quality of complaint and the absence of study, emphasizing the need for media education in schools. Kellner (2002) argues that because of massive changes in technology and our social and political worlds, education needs to respond accordingly. He writes, "the demands of the new global economy, culture and polity require a more informed, participatory and active citizenship, and thus increase roles and challenges for education" (p. 91). A common belief among scholars–who otherwise might not agree on how to implement media studies–is that they unequivocally need implementation.

Overall, it is believed that including media studies will contribute to young people's citizenship and participation in democracy and there is a need for formalized study of the media. Participatory democracy relies on an informed citizenry. Citizens gather most of their information from the media (or, less directly, from other citizens who gather their information from the media). If citizens are not media literate, how can they be properly informed? An uninformed or complacent citizenry strengthens neoliberalism while an informed citizenry weakens neoliberalism. It is in the citizens' interest to be informed and in private enterprise's interest to keep the citizenry docile in order to seamlessly perpetuate hegemony. Many scholars have myriad concerns about implementation and intent; the massive overhaul needed demands careful exploration of broad ideas and particular details. Repeatedly, authors write that despite the quantity of media in the United States, the study of them has never been formally established (Domaille & Buckingham 2001; Furness 2007; Kellner 2002; Kellner & Share 2007; Kubey 1998; Tyner 1998). There appear many reasons why media studies are absent from the primary and secondary school curricula, including cuts in budgets and social services as well as over-packed schedules and expectations. As media change and become, on some level, more accessible to more people, they are more difficult, if not impossible, to 'contain' within classroom space and it is increasingly difficult to overcome the pressure to keep up with the latest advances in technology. The possibilities and needs are overwhelming, it feels, and the absence of media education reflects this. Media education can and does cover so much material and cuts across subjects and fields of inquiry; it is necessarily interdisciplinary. Trend (1994) writes that because of its role as an interdisciplinary subject devoted to the study of popular culture, media literacy is perceived as an "educational frill" (p. 237). Media courses and their inherent interdisciplinary quality directly challenge traditional, conservative and test-model curricula.

There are significant geographic and organizational obstacles to including media studies in the school system. State-run, local school boards with little to no federal curricular authority, covering 50 states and 3.6 million square miles "has led to greater isolation of media education in the U.S." than in other countries (Kubey 1998, p. 59). The United States has 65 million school-aged children in more than 15,000 independent school districts, resulting in a "wide disparity among various cities and states in the implementation of media education initiatives" from states or schools making significant progress to little or non-existent progress in other states or schools (Domaille & Buckingham 2001, p. 75). A key characteristic–and long-running debate in United States education–is the local organization of schools with little common conversation between them across the nation. As will be shown in Chapter Two, this not only impacts pedagogical organization, but also how to provide basic education to the nation's vast variety of learners. One reason why Great Britain has successfully implemented media education is due, in part, to their nationalized education system. This does not mean that their methods are perfect or that the United States should simply give up or blame its individual, independent ideologies. What Great Britain and the United States share is an absence of teacher training, assessment and outdated content. As Kubey points out, the United States is not particularly known for its self-reflexivity. Kubey observes the United States is "relatively isolated geographically and culturally" and engages very little foreign media product (p. 60). Without that influx of 'other' media, there is little incentive for examination and we easily succumb to the belief that the media we know are 'naturally' present.

Within schools, there is perceived to be an absence of time in the day or school year for another subject to be added. Both Kubey (1998) and Jenkins *et al.* (2006) discuss the over-full American school day. Kubey writes about curricular additions, such as "drug education, AIDS prevention, antibullying and peer support programs and computers" against which media education must compete (p. 62). While the curriculum has grown increasingly crowded, budgets across the nation in all manner of school districts have been–and continue to be–slashed dramatically, directly translating to cuts in social services and coursework deemed non-essential. When the nation is in crisis, 'essential' coursework often takes on protective proportions, arming children against dangerous outside forces that are treated as discrete elements–hence, increased health education in the face of the AIDS crisis, but no corresponding comprehensive sex or wellness education. Jenkins *et al.* (2006) posit, "much of the resistance to media literacy training springs from the sense that the school day is bursting at its seams" and they caution against media literacy as "an add-on subject" which could easily succumb to budget cuts (p. 57). Instead, they see opportunity in struggle, calling for a "paradigm shift, one that, like multiculturalism or globalization, reshapes how we teach every existing subject" (p. 57). Instead of treating media studies as an extracurricular or elective course, it helps reshape methods of teaching and expectations of the classroom and becomes fused within all subjects. Given the current economic crisis, paradigm shifts crop up in many environments as people look for new, innovative ways to solve problems and make improvements. However, as critics of neoliberalism argue, this could also be the space where private enterprise rushes in (Giroux 2007; Harvey 2005; Klein 2007). Writing about the aftermath of Hurricane Katrina, Giroux (2007) makes connections between slashes in social services and corresponding decreases in educational opportunities. He writes:

> The coupling of the market state with the racial state under Bush means that policies are aggressively pursued to dismantle the welfare states, eliminate affirmative action, model urban public schools after prisons, create further barriers for immigrants, and incarcerate with impunity Arabs, Muslims, and poor youth of color (p. 232).

In this paradigm shift, tragedy was exploited for the greater good of private enterprise. If this destructive paradigm shift was possible, there must be a way to make socially just shifts.

Beyond Fascination with Technology

In his discussion of the obstacles facing American media education integration, Kubey (1998) writes that, "Media education has yet to obtain popular support. Far more parents, for example, will say that they want their children to be computer literate than will say they want their children to be media literate" (p. 60). This introduces a major concern within media education: the focus on–indeed, fascination with–technology.

Technology education is *not* a synonym for media education, and yet, in practice it often becomes so. Trend (1994) writes that, in an effort to compete and advance, "corporate educational reformers reach for technological solutions to school problems" and warns "we should not delude ourselves that these new technologies by themselves have the capability to changing social relationships or economic structures" (p. 234). Technologies certainly contribute to new relationships, alliances and increased cultural production, but not by themselves. Technologies, by themselves, do very little. They are not neutral scientific tools, but rather grow through "the interplay of complex social, economic, and political forces" (Buckingham 2008, p. 11). There remains unanswered the question of what to *do* with technologies, which, when put into classrooms, often remain unused. Kellner (2002) argues the question is not whether computers are good or bad in the classroom or more broadly for education. Rather, a more complex series of questions needs asking:

> what useful purposes can computers serve, what sort of skills do students and teachers need to effectively deploy new media, computers and information technology, what sort of effects might they have on learning, and what new literacies, views of education and social relations do we need to democratize and improve education today? (p. 92)

An infusion of technologies has not proven to solve problems and technological prowess itself involves many unheralded skills. Computer literacy, for example, demands "refined reading, writing, research and communicating ability that involves heightened capacities for critically assessing, analyzing, interpreting, processing and storing both print-based and multimedia material" (Kellner 2002, p. 96). This cannot happen 'just' by putting computers in classrooms.

As Western, post-industrialized nations move confidently forward with digital technologies, there remain many questions about their inclusion in pedagogical conversations and action. Fascination with technology has little foundational support. Kellner and Share (2007) write that despite "significant public support," fascination with technologies "lacks a critical-analytical framework to analyze these new tools" (p. 18). The emphasis, thus far, Buckingham (2007) writes, "has largely been on providing *access*," assuming that inclusion of technology needs no corresponding education and that "now that the initial euphoria surrounding computers in schools has begun to wear thin" what young people learn from those technologies needs closer examination (p. 111, italics in original). Digital media technologies are not neutral, functional objects. Most young people are well adept at their personal use of technology and do not *need* school to access or use technology (Buckingham 2007). While it once might have been fascinating to have computers in classrooms, for many young people, personal home computers are better–and have greater, less restrictive, Internet access–than what they encounter at school. Young people navigate conflicting, contradictory messages: at home, they are experts, authorities and in control of their own activities while at school, they are automatically, instantaneously perceived incompetent and incapable of critical judgment. Jenkins *et al.* (2006), who encourage and support young people's digital media construction, do not adore the computer. They shudder at policy conversations, which, in their estimation, focus on the tools of technology rather than their vast social infiltration and the ways in which technologies participate in societal shifts. To be responsible, putting a computer in a classroom must have a purpose and clarity of mission; its presence will alter the classroom and the use of space. Furthermore, the conversation not only begins with the idea of putting a computer in a classroom, but rather must be about all the technologies, access points and fluid data that are part of the contemporary computer system.

Conclusion

To include media literacy in any capacity is to assume, on a certain level, that it *works*. Those who believe in discrete media classes assume that courses focused on analysis and production will be successful. Those who believe media studies should reframe the educational paradigm and be integrated across the curriculum believe a radical restructuring of pedagogical methodology will be successful. Those who believe in protecting children, celebrating them, or some point in between, believe their way will be successful.

But what does effective media literacy education look like? How is it known that a student is media literate? Much of the literature covered thus far spends most of its energy discussing what students need to learn to be competent, effective citizens, as activists, critical thinkers, critical consumers, or active rejectors of the media. What is missing in the inquiry thus far is what it means to be competently media literate. How is it known that a teacher is media literate enough to share the information with his/her students? How is it known that a student has learned from, but not blindly internalized, lessons in media analysis and critical inquiry? Questions of effectiveness and assessment, teacher training, and expanding notions of literacy will be shown to be conspicuously absent from young people's understanding and awareness of their own experiences with media education and will be discussed at greater length in Chapter Seven.

Given the current sociopolitical and socioeconomic environment, one might expect *less* media education in action, even if it is a primary concern among educators, which leads to the question of what role education plays in young people's lives. One major reason why media education has struggled in the United States is because our education system is in continuous struggle to identify itself and stake a claim. Ours is a country that holds great faith in education, without always a corresponding ability to articulate the parameters of that faith or why we hold it so dear.

Chapter Two examines a slice of the broad urban education environment, looking closely at significant shifts in the New York City public school system. The New York City public school system has followed a similar rocky path as media education in the United States: both are vitally important, unduly complicated, projects whose intent is to better the circumstances of its participants and open doors to critical awareness and active citizenship. Media education has no fixed location, no clear ideology and no definitive recipients; it is subject to the whims of a financial market bigger than itself. Media educators desire classes for all students – but in what capacity? The New York City public school system shares some of the muddled terrain of media education.

Currently, New York City schools are at a potential point of reflection after a massive overhaul to the system, the first of its kind in over three decades. Although the changes in the New York City public school system ostensibly embrace radical pedagogies, traditional methods, especially standardized testing, continue to flavor most new school reform. In this way, New York City schools fit within neoliberal orthodoxies that focus on private enterprise and individual responsibility. The face of new school reform in New York City is mayoral control over development of small, theme-based schools, whose changes at this point have proven to be largely rhetorical. When alternative themes, such as media studies, are the focus of a school, they are often included without cautious application and, after an initial spark, become diluted. Chapter Two's task is to explore key points of New York City's public school history and bridge this information with understandings of media education in the United States, to better understand how media education operates within one particular New York City public school.

Notes

[1] Both Canada and Australia have rich, nuanced media studies programs integrated into their primary and secondary curriculum and are global leaders in the media education movement. They are not 'left out' of this study with any malicious intent. Rather, my personal research and training has been grounded in the British model and it is what I draw from to develop a media literacy curriculum in high school, undergraduate and graduate courses.

[2] Wendy Chen provided this information, culled from January 2008 interview data with media educators based in Great Britain and textual analysis of official course materials.

[3] Bazalgette (1992) subdivides the key aspects with the following questions:

Agency: Who produced this text and why? What is the role of the producer? Who has control over the text (audience/producer)? Who else is involved in the chain of production?

Category: What sort of text is it? What difference does this sort of categorization make to the way I/the audience thinks about this text?

Technology: How was it produced? What technology is being used? How much control do I/the producers have over the technology? What technological choices are available?

Language: How do I make sense of it? What choices do I/the producer make about this text?

Audience: Who is the intended audience? In what context will they see it? What response is anticipated/hoped for?

Representation: What does it say about [the subject]? What do I/the producer want to show? What attitude is conveyed?

[4] Buckingham (2003) details the four concepts with following discussions:

Production: Media texts are consciously manufactured. Most are produced by groups of people, for commercial profit; this means there are economic interests at stake. Increasingly, questions about the global reach/impact of media must be discussed with production (local vs. foreign production and reception; use/location of geography for production).

Language: Every medium has its own combination of language that is used to communicate meaning. Verbal, written, moving images and sound languages are used in familiar codes and conventions, generally understood by audiences (even if they are unfamiliar with the particular show, they can easily figure out what it's about because of the familiarity of codes and conventions). Within language, should study meanings, conventions, codes, genres, choices, combinations, technologies. Studying language involves 'making the familiar strange' – challenge students to look at their favorite texts, or texts with which they are greatly familiar, as 'new' viewer/ reader/ listener/ player.

Representation: Production involves making events into stories, creating characters. Media representations invite us to see the world in a particular way (and restrict other views). Representations tell us that even in fantasy, we can learn about reality. When studying representation, look at: realism, telling the truth, presence and absence, bias and objectivity, stereotyping, interpretations, influences. Analyzing representations involves questions of ideologies and values.

Audiences: Involves learning how the industries operate, who they target (who they resist). Should involve self-reflection and first-hand research: students can keep 'media diaries,' compare their choices with peers, family members; brings up questions of methodology, especially validity and reliability of data gathering, social differences of media use. When studying audiences, should examine targeting, address, circulation, uses, making sense, pleasures, social differences.

[5] Similar to the BFI, the Canadian Association for Media Literacy details eight concepts, including construction, interpretation, commercial interest, ideology, language, commercial implication, social and political implication, and form and content are connected. See aml.ca/whatis for discussion of the concepts.

[6] See *'Acme Teaching Resources'* at acmecoalition.org; *'Classroom Resources'* at namle.net; *'Read, Write, Think'* at readwritethink.org and *'The Lesson Plan Library'* at medialit.org for examples.

Chapter 2

To Whom Does School Belong?
Urban Public Education and Neoliberalism

For most of American history, youth were seen as the promise of the future and school was the place where they would be guided to a socially just, civilized, intellectually productive existence as functional members of a workforce. The social construction of childhood dictated that young people be protected from the dangers of the adult world while simultaneously being better prepared for it upon age- and intellect-appropriate entry. School was seen as the primary location where these things would occur, and by the mid-20th century, more American children were going to school and staying in school for longer periods of time (Ravitch 1983; Palladino 1996). Admittedly, this romantic vision of school as the protector of childhood leaves a lot of important details out: whose children should be protected and educated? Do all children–irrespective of race, religion, economic status, geographic location or learning ability–deserve an equal education? Who is responsible for determining what should be learned and how learning should be funded? While these questions have been the subject of continuous debate over the years and no singular answer has emerged, one very clear deterrent has arisen since the late 20th century: the rise, and inclusion, of neoliberal philosophy that has significantly impacted education.

With the rise of neoliberal orthodoxies, young people are no longer an unencumbered promise of the future, but rather a threat to be contained. Neoliberalism helped strip the belief in youth as the promise of the future and reshape them as the private enterprise of the future. Specifically, young people of color from urban neighborhoods are perceived as the biggest threat. When neoliberal orthodoxies find their way into education, clear categories are created that determine who deserves what kind of education and only those already primed to succeed will do so; neoliberalism unequivocally harms the education of poor students of color, no longer providing them with a decent shot at a democratic education. According to Leistyna (2007), "educational policies and practices informed by the logic of neoliberalism" exacerbate rather than ameliorate negative social and economic conditions (p. 97). Just as an earthquake's aftershocks negatively impact those further from the epicenter, so too do the aftershocks of neoliberalism impact education and the lives of the poor. Neoliberalism, with its focus on private enterprise, capital accumulation and individual achievement in defiance of community development, is the antithesis of the radical pedagogy needed to dramatically restructure the education of the oppressed articulated by Freire (1970/2000).

In his introduction to the 30th anniversary of *Pedagogy of the oppressed*, Macedo (2000) points out that Freire continuously denounced neoliberalism throughout his writings, critiquing "the false notion of the end of history and the end of class" (p. 13). History and class cannot be eradicated by free market principles and an examination of the current state of education through neoliberal philosophy shows that history and class are now *more* prevalent. Neoliberalism impacts all sectors of society–and admittedly, aids a select few with incredible wealth–but it negatively impacts oppressed members of society, furthering their oppression and strengthening their oppressors. Neoliberalism encourages dehumanization, which, as Freire (1970/2000) writes, "is *not* a given destiny but the result of an unjust order that engenders violence in the oppressors, which in turn dehumanizes the oppressed" (p. 44, italics in original). Critical pedagogy endeavors to counter this discriminatory hierarchy, working *within* sites of oppression to understand lived experience, rather than *outside* oppression, allowing it to fester.

Neoliberalism has taken its hold in primary and secondary schools, with an increased focus on standardized testing, rigorous 'zero tolerance' security measures and increased Byzantine divisions within school systems that obfuscate the learning process. In the special issue of *Workplace: A Journal for Academic Labor* (February 2004), contributing authors Leistyna, Carlson, Aronowitz and Giroux argue against the tidal increase of neoliberal politics that negatively impact schools and the students within. Struggling students are systematically left out of an adequate educational experience; the list of things they encounter on their way to school is itself overwhelming. In his introduction to *Workplace*, Leistyna (2004) writes, "… class warfare, racism, and other oppressive and malignant ideologies that inform actual educational practices and institutional conditions play a much more significant role in students' academic achievement" than the content or evaluation in their classes (¶ 3.7). In neoliberalism, Leistyna specifies, the victim is blamed "for having a poor work ethic, being financially irresponsible, having bad family values, having little interest in education and advancement, and/or (in some genetic twist) not having the necessary smarts" (¶ 4.3). A clear example of this comes from Alonso *et al.* (2009) who do not explicitly use the word 'neoliberalism,' but do speak of its ramifications. They write, "White pundits imply that African American and Latino students *choose* to drop out because they lack educational values" (p. 5, italics in original). In their discussion of how their participants understand what constitutes a 'good' student, Alonso *et al.* (2009) share one participant's answer, "… being a 'good student' meant paying attention, doing your homework, and passing tests" (p. 136). In neoliberalism, academic success is singularly defined as the ability to pass standardized tests.

Neoliberalism has not proven to create the highly productive, highly competitive schools from the ashes of 'government funded' (i.e., public school) education that conservative economist Milton Friedman (1955) imagined. Neoliberalism offers up public education to for-profit enterprises and increases the drive for individual achievement–or failure–against community development. The result, according to Chomsky (2000), is "a general assault in the last 25 years on solidarity, democracy, social welfare, anything that interferes with private power" with education as a primary target of this assault. Chomsky argues the public education system is one premised on the principle that citizens care about the welfare of other people's children, which is currently undermined by a self-directed private power to which "everyone else has to subordinate."

Tracing the history of the urban school system, I highlight how neoliberalism is intimately woven into the thoughts on how to educate poor children of color and how it inflects all aspects of education. This chapter examines the post-World War II decline of the urban school system in the face of increased suburbanization and shows how civil discontent in 1960s New York City led to community uprisings that significantly changed the education of poor students of color. Poor black and Latino families wanted greater connection to and control of their children's education when they believed that the larger system had ignored them. Unfortunately, the protests, which began with clear intent, resulted in a murky educational environment for over three decades where poor students of color were systematically ignored. Today, New York City schools are going through another wave of change as No Child Left Behind matures, the economy falters, and the city becomes more, not less, segregated.

How did the city school system, once a model of success, fall into such seemingly irredeemable failure? I argue that neoliberalism, both implicitly in epistemology and explicitly in local and federal policy changes, helped destroy urban schooling. Education does not occur only in the classroom, but is rather part of the broader structure and organization of society and culture.

How one views education, in and out of the classroom, is analogous to how one views the responsibility of society to its most vulnerable members.

Development and Decline of the Urban School System

Pre- and Post-World War II Changes

America at the beginning of the 20th century witnessed the development of the modern metropolis, one organized by the distribution of wealth via industry. As industry developed, modern class stratification and class inequalities crystallized. America developed largely in part because of and surrounding its immigrant population, whose labor and domestic settling contributed to the development of the cities (Cremin 1988). Situated within this development was the school and its responsibility to train and educate future laborers and intellectuals. The changes in American living and working patterns inevitably impacted the development of schools and education. School and schooling took on increasing importance: more children were going to school and staying in school longer; school became the primary socializer of young people and was believed to be the route to financial security, active citizenship and the place to train young people to be adept laborers or thinkers (Cope & Kalantzis 2000; Cremin 1988; Kalantzis & Cope 2000; Palladino 1996; Ravitch 1983). The city school system was strong and the financial, staffing and curricular model against which the rural school system was seen as inadequate (Ravitch 1983). New York City schools, in particular, thrived on a legacy of success, especially the legend of attention to children of immigrants, long after they were, in practice, failing (Ravitch 1974/2000).

After World War II, the nation and its schools went through dramatic restructuring of geography and intent. Increasing numbers of Americans were living in cities and by 1950 almost two-thirds the 151 million person population lived in cities (Cremin 1988). As densely populated urban areas grew more crowded and clearly separated from the newly developing suburbs, the conversation about how to educate the poor grew increasingly pertinent. The 1945 Senate Committee on Education and Labor convened a hearing regarding a proposal for federal aid to education in part out of concern for poor districts whose families could not finance quality schools from the local taxes (Ravitch 1983). According to Ravitch (1983), inquiry into federal aid consistently faltered for three reasons: "race, religion and fear of federal control" which manifested in questions of funding segregated southern schools, who should fund religious private schools, and fears of government domination of the school system (p. 5).

'Crisis' marks much of the impetus for change in the public school system. Post-World War II population and immigration increases, especially in the city, marked the crisis of the late 1940s. Bestowed on the city school was the responsibility to "provide the social discipline essential to life amidst crowded conditions" (Cremin 1988, p. 7). Tyack (1974) writes the overwhelming worry and inquiry was "about the critical shortage of funds" and "how the cities would ever hire enough teachers and build enough schools to educate the multitude of children born during the war" (p. 269).

1960s: Urban Unrest

A third, ultimately successful, school model entered the conversation soon after World War II and by the 1960s, the city school lagged significantly behind the success of the suburban school. According to Tyack (1974), this lag occurred because cities "contained a disproportionate number of the old, the poor and the unemployed" (p. 278). Industries whose labor needs had helped build cities prior to World War II were now themselves branching out to the suburbs, leaving city labor needs depleted. The suburban school system has since been the pinnacle against which urban and rural schools are unfavorably and unsuccessfully compared (Anderson & Summerfield 2004). The city school grew overcrowded, there was little maintenance or upkeep, its teachers grew tired and uninspired, and its predominantly black and Latino students grew increasingly poor (Anderson & Summerfield 2004; Anyon 1997; Goldstein 2004; Podair 2002; Ravitch 1974/2000).

The 1960s marked the time when New York City public schools' enrollment became majority black and Latino and the schools were failing these students of color. By the mid-1960s, according to Podair (2002), black students constituted 30% of public school students "but earned only 2.3 percent of the academic diplomas" (p. 154). Black and Latino students together made up more than 50% of the public school population (Ravitch 1974/2000). Black and Latino students continue to represent the majority population of New York City public schools and contemporary schools are socially and geographically segregated (Orfield & Lee 2005). By 2004, 73% of African American students and 77% of Latino students attended majority nonwhite schools while only 12% of white students attended majority nonwhite schools (Alonso et al. 2009).

Though urban schools claimed to be 'color blind,' they were not wholly successful and majority black and Latino schools were both failing and ignored. In 1957, the first ethnic census of the school system shed light on the deplorable treatment of poor students of color (Ravitch 1974/2000). Fully embracing the *law* of desegregation, neighborhood schools remained socially and geographically segregated. Kenneth Clark, a psychology professor at City College, saw the results of the census and "charged that the New York City school system was maintaining segregated schools where Negro children received inferior education" (Ravitch 1974/2000, p. 251). The new face of segregation was found in the neighborhoods and communities where the majority population was of color. In New York City, the frustration and anger over the treatment of young people of color grew over the decade after the census, culminating in a series of changes that would dramatically alter the school system as a whole.

NYC Points of Transition

Ocean Hill–Brownsville and the Process of Decentralization: 1967-1970

One the most dramatic shifts in the history of the New York City public school system were the Ocean Hill-Brownsville strikes of 1968-1969 that led to the decentralization of New York City's massive public school system. The seeds of the strike are undoubtedly found in the public revelation of the deplorable treatment of poor black and Latino students and the failed promises of *Brown v. Board* (1954) and the Civil Rights Acts (1964). *Legal* desegregation, it was soon realized, did not make schools better for poor children of color and the Civil Rights Movement did not end racism. What was law on paper did not automatically translate to changed beliefs or behaviors and no one felt that more acutely than those for whom the law was to protect. Riots in the summer of 1964 and 1965 expressed discontent at deplorable conditions in living, working and education environments. In 1966, the New York City Board of Education released reading scores for the entire city for the first time "and most reading failure was concentrated in ghetto schools" (Ravitch 1974/2000, p. 309). Poor students lived and went to school in poor neighborhoods with poorly funded, inadequate, overcrowded schools, revealing a citywide geographic segregation. Well-meaning liberal white families who supported desegregation and the Civil Rights Movement did so with the luxury of knowledge that their children would not be unduly impacted. Full racial integration in schools was deemed impossible because white families did not want to send their children into dilapidated schools and, by the mid-1960s, the population of black and Latino students was well over 50%, so there were not enough white students to equally balance the numbers (Orfield & Lee 2005; Ravitch 1974/2000). The dilemma remained: parents in poor neighborhoods wanted better educations for their children and in unveiling dilapidated schools, wanted greater connections to and control over the process of schooling. Parents who wanted greater involvement in their community schools believed there was more than one way to educate children and believed community schooling should draw from all of the community's offerings.

School officials and experts also pondered the need for change in what was becoming an unwieldy school system. The thread of inquiry within the Board of Education, circa 1967, focused on decentralization, which, ostensibly, would give more control to local communities. In April 1967, the Board of Education (1969) declared:

> All members of our board are committed to the principle of decentralization of operations. In a city as large and varied as New York, we believe it is essential to have as much flexibility and authority at the local level as is consistent with our need for centralized standards (p. 17).

Decentralization, it was believed, would give more control to district superintendents, principals and local school boards and community involvement. What seemed like a good idea initially had disastrous results that impacted the school system and its most vulnerable constituents for over three decades.

Between 1967-1968, parents whose children attended segregated schools began to gather to protest poor school conditions. These gatherings occurred around the city, especially in Harlem, the Lower East Side and Ocean Hill-Brownsville. Ocean Hill-Brownsville, a particularly dilapidated part of Brooklyn, was situated between predominantly white neighborhoods and for two years families had been without representation because the white communities had all the seats on the local school boards (Podair 2002). Literacy rates and school attendance in Ocean Hill-Brownsville were decreasing while dropout rates were increasing. The school buildings in the community were deemed unsafe. The community wanted to make change, believing there was more than one 'correct' way to educate children and poor children of color deserved a solid education (McCoy 1969).

When the Ocean Hill-Brownsville families gathered together, they created their own board to plan the takeover of their schools. This board was made up of parents–primarily mothers, with little formal education themselves–who challenged the school professionals' assessments and argued against black and Latino families being educated and judged by white standards. Teachers were opposed to community control and especially what they deemed the unauthorized parent board in Ocean Hill-Brownsville. The parents wanted respect from the teachers, but there was significant, seemingly irreparable, miscommunication between each party's desire, intent and perceived treatment (Podair 2002). An underlying tension was the belief among teachers that the black and Latino families were anti-Semitic and a corresponding belief among black and Latino families that the teachers were racist (Podair 2002; Ravitch 1974/2000).

Rhody McCoy, a long-time New York City public school educator and principal, was appointed the unit administrator of the board, which oversaw the eight schools in the community (McCoy 1969; Podair 2002). The Teachers Union deemed both the board and McCoy's position as unit administrator illegal. McCoy, however, supported the parent board and accepted the position because he saw the opportunity for intervention in what had become a catastrophic educational environment for poor black and Latino children. McCoy believed white values prevailed in formal conversations, a standard to which poor children of color were unable to achieve; there was no respect for the poor family of color's values or for work done to improve communities from within. Speaking of the alienated community at the Harvard Educational Conference (January 1968), McCoy stated:

> In Ocean Hill-Brownsville, there are people groping in the dark; they are people who for a long time have felt themselves outside the mainstream of public concern. The city takes no notice of them. These people are obscure, unnoticed–as though they do not exist. They are not censured or reproached; they simply are not seen. They are the invisible residents of a demoralized, poverty-ridden inner city. To be ignored or overlooked is a denial of one's rights to dignity, respect, and membership in the human race. These residents have been frustrated at every turn in their attempt to reverse the process (p. 52).

Both the desire and need for change were palpable, but action and implementation were unclear.

School strikes were threatened or occurred in various parts of New York City throughout 1968. Throughout New York City and beyond, massive feelings of unrest and anger were on the rise, particularly in the wake of the assassinations of Martin Luther King, Jr. and Bobby Kennedy. More than ten years since *Brown* and four years since the Civil Rights Act little had changed, other than making the situation for poor families of color more obvious and more awful. Teachers felt their authority and expertise were inappropriately challenged. The first strikes in Brooklyn occurred in the spring of 1968 and by the time the school year ended, "students had missed almost 7 weeks of school" and disputes between the Teachers Union and the Ocean Hill-Brownsville parent board were unresolved (Ravitch 1974/2000, p. 362). Parents felt their children's education remained in jeopardy while teachers bristled at racist labels pinned to them. In the fall of 1968, teachers returned to school and immediately went on strike; indeed, almost all of September was struck (Ravitch 1974/2000). According to McCoy (1969), who clearly favored community rights, and the New York Civil Liberties Union (1969), who monitored the strikes, the cause of the strike in the fall of 1968 was the angry, reactionary Teachers Union. The New York Civil Liberties Union favored decentralization and community control as a way to give "ghetto communities equal access to the process of making decisions vitally affecting the education of their children" (p. 104). After September 1968, students went back to school, teachers went back to work, and there was an uneasy rest as the Board of Education initiated the formal process of decentralization (Advisory & Evaluation Committee on Decentralization 1969). There was no clear victory for either side.

By 1969, New York City public schools were decentralized, but still chaotic. The Board of Education was made up of seven people, appointed by six different elected officials: Two by the mayor and one by each borough president. Control of the schools was divided between a central administration, who oversaw all high schools, and community school boards who selected district superintendents and principals. The central administration regulated budgets, staffing and resources (Ravitch 1974/2000). It was an undeniably complicated system that would remain in place, with little official change or clarity, for 34 years.

As the largest public school system in the nation, the decentralization of New York City schools was believed to influence urban school districts and political perspectives across the country. Berube and Gittell (1969) comment:

> on trial were some of our most cherished concepts: politically, the public's right to determine the policy and course of education; educationally, the moral imperative to pro-

vide quality education for all in publicly supported schools; and socially, the egalitarian ideal of a just, interracial society (p. 3).

The Ocean Hill-Brownsville crisis illuminated the role of the community in schooling, the irreparable division between 'expert' and parent and the awareness that for a black or Latino person to succeed, they would need to embrace white, middle-class values, essentially an impossible task. Contrasting egalitarian theories of public education for all, Tyack (1974) writes, "the ghetto parent saw that his child's school was segregated, that he had little voice in determining school policies, and that his child would graduate woefully ill-prepared to compete in a complex technological society" (p. 284). Born of–but ultimately devastated by–the Ocean Hill-Brownsville crisis was the desire for community control and significant participation in the supposedly democratic process. What poor black and Latino families made public was their rejection of white middle-class standards as the singular correct model of pedagogy.

The ideal of community schools was to draw from the best and most relevant parts of the community and bring that to the classroom. Decentralization was less than ideal, and in it can be seen the seeds of neoliberal educational philosophy. Neoliberalism demands attention to the individual and privatization of industry; it denies community activism or connection to the democratic process. Unfortunately, the process of decentralization served neoliberalism more than it served communities in this situation. Writing on the desire for community control, Berube and Gittell (1969) comment:

> If school professionals succeed in halting the political drive of the black communities, we can anticipate the end of public education. Most probably, the energies of the black and white underclass would be redirected toward establishing alternative forms of school systems that are more attuned to their needs (p. 6).

Decentralization in practice *did* halt the political drive of the black communities with the development of the labyrinth Board of Education where there was little clarity in negotiations and, because of its complex web, little to no place to locate responsibility or make change.

The In-between Years: 1970-2002

For roughly 34 years, the largest public school system in the country saw no significant changes, other than an increased segregation within schools and decreased equality for poor black and Latino students. Throughout this time, individual schools, school administrators, and board members made small, independent changes, largely beyond the official purview of the Board of Education. What most clearly categorized these 34 years were individual, independent changes; absent a structural overhaul of the system, individuals made changes for a finite number of students. Far from rejecting neoliberalism, these changes unintentionally supported neoliberalism: when individuals made changes, the system could easily abdicate responsibility.

The Board of Education's clear points of failure were bolstered by individual initiative and outside funding. In the 1980s, Schools Chancellor Joseph A. Fernandez engaged in small school experiments, believing that most New York City high schools were "too big to be effective" (Ravitch 1974/2000, p. *xxvi*). More than 100 schools, with enrollment capped at 500 students, were established and received waivers enabling individual administrations to select faculty and control curricula and grade promotion guidelines. Small schools were believed more likely to succeed because more intimate, direct relationships could form between teachers, staff and students. In 1994, New York City received a $100 million grant "to replace some of the city's larger, overcrowded neighborhood schools with 50 small, experimental schools" (Celis 1994). Some of the small schools were opened with "unusual collaborations," including sponsorship by "educational reformers working with organizations like community groups, colleges, churches and even a labor unit" (Gonzalez 1995).

Any discussion of individual attention, smaller schools and more money inevitably turns to Deborah Meier, the principal of the Central Park East Secondary School (CPESS), long heralded as a small school success story. CPESS had a 90% graduation rate when Meier was in charge, more than double the city rate (Celis 1994). Tyner-Mullings's (2008) analysis of CPESS shows that at its inception, it had fewer than 600 students in grades 7-12, making it one of the smallest schools in the city. The curriculum emphasized critical inquiry, group work and portfolio rather than test evaluation. CPESS "represented not only an alternative approach to education, but a shining example of the possibility of social change" (Tyner-Mullings p. 3). Meier's model and success were not easily replicated by those with less educational experience, less tenacity for fundraising, the attention of fewer influential individuals, and less focused drive. CPESS was not self-sustaining without Meier and when she departed the school, its success declined and the "institution that once developed the premiere alternative pedagogical philosophy ... has maintained very few, if any, aspects of this alternative approach" (p. 4). Tyner-Mullings determines that the school suffered from "problems of succession and isomorphism, as well as goal displacement, role conflict and the dispersion of CPESS faculty, staff, students and parents to the new schools that the CPESS model created space for" (p. 4). Passionate and effective teachers and staff under Meier's guidance did not operate as proficiently without her when they set out to start their own schools.

What is learned from CPESS and the intervening decades after decentralization is that individual efforts by those with a great deal of experience and the tenacity to navigate the school system can result in highly successful schools for selections of New York City youth. Neoliberalism 'won' by showing that a manipulated, highly dysfunctional form of 'community control' had failed. Private control would rescue the community from itself. By 2002, with the election of Mayor Michael Bloomberg, the presidency of George W. Bush and an increased interest in standardized tests, the city was primed for recentralization and a more organized effort to implement neoliberal principles.

Mayoral Control: 2002-Present

The takeover of the school system by Mayor Michael Bloomberg grew from one of his main campaign promises and was initiated by shutting down the Board of Education and replacing it with the Department of Education (Goodnough 2001, 2002; Hartocollis 2002; Steinhauer March, 2002). The 2002 change marked the point when, on a large scale, factory-style comprehensive schools began to be systematically dismantled and replaced with small, theme-based schools. Schools with reputations for significant drug, crime, high dropout and high teacher turnover problems were targeted. It was also supposed to represent a shift from obtuse bureaucracies to a seamless structure. Bloomberg and his appointees did not come from political or pedagogic backgrounds, but rather from business and corporate environments; they were men with little to no experience in the classroom (Goodnough 2003; Hartocollis 2002). Bloomberg's focus on radical change were undoubtedly inspired from the small, under-the-radar changes during the 34 years of decentralization.

Many politicians before Bloomberg wanted control of the school system, but he was the first with such a rapid succession. Quickly into his first term, with the city still reeling from the September 11th terrorist attacks, the questions began whether Bloomberg would capitalize on his campaign promise to overhaul the school system; after five months of negotiations with the Board of Education and seven months in office, he took over the school system. The timeline of events reads remarkably quickly, given the unwieldy bureaucracy that exemplifies New York City public schools and the following discussion draws primarily from *The New York Times*' chronicle of Bloomberg's takeover and significant shifts in staffing. Within two weeks of taking office, Bloomberg scheduled a lunch with Schools Chancellor Harold Levy to "discuss pressing issues in the school system" (Goodnough 2001). A *New York Times* opinion piece stated "New York's political leaders are finally ready to begin streamlining the city's unmanageable school system" and observes that mayoral takeover would either make the schools successful or make it very clear where to locate blame (*'Mayor Bloomberg's Public Schools,'* 2002).

Bloomberg's desire was full control of schools, the power to appoint–and fire, if needed–a Chancellor, to dismantle the ossified Board of Education, and to have parents and communities more involved in their neighborhood schools. Bloomberg never appeared to doubt that he would gain control of the schools (Steinhauer March, 2002). By early June 2002, then-Governor Pataki agreed to Bloomberg's terms and, within a week of the first tentative agreement, signed the changes into law (Goodnough June, 2002; Steinhauer June, 2002). The consensus was that decentralization was not working and its confusion had "provoked near constant infighting and hidden the blame for the city's failings" (Goodnough June, 2002). The Department of Education would have a 13-person board, of which Bloomberg would appoint eight members and a 20-member task force was formed to devise replacement plans for the 32 community school boards (Steinhauer June, 2002).

While then-Schools Chancellor Levy could have stayed in his appointment through December 2002, he resigned in August after Bloomberg appointed publishing executive and lawyer Joel Klein. A *New York Times* opinion piece comments on Levy's graceful exit–a rarity in the New York City political machinery–and defends the outgoing Chancellor whose establishment of peace with the Mayor's office "was an achievement in itself" (*'Chancellor Levy Exits,'* 2002). Bloomberg's changes, it is implied, will be seen through the lens of history as beginning with Levy, who had begun to streamline the Board of Education bureaucracy, helped increase the number of certified teachers, recruited non-teachers into education, improved teacher contracts and increased summer school programs (*'Chancellor Levy Exits,'* 2002; Goodnough August, 2002). In contrast, Klein had minimal education experience. He studied education "for a bit" and taught math to sixth graders in Queens before joining the Army Reserve (Steinhauer July, 2002). Klein was most well known as lead counsel on the antitrust prosecution of Microsoft, run by Bill Gates, whose eponymous foundation has given New York City public schools a significant amount of money.

By August 2002, *The New York Times* was questioning whether the looming school year would feel any different and that question continues to be asked. Steinhauer (August, 2002) writes, "Now that the Department of Education is one of the Mayor's agencies, rather than a whipping post, parents may be moved to think that their schools are working better right away, if for no other reason than that City Hall will stop telling them how awful they are." In the seven years since Bloomberg took over the school system, precious little has actually changed. While he has created more small schools, they are often opened within the space of already existing larger high schools, therefore not diminishing overcrowded conditions (Gootman 2003). New York City schools are increasingly segregated and schools established with special, attractive educational opportunities draw young people out of their communities rather than working on integration and betterment within the community (Robinson 2004). Graduation rates have increased but critics question whether it is because smaller schools enroll fewer special education or special needs students (Herszenhorn 2006) and more students are being discharged or directed to GED programs than graduation (Gotbaum November, 2002). Fast-track intensive principal training programs put more individuals in schools, but with less educational experience who are often overwhelmed by the responsibilities and not trusted by their faculty (Gootman & Gebeloff 2009). As Mayor Bloomberg focused on re-writing term laws to garner a third term in office, he forgot about the school system and in July 2009 did not renew his own mayoral control law. Communities and parents expressed discontent in a space where there is no official control (Barbaro 2009; Fertig 2009; Hernandez 2009; Sulzberger 2009). While he rapidly fixed this oversight, its occurrence and his contested, vituperative third-term bid illustrated significant fault lines in his heretofore seamless control.

Urban Concerns: How to Educate Poor Students of Color?

At no point in history has the education of the urban poor been an easy task; the majority of New York City youth in the public school system are from poor families of color and despite being part of the largest public school system in the nation, are easily forgotten. For myriad reasons, city schools cannot and do not follow the successful suburban school model. City school systems are racist and classist and were so at a moment in time–post-*Brown*, post-Civil Rights legislation–when, as seen through the lens of history, they could have made significant beneficial changes. Deconstructing the ramifications of Ocean Hill-Brownsville, Berube and Gittell (1969) comment, "The failure of city schools to educate a predominantly black population is a national disgrace ... Most of America's schools function behind a curtain of ignorance" (p. 3). Poverty and race are inextricably linked in the urban school system, especially when institutional racism and classism enable options for wealthier, white families. Families within impoverished communities are acutely aware of their environments and are often eager to make change, though their requests often go unheeded. When it was made clear that education was not fulfilling the expectations of the Civil Rights Movement, especially desegregation of schools, families and communities lost faith in schools.

Educating the poor inevitably involves confronting issues of racism. The schools attended by poor young people of color "are woefully inadequate" diminishing their chances to attend university and increasing their social and economic exclusion (Fine, Bloom & Chajet 2003, p. 14). Contemporary, modern-day racism is not an overt binary opposition between two forces, one significantly more powerful–and more willing to engage that power in negative ways–than another. Modern racism is less about direct, obvious displays of hatred based on one's skin color and more about an unwillingness or inability to think and operate with race as a still-significant social construct. Modern racism is subtle and therefore insidious, written into policies that dismantle social systems (often while claiming to heal them) and denying multicultural perspectives.

'Racenicity,' which bridges race and ethnicity as interconnected social constructs, is a term Leistyna (1999) constructs to frame contemporary racism. Racenicity is the "result of the antagonistic social relations caused by the unequal distribution of power throughout society along racial lines. It is the product and driving force of an ideology in which 'whiteness' ... has been a socio-politically and institutionally sanctioned marker of status in the United States" (p. 66). Racenicity does not imply that whites are without ethnicity, but rather are "for the most part, not only unconscious of the ideologies of power relations that shape and reproduce racialized patterns but also unable to clearly and profoundly define what those patterns are and why exactly it is they hold so tightly to them..." (p. 77). White people no longer need to *intend* to be racist or be explicit in their racism, they simply need to be ignorant of their invisible privilege and its ensuing unwritten benefits to perpetuate contemporary racism (*cf* King 2007; Lipsitz 1998).

A major impetus for the education of the poor is to provide methods for escaping poverty. The current urban education system does not adequately provide these methods. Urban schools, who educate one-third of the nation's youth, continue to be racially segregated, receive fewer financial resources than corresponding suburban schools and are believed to be the worst schools in the nation (Alonso *et al.* 2009; Anyon 1997; Goldstein 2004; Greene 1988; Noguera 2003; Orfield & Lee 2005). Noguera (2003) observes the children of economic and social privilege are given more while "we provide substantially less to those with the greatest needs and relegate them to the least desirable schools." The threads of invisible privilege travel far. Often, young people in urban environments have family and work priorities that contribute more immediately to their short-term survival than the long-term benefits of sustained education and school cannot always be their first priority (Goldstein 2004). Yet these students, who cannot prioritize school, are injured for prioritizing survival. Kalantzis and Cope (2000) write, "Undeniably, you get a better education if you are wealthier; if you speak the national language; if you belong to the most powerful ethnic group; if you live in the right neighborhood or the right country; of if you are a male" (p. 122). Superior education should be made available to all bodies, irrespective of social or economic situation; anything less is hypocritical and an insult to democracy.

School Reform

The list of topics under the broad umbrella of 'reform' feels infinite. There are concerns with curriculum and defining the pedagogical goal of school or with access to school by students and communities of different race, gender or economic class (Freire 1970/2000; Kliebard 1995; Grant & Murray 1999; Greene 1988; Tyack 1974; Zimmerman 2002). There are concerns over where reform should originate, ranging from individual curricula to the larger communities in which schools are located, or to movements toward nationalized curricula (Anyon 1997; Dillon 2008; Greene 1988; Lewin 2008). Some scholars argue that schools themselves are sources of continuous oppression (Greene 1988; Hill 2004; Yonezawa & Wells 2005). There is a continuous, conservative desire for increased standardized testing and a reemergence of a traditional, classics- and skills-based curriculum (Kilpatrick 1992; Sykes

1995) bolstered by federal policy in the name of No Child Left Behind (NCLB) (Aronowitz 2004; Giroux 2004; Leistyna 2004, 2007). Liberal scholars point out that the conservative position on standardized tests, NCLB and neoliberal policies fail students more consistently than they develop them (Aronowitz 2004; Carlson 2004; Giroux 2003, 2004, 2008; Leistyna 2004, 2007). While President Obama's Race To the Top initiative works to counter some of the high-stakes stringency of NCLB, it is as yet untested. Its name alone and its financial awards based on improvement are redolent of neoliberalism's emphasis on hyperindividualized competition (*Remarks by the President on Education* 2009).

School reform is not found in isolation, but rather within communities that have expressed discontent or demanded change, though the reform that is asked for is not necessarily the reform that occurs. Contemporary reform is inevitably linked–either in support or rejection–to neoliberal philosophy. Anyon's (1997) adroit analysis of the Newark, New Jersey school system shows the disastrous decline of the schools was in lock-step with an equally disastrous decline of community. Anyon argues that until politics, economics and cities work together, "educational reformers have little chance of effecting long-lasting educational changes in city schools" (p. 13). Both Giroux (2004) and Aronowitz (2004) are concerned with the long-term impact of educational bias against the urban poor. In the current geo-political environment of terrorism and genocide, Giroux (2004) constructs urban school reform as a metaphor for war where the children in most need of schooling are destroyed by the system. The "chronic state of crisis" of American education is exemplified in the increased importance of standardized testing which bolsters strict and harmful class distinctions through its punishment of those who cannot conform to the appropriate ideology (Aronowitz 2004, ¶ 1.3).

The current face of New York City reform developed out of Bloomberg's changes first started in 2002. The changes include the re-organization of the structure of the school system; adherence to federal movements including vouchers and NCLB; and increasingly, concerns with security, overcrowding and graduation expectations as ways to funnel young people through the system. All these changes connect to neoliberalism and its emphasis on the individual and private enterprise.

Small Schools

The variety of New York City schools range from selective, academically competitive programs to specialized programs designed to help students with acute needs. Small schools, representing grades 9-12, "enroll about 500 students and provide classes designed to ensure that all students meet high standards and graduate" (New York City Department of Education, *Choices*). There is little to no discussion on *how* these schools are 'designed to ensure' standards and graduation rates; tautologically, small schools are believed to be inherently better than large schools *because* they are small.

While the idea of small schools is profound, the reality of them is problematic. As part of the development of small schools, principals were given greater autonomy and personal discretion on how to spend their allocated dollars[1]. The reputation of small schools–where more money is spent on instruction rather than administration–may be undeserved. According to the National Center for Educational Statistics, "the percentage of expenditure on instruction is virtually identical regardless of the geography and demography of school" (cited in Anderson & Summerfield 2004, p. 32). Because school budgets are based on the number of students, small schools equal small budgets, irrespective of *how* the money is spent.

Real estate is at a premium in New York City and the new small schools were moved into floors, hallways, or specific classrooms in already-structured and sometimes still-occupied school buildings. The idea that students would be grouped into close-knit communities is dismantled when they enter and exit a school building with thousands of other students, with whom they are not allowed contact. From the outside, passersby see no difference in structure.

As part of the construction of these small schools, curricula and pedagogy were formed around themes that were to be integrated into the curriculum. Theme-based education was believed to focus student learning and provide an accessible entry point to otherwise unfamiliar material. The themes cut across a variety of philosophies and subjects. Some themes, such as math or arts and letters, easily fit into the broader graduation requirements of the public schools; more esoteric themes, such as sports, environmental studies, law and justice, or media studies are more difficult to integrate with traditional subject matter. In theory, the themes are strong ideas and may provide young people with non-traditional educations that combat the negative environments in which they were raised. However, schools with themes are not exempt from expected course completion and there are no official training or professional development programs for teachers to instruct them on how to incorporate the theme into their curricula. Furthermore, there is no teaching certification for non-traditional subject matter, which means schools must make a choice to have non-licensed teachers in the classroom, to not have courses specific to their theme, or to have teachers untrained in the theme teaching classes. Because the autonomy of small schools is encouraged, they are subject to the twists and turns of neoliberalism; if a small school fails, it is the school's fault, not the structure where the school is found.

Vouchers

Increased frustration with broad-scale school inequalities led people to look for alternative methods. Vouchers, initially proposed in 1955 by Milton Friedman, in his essay *'The role of government in education'* were first tested in the 1970s, under the Nixon administration. According to Friedman (1955), a government that paid for its schools was treading dangerously close to socialism and the best way to make American schools strong was to privatize the entire system, give parents choice of where to send their children and encourage competition to make schools better. He writes:

> Governments could require a minimum level of education which they could finance by giving parents vouchers, redeemed for a specific maximum sum per child per year if spent on 'approved' educational services … the role of the government would be limited to assuring that the schools met certain minimum standards such as the inclusion of a minimum common content in their programs, much as it now inspects restaurants to insure that they maintain minimum sanitary standards (pp. 4-5).

In neoliberal education, the government plays the role of inspector and schools become private enterprises. Vouchers are, quite literally, the ticket out of struggling communities.

Though Friedman is most well known for his radically conservative economic policies that helped bring to fruition neoliberal orthodoxies of modern government and foreign policy, he clung to his belief of privatized education throughout his public career (1995, 2002, 2005). Most abhorrently, he capitalized on Hurricane Katrina's August 2005 physical destruction of the deeply troubled New Orleans school system as a way to start a 'clean-slate' project in large-scale privatized schooling (Klein 2007). Defenders of Friedman argue that his plan is especially helpful for poor students because, as William F. Buckley, Jr. (June 2005) writes, "competition inevitably encourages quality and students who are free to opt for alternative schooling would flock to do so," speaking of students as some sort of eager wild pack animals.

Vouchers are a deceptive entry into neoliberal philosophy. School choice and enabling parents to send their children to successful, highly functioning schools sounds like a good plan; on the surface, it sounds like democracy in action. No parent would willingly, eagerly send their children to unsafe, failing schools. In reality, vouchers encourage parents to make a choice between participating in, or giving up on, their communities and, in choosing vouchers, invite their continuous subservience to capital enterprise. While Friedman (1955) had a specific vision for vouchers as a way to privatize education, Tyack (1974) constructs a more complicated terrain where vouchers may be seen as an empowered solution in the face of disillusionment. Parents in struggling communities who wanted a better future for their children saw school as a site of change and wanted greater connections to and control over their neighborhood schools. Angered and disillusioned at their lack of control, parents wanted radical change and were well aware there were better schools in (nearby) better neighborhoods. Post-Civil Rights disillusionment and despair led many parents to "question both the ideology and the institution of public education" (p. 270). Teachers, too, were dissatisfied with work and school conditions and personal and professional disillusionment culminated in social unrest and grasps for change. Tyack writes that by the 1970s, teachers, students and families were frustrated with the state of education and "people on both ends of the ideological spectrum began to propose basic alternative structures of schooling," vouchers among them, to make change (p. 272). The voucher system was a solution developed out of frustration.

Milwaukee, Wisconsin has the longest running large-scale voucher program, in operation since 1990, and stands as a model both for other cities and for critics of the voucher system, who see Milwaukee's experiment as a dismal failure. Voucher schools divert money from public schools to pay for testing, assessment, school choice procedures and a slew of other plans and remedies that have not actually contributed to school betterment, and in fact, have contributed to the continuous decline of the public school system (Aronowitz 2004; Giroux 2003, 2004). Barbara Miner, writing regularly in *Rethinking Schools*, is a fierce opponent to the voucher system who counters both Friedman and neoliberalism's cheering of school choice and vouchers.

She writes, "conservatives have spinned vouchers as a way to increase achievement for low income families" but this does not actually happen (February 2002). In Milwaukee, voucher schools "receive public dollars but operate as private schools" and are not required to provide services for special education or special needs students (Winter 2003). Miner believes that the promise of competition is unmet and because voucher schools do not have to follow public school guidelines, can hire uncertified teachers and do not have to release student data achievement, therefore making them publicly unaccountable (Fall 2005).

No Child Left Behind and Testing

The 2001 educational initiative, NCLB, set forth by President Bush, put in motion a well-organized method of neoliberalism. In the spirit of 'compassionate conservatism,' NCLB increased state grade- and standard-promotion tests, held teachers and schools accountable for significant improvement with the promise of more money for success and the threat of decreased funds in the absence of improvement, and made it federally legal for parents to remove their children from struggling neighborhood schools and transfer them to more successful schools. Through NCLB, "standardized curricula and high stakes testing have been officially embraced as the panacea of academic underachievement in public schools in the United States" (Leistyna 2007, p. 98). Aronowitz (2004) writes that standardized tests "are the antithesis of critical thought," where students are taught to "regurgitate information and to solve problems according to prescribed algorithms" (¶ 1.4). Under NCLB, "marginalized urban youth will get left behind and locked out of opportunities for developing their fuller potential" according to Carlson (2004) because the reform "includes steep and continuing cuts in financial support to urban schools" (¶ 1.1).

Poor black and Latino students are disproportionately hurt by NCLB in various ways. While NCLB claimed to be about 'choice' and 'flexibility' for the 'neediest children,' Fine *et al.* (2003) find those words put to action the "cruel betrayals" of the children it was supposed to serve most (p. 12). Mashburn and Weaver (2007) argue NCLB's "premise and primary elements are contradictory" (p. 560). Students in struggling schools who could not compete with privileged schools are punished if they do not improve *enough*. The message is that these students not only are not good enough, their efforts will not *be* good enough. NCLB federally sanctions the removal of children from their communities and neighborhoods, fostering the idea that their communities are bad and are unable to be fixed. NCLB systematically undoes work done within and on behalf of communities, deletes civic participation and public debate and encourages individual enterprise. NCLB is a large step towards increased privatization and dismantled social services. In effect, Bush used the rhetoric of improving the education of the poor as a smokescreen to further disempower the poor.

NCLB opens the doors to increased inclusion of and dependence on testing. A school hobbled by NCLB has little room or flexibility for any curriculum that does not involve testing or test preparation. Increased testing becomes the measurement of intellectual competence and school success. This "mechanical approach" to education "has focused primarily on the transfer of skills from the instructor to the student through mindless drills and rote memorization of selected 'facts' that can easily be measured by standardized testing" (Leistyna 1999, p. 7). Testing trains the student–and the school–in non-creative, non-inquiry based 'learning' and further trains teachers to be data managers. Increased testing forms teachers and schools into factories churning out automatons. Giroux (2003) writes testing has "become the new ideological weapon in developing standardized curricula that ignore cultural diversity by defining knowledge narrowly in terms of discrete skills and decontextualized bodies of information, ruthlessly expunging the language of ethics from the broader purpose of teaching and schooling" (p. 88). Bowing to the pressures and expectations of standardized testing, "many school administrators have been forced to drastically narrow their curriculum and cut back on anything and everything that is perceived as not contributing to raising test scores" (Giroux 2003, p. 99). Foreign language, arts, sports, and alternative extracurricular work are cut, education is reframed as 'back to the basics' and struggling students who may need extra help or alternative teaching methods are discarded (Giroux 2003; Leistyna 1999). Increased testing piles federal tests onto state tests, onto achievement tests, onto placement tests, all of which put great pressure on students whose schools do not or cannot adequately prepare them for such testing. However, in the spirit of neoliberalism, testing conditions students to believe there is one, single path to academic success. Alonso *et al.* (2009) share one participant's assertion that "listening to the teacher, taking notes, doing homework, and passing tests are characteristics of being a 'good student'" (p. 123). Demurring to the invisible power of neoliberalism, this student has learned that if he cannot follow this route, it is his fault. A one-size-fits-all educational model where the two options are participate or perish flourishes.

Testing is not an infallible measure of improving schools and while tests are not creative, their results can be creatively measured. Noguera (2003) writes that rising test scores do not unequivocally mean schools or students are improving but rather, schools train "teachers to teach test-taking skills and by limiting the curriculum to material that would be covered on the tests." More disturbing, Noguera (2003) observes that schools raise test scores "simply by pushing out the neediest students who were likely to bring their scores down." Standardized tests measure rudimentary, socially sanctioned 'correct' knowledge that generally reflects middle class values and statistically guarantees that half of test takers will always be below average (Giroux 2003; Leistyna 1999; Miner February, 2001).

Increased Security

An unproven, yet increasingly adopted, method of control of youth is increased security and surveillance in the form of metal detectors, police presence and closed-circuit cameras. As such, schools–especially those in disenfranchised areas–begin to look and operate like prisons and students are actively denied any civil rights when their bodies, possessions and movements are subject to constant scrutiny (Cassidy 2002; Giroux 2003; Goodman 2003). An increasing number of arrests in schools for disciplinary infractions or suspected criminal behavior reveal both racism and the stripping of authority from school officials in favor of police officials (Cassidy 2002; Lewin 2003; Rimer 2004). Students of color and students attending schools in impoverished neighborhoods are disproportionately targeted by searches, arrests, and harshly disciplined by law enforcement rather than school officials (Advancement Project 2005; Miller 1996; Polakow 2000; Polakow-Suransky 2000; Rivera, Huezo, Kasica & Muhammad 2009).

In response to the Columbine shootings (1999), increased security in schools was given greater support, or, at the very least, resigned acceptance. The belief that schools are growing increasingly violent is, in reality, not the case and reactionary responses to school violence do little to actually address the root causes of violence and discontent (Noguera 2000, 2004). Noguera (2000) observes that violence controlled through the removal of individuals "treats violence as a form of individual deviance that can be rooted out through punitive and exclusionary measures" (p. 133). Treating youth violence with violent measures does not curb or heal violence but rather teaches young people that authoritative violence is acceptable and in so doing, may actually reinforce violent behaviors. Symbols of violence–metal detectors, security cameras, uniformed police officers, locked doors–are lessons in acceptable violence, not deterrents, and teach students they are already guilty (Noguera 2000). School safety *is* important and no student *wants* to attend an unsafe school. But who determines safety? 'Zero tolerance' policies in schools are the "easiest route" to safety (Advancement Project 2005) but there is little to no evidence they increase the safety or security for students (Advancement Project; Polakow-Suranksy 2000).

In New York City, School Safety Administrators (SSA) and school-assigned police officers are not part of the Department of Education or under the purview of school principals, but rather are employed by the New York City Police Department. Mukherjee and Karpatkin's (2007) exploration of police activity in schools writes that New York City's system makes the school policing program "out of step with virtually every other large school district in the country, where school safety officers are generally under the supervision of educators, not police departments" (p. 6). Between 1995-1996, then-Mayor Rudy Giuliani worked to unify all branches of safety officers, including SSAs, under the umbrella of the New York City Police Department. Giuliani believed school safety was "poorly managed" and in need of greater organization and authority (Mukherjee & Karpatkin p. 8). By 2001, the majority of principals surveyed said there was no significant change in school safety (Mukherjee & Karpatkin).

Mayor Bloomberg's Impact Schools Initiative (2004) made all middle and high schools subject to roving metal detectors and many schools, especially overcrowded schools in impoverished, neglected areas, have permanent metal detectors through which all students must enter. Bloomberg claims that incidents of school violence have decreased dramatically, but outside research has found no statistical significance to support this claim (Mukherjee & Karpatkin 2007). Noguera (June 2004) warns against the increased police presence and metal detectors in schools, which "may end up creating an environment that is so repressive that it is no longer conducive to learning." Overall, the victims of increased school safety measures are the students, especially students of color who are put into the awkward and irreconcilable position where they know their own behavior will not be tolerated, but adult violence in the name of authority and safety is not just tolerated but encouraged.

Overcrowding

A major concern within New York City schools is overcrowding. Efforts to create small schools have not solved the overcrowding dilemma because there are not a corresponding number of new places to put schools. New small schools are fashioned within hallways, floors and reconstructed spaces within already operational or phased-out comprehensive high schools. In the 1980s, the typical comprehensive high school enrolled between 2000-4000 students; only the selective examination schools kept their enrollment at capacity (Ravitch 1974/2000). Today, in the face of small school development and school reform, some buildings operate at 175% to 300% capacity and "some schools meant for 1200 students instead enroll 3000" (Alonso *et al.* 2009, p. 152). These overcrowded schools are not well maintained, so in addition to having too many bodies, they are dangerous and do not enhance student learning (Alonso *et al.*; Gootman 2003). Public Advocate Betsy Gotbaum (June 2002) argues that demographics need to dictate the building of new schools "in districts where overcrowding is most severe."

Graduation

'Graduation' is a mysterious enterprise in New York City. There is no singular, clear definition of what graduation means; it can range from a high school diploma to a GED (General Education Development), depending on source consulted or statistic desired. Young people who get a GED or alternate certificate are often considered 'graduates' (Alonso *et al.* 2009). There is a distinction between 'discharged' and 'graduated' students. To be discharged is to release a student from a school in order to enroll in another education setting or GED program. Gotbaum (November 2002) found that in the 2000-2001 graduating school year, New York City discharged more than 55,000 students and graduated 33,520 students. She believes because of increased stringency in graduation rates, more students are funneled toward GED programs or choose to drop out (*cf* Haney, Abrams, Madeus *et al.*, 2005). New York City aims for a 55% 4-year graduation rate; in the 1990s, 50% of students graduated with a diploma in 4 years (Ravitch 1974/2000) and New York is believed to be "the worst state" for 4-year graduation rates (Losen 2006). Graduation rates disproportionately punish black and Latino students. The class of 2001 graduated approximately 28% of its Latino males and less than 30% of its black males with a diploma (Losen 2006). The average 4-year graduation rate for African-American students it is 42% and for

Latino students, 38% (Ravitch 1974/2000). For many years, New York City followed an unofficial social promotion model where underprepared students were moved on to the next grade, and ultimately graduated with a diploma, "even though they had not mastered the work of their grade" (Ravitch 1974/2000, p. *xxv*). The logic behind social promotion was that students would drop out if held back, while critics argue they would drop out, even if promoted, when they no longer understood the material.

All New York City youth are entitled to an education and cannot fail out of the system. However, students over the age of 16 may choose to drop out of school; students aged 17 and above may opt for a GED instead of a traditional diploma; and students who are consistently held behind end up shuffled through the system until they age-out at 21 years. NCLB requirements, increased stringency in graduation requirements, decreased money for at-risk youth and absent support service options make it harder for students to move successfully through school and disincentivize struggling students. Discharges are increasing faster than graduation rates (Gotbaum November, 2002). Currently, New York City public school students have three 'graduation' options: a high school diploma, which means completing the required credits[2] and passing Regents exams; an advanced diploma, which includes Regents in a foreign language; or a GED, which may or may not mean they have completed a traditional high school curriculum but have not taken or passed Regents exams (New York City Department of Education, *Getting to Know High School*; Gotbaum November, 2002). Regents exams, the New York State achievement tests which are required for graduation, have a constant presence in high school and, according to Alonso *et al.* (2009), condition students to "believe that tests are the only important measures of academic success" when they are the only legitimate route to a high school diploma (p. 123). Students used to have the option of a 'local' diploma, which meant they had not passed or taken Regents exams, but had still graduated from high school with a diploma; this is no longer an option and more students are having difficulty meeting the requirements.

Conclusion

As has been shown through Chapter One and Two, both media education and urban education reside in a precarious position in the American conscience and in the American pedagogical landscape. How are young people learning? How do they understand their education? How do they convey their understanding? Chapter One explored the current media education environment in the United States and claimed that both urban education and media education follow similar, uneven terrain. Similar questions about who deserves what kind of education and who deserves what kind of media education are asked of both; there are no clear, critical answers to either.

The development and decline of urban education in New York City has hindered the intellectual opportunities of poor children of color for an insufferably long time. In modern-day racism and classism, these bodies are not explicitly oppressed, but rather, they endure the subtle oppression of 'racenicity': they are the subject of much benevolent conversation, where their institutional disadvantage is used to promote rhetorical, but not actual, change; and their experiences with and understanding of segregation, security and pedagogical achievement are from within a negatively labeled space in need of fixing. They are encouraged to leave their communities rather than fix them; they are encouraged to aspire to a white, middle-class model rather than to respect and understand their own multidimensional model.

Armed with this literature, I now shift into the methodological discussion that frames the organization of the primary data of this study. How do young people themselves understand their schooling and experiences with media education? What role do they play in the classroom and how do they articulate this role? What can be further learned–perhaps clarified–about both media education and urban education by speaking with and listening to those most directly impacted by the experience: the students themselves? Chapter Three discusses the methodological stance and methods taken in this work in order to better answer these questions and provides an initial introduction to the participants and shares the stories of four participants who trusted me with their most intimate, sometimes detrimental, stories to share how knowing participants on a long-term, intimate level may engender a trust otherwise unavailable in qualitative research.

Notes

[1] A systematic part of NYC school reform was the development of the Empowerment Zone (originally named the Autonomy Zone), a formal support connection between small schools and the DOE, providing professional support and development. Many of the newly formulated small schools joined the Empowerment Zone, which ostensibly gave principals and school staff greater autonomy; in exchange for this autonomy, principals sign a performance contract and their schools are reviewed formally after five years. Over five years, principals must achieve the following: 90% school-wide average daily attendance; <4% dropout rate annually; 80% course pass rate across all students in English, Math, Science and History; 90% of 9th and 10th graders promoted to the next grade; 80% Regents pass for ELA and Math; a choice between 70% of cohort graduate after 4 years or 55% graduate after 4 years and 75% graduate after 5 years; and 90% of all graduating students accepted to a 2- or 4-year college. In the 2007-2008 school year, 500 schools were part of the Empowerment Zone and according to the Department of Education, an overwhelming number of principals are remarkably happy with their experience. However, the Empowerment Zone benefits are largely diluted. Because all schools are now required to partner with a support organization, the impact of the support of Empowerment participation is less important. Empowerment schools are still expected to achieve the permutations of their signed contract (see the New York City Department of Education's *Empowerment Schools* at http://schools.nyc.gov).

[2] New York City Public School students are expected to complete a certain number of credits in a fixed number of categories. A full credit represents a full semester's worth of work. Students are required to take 8 credits (4 years) in English and Social Studies courses and 6 credits (3 years) in Science and Math courses. Students need 2 credits in art, music dance or theater; 2 credits in a foreign language; 5 credits in health or physical education; and 7 credits in electives. To graduate from high school, students need to take and pass, with a minimum score of 65, a certain quantity of State Regents exams. To receive an Advanced Regents Diploma, students must take 6 credits in a Foreign Language, which then decreases their quantity of electives (for further discussion, see the New York City Department of Education's *Getting to Know High School* Report at http://schools.nyc.gov).

Chapter 3

Knowing Participants:

Ethical Questions of Feminist, Qualitative Research

In *'The politics of feminist research'* McRobbie (1982/1991) writes that questions asked in scholarship "are always informed by the historical moment we inhabit–not necessarily directly or unambiguously, but in more subtle ways" (p. 121). This chapter discusses the 'subtle ways' we learn the 'answers' to research inquiries when engaging in qualitative methods, doing the best to know the parameters of the inhabited historical moment. The questions asked and answered shift over time; the questions asked can only be worded in such a way and, in turn, will only be answered in a certain way, based on the occupied historical moment. This chapter shares the methodology for this study and provides an initial introduction to the 21 participants. When engaging in qualitative methods, especially when the primary data is drawn from interviews, the research fluctuates and breathes, based largely on the knowledge of participants as they tell their stories about their lives and the multiple influences on their development. While a great deal of direct, tangible data is learned, a greater quantity of subtle data is learned which, when listened to closely, reveal and contribute to the multi-dimensional complexities of real life. The researcher is informed by and learns from his/her participants and the questions asked are framed as they are by the particular intersection of space and time.

For example, during the time I conducted the interviews, Barack Obama was, at best, a *possible* contender for the presidency; the economy, though showing cracks for those who knew where to look, was believed strong; and few people outside judicial circles knew of Sonya Sotomayor. The historical moment consisted of few contemporary public figures of color known nationally for their intellect rather than their physical or artistic prowess. While the structural roots of gender, race and class have not changed, there are important additions to the conversation. Were I to conduct the interviews today, asking the same questions, I imagine these shifts would be part of the conversation and contribute to the knowledge constructed of the present historical moment.

My concerns with media education as problematically infused in urban education occur now because of the shifts and obstacles within media studies and education. These concerns will become part of a larger tapestry informing media and urban education. When engaging in quasi-ethnographic methods, especially participant-observation and interviews, the data learned often travel beyond the scope of the initial research questions. My initial focus was to learn how young people made meaning of the media and experiences with media education. What I learned was that their understandings of media and media education were deeply and inextricably linked with their understandings of school and their social environments. This is not surprising–adolescents spend a significant portion of each day in school–but it does influence the data in important ways. My initial intention to focus on media knowledge and media education awareness needed expansion to include the vital imbrication of school, social location and self-awareness. What the participants know about the media is connected to and informed by what they do in school, how they live as adolescents and their developing world knowledge and worldview.

The data shared here tackle the methodological questions explicit to this research as well as broader questions connected to qualitative data gathering and familiarity with participants. At the outset, my naïveté told me that media education could easily be enfolded into school, especially within the frame of new school reform; this naïveté was systematically stripped and replaced with knowledge of the New York City public school system and its bureaucracies both within the larger system and within the walls of individual schools. My naïveté was further undone as I engaged in quasi-ethnographic research, asking young people how they understood and made meaning from the media and media education. What I thought was most important to their education was not always shared by the participants, some of whom worked very hard at basic survival. To learn about media understanding and media education experience, I needed to learn about their lives, their interests and skills, and they ways in which education and their school fit into their lives; only then would I learn about the media and media education. These young people lived *within* new school reform. They did not see it as something special, different, or troubling; they were unable to articulate its parameters because they were absent the critical distance necessary to do so.

I conducted interviews to learn from those most directly impacted by new school reform how they understood the construction and implementation of media education in their school. In so doing, I was confronted with the emotional realities of the participants' lives and how their experiences extended far beyond the walls of the classroom and inevitably impacted their classroom experiences. Education does not occur just within the classroom walls and life's challenges and difficulties do not wait patiently for students to be 'ready' to deal with them. I was confronted with the methodological question of what it meant to gather data from young people I knew and whether or not my knowledge of them influenced their willingness to share their stories.

The logical, cognitive awareness that personal information will be learned during the process of data gathering is quickly subsumed by the emotions unveiled, especially when the participants are well known to the researcher. Through interviews, I learned a great deal of intensely private information from the participants and because of my position in their school where I was not a traditional or easily categorized authority figure, I was confidante to students beyond the scope of this research. What are the ethical implications of engaging in qualitative research, specifically semi-formal interviews, with a youth population with whom I was familiar and in many cases, with whom I was already intimately involved? As a media studies scholar employing feminist and cultural studies methods to better understand the integration of media education into a small, theme-based New York City public school, what are the unintended consequences of this work? What is the subtle knowledge learned in the research process and how does it influence the data? The initial unintended consequence was how much their awareness of school infiltrated their answers. Had I conducted the interviews outside of school or had I not known the participants prior to the interviews might have altered the organization of answers and revelations of personal data. Therefore, the subtle knowledge learned is the multiple ways in which researcher/ed influence each other and the formation of data. It mattered a great deal to the construction of the historical moment that I knew, and more importantly, was trusted, by the participants.

My initial interview protocol to study young people and media education revealed itself to need more complexity than initially imagined. The participants needed to talk about their school–including and especially their frustrations with it–and needed, in some cases, to share deeply personal data as a form of self-reflection, which revealed a developing self-awareness. As far as I could determine, the participants told me a/the 'truth' about their experiences. Given the personal and potentially detrimental nature of some stories told, I assumed that it was *because* of my prior knowledge and that I worked in their school for two years that served as the initial invitation to trust me. I asked the participants if their knowing me influenced their answers, especially their willingness to share intimate information and many of them acknowledged that yes, knowing me determined, to a degree, their comfort level.

Simultaneously, what I thought was my major concern, the integration of media education, became much more involved as I learned from the participants the layers of social learning with which they struggled. While engaging with the research, my concern with neoliberalism and its influence on poor urban youth of color who, because of their social and ideological locations are considered less deserving, grew. The invisible social privilege that these participants do *not* possess became a layer of concern that called for further examination and exploration on my part to learn with what these young people were struggling and why those struggles feel so insurmountable.

In this chapter, I share the methodological foundations of the project, broadly introduce the 21 participants and detail the articulations of four participants, Marlo, Joan, Lucy and Alvin, on why and how they chose to trust me with private stories. These four young people shared a great deal of information beyond the scope of the research, information that made them vulnerable to my confidence, which articulates the parameters of trust. While prior to conducting this research, I absolutely believed that trust between subject and researcher was important, this research provided me the opportunity to articulate that importance, largely informed by feminist methods that ask the researcher to continuously (re)examine his/her roles and, as McRobbie (1982/1991) discusses, be available to the 'subtle' moments as they present themselves. In conducting this research, I undoubtedly and indelibly became a student of the educational process and was further reminded that all the threads of our identities are woven closely together: I could not ask questions about the media without also and necessarily asking about school, social location, identity development and social awareness. Furthermore, while I had read literature on feminism and on white privilege and could easily intellectualize my position as a white, female, feminist scholar with a great deal of unearned privilege, this research enabled me to understand, on an emotional level, the implication of those bits of privilege that cannot be undone. I focus an entire chapter on methodology as a way of highlighting the dance between intellectualization–which allows an emotional distance–and emotional fusion–which undoes intellectual rationalization.

Framing the Research: Methods and Organization

Over the course of six months, I interviewed 21 students in both group and private interviews. The 11 male and 10 female participants represented grades 9-12 from ages 14-17[1]. Some participants engaged in only group or private interviews, while others engaged in both group and private interviews. I strove to interview as broad a cross section as possible, across ethnicity, age/grade, and school participation[2]. Twenty of 21 participants self-identified as Latino/a and/or African American; one male participant self-identified as mixed Latino/White ethnicity. Though we did not discuss family income in detail, given the broad mission of small schools and the participants' own understanding of their family income, it can be safely stated that all 21 participants struggle economically in low-income and working-class environments. The participants' concept of money and the economy is located in whether they live in public or private housing, whether they and/or their parent/guardian is employed and whether they can be conspicuous enough consumers to not *appear* struggling. I interviewed incredibly motivated, highly functioning, straight-A students as well as students in academic peril and with behavioral problems. I interviewed students with drug problems or who were drug dealers, those with prison records, experiences of homelessness, domestic shelters and sexual abuse. Some students had a long record of extra-curricular activities, others focused on after school jobs or solely on school. I paint a portrait of each participant when they are introduced not with voyeuristic intent, but rather to show them as complex, multi-dimensional characters who live beyond the labels attached to them. Some of the participants absolutely 'fit,' while others challenge, the stereotypes with which they are labeled. Some participants who engage in problematic behavior or who have been involved in unhealthy, negative or detrimental activities shed light on the motivations, context and rationality of their choices. While I had contact with just under 400 students, I kept the number of interviews small; I wanted to make sure that I got to know the participants thoroughly and get in-depth stories about their experiences.

To best understand the parameters of new school reform, especially the implementation of alternative curricula, I engaged in qualitative, quasi-ethnographic methods that privilege data drawn directly from the site of research, specifically participant-observation and interviews with students (Fine 1998; Fine & Sandstrom 1988; Guba & Lincoln 1998; Lindlof 1995; Schwandt 1998). I strove to learn as much about the participants as they were willing to share and interrogated their stories against the social norms of larger society (Fisherkeller 2002; Steinberg & Kincheloe 2004a; Way 1998). In respect to feminist and cultural studies methods, the oppressions and struggles faced by young people must be challenged and mapped against systemic ideology (Buckingham & Sefton-Green 1994; Gorelick 1996; Kellner 1995; Steinberg & Kincheloe 2004a). Because I knew the participants and shared in their school environment, I relied on that connection to contribute to the analysis of their stories (Fine 1998; Heldke 1998).

I aim to uncover the taken-for-granted reality (Alvesson & Skoldberg 2000) of young people as they negotiate their way through their lives, focusing on their understandings of an alternative media studies curriculum and its connections to new school reform. Listening to young people's stories develops inroads for understanding their self-perception and provides insight into what is needed to more thoroughly integrate media studies education into school reform from those who experience it directly. Listening to young people's stories breathes life into the historical moment they occupy. Listening to young people helps undo monolithic oppressive labels and in so doing makes space for more thorough, multidimensional understandings (Alonso *et al.* 2009; Fine *et al.* 2003; Noguera 2000). The very nature that young people are different in age and critical awareness from the researcher forces scholars and pedagogues to step outside of their familiar spaces and look at youth concerns with a new approach. Some participants share stories of dangerous and potentially harmful behavior, which I do not justify and work not to rationalize. Rather, I work to show their behavior through their perspective. When young people say they have 'no choice' or 'no option' or 'that's just the way things are,' what is the trajectory that led them to this belief? When young people who are otherwise and oftentimes ignored are actually listened to, we can hear ways to thoroughly work on their behalf, especially their concerns about school quality, educational progression and safety (Alonso *et al.* 2009; Fine *et al.* 2003; Noguera 2000; Polakow-Suransky 2000). While I did not live amongst the participants, I worked in their school and participated in their school lives for two years. This is simultaneously heartwarming and heartbreaking: I got to know and become involved in the lives of amazing people. However, getting to know those students sometimes means entering a world of serious pain and suffering and it is impossible to leave that knowledge 'in the field,' especially when that knowledge is potentially detrimental.

Feminism and cultural studies converge in this study to examine young people's self-awareness of their social positions within the larger society, manifest through their media knowledge and educational experiences. There is space for research that directly interrogates young people's understandings of their education, experience of alternative pedagogy and articulation of social development. Alternative pedagogies compete for top priority with increased attention to the stringent neoliberalism emphasis of standardized tests as the measure of school, intellectual and student success. This research originates in the classroom, a place that in American ideology is the foundation of a successful nation. Classrooms are grounds for intellectual and social learning and deserve continuous examination. As discussed in Chapter Two, schools are believed to be the primary location for social development and the most surefire route out of poverty. This is more tumultuous in action than in rhetoric, of course, and classrooms are also host to the social, psychological and biological development of young people. While learning about the experience of media, media education and the value of school, I also learned about the very real lives of young people. Sometimes school is not–cannot be–their top priority. When the laboratory is the classroom, the study is anything but sterile.

Conceptual Methodological Frames: Cultural Studies and Feminism

Hall (1992) called McRobbie's (1976) studies of girls' subcultures an 'intervention' that awoke cultural studies to feminism. McRobbie (2008) further converges cultural studies with feminism and, in acknowledgement of her own intellectual oversights, demands scholars continuously and cautiously (re)examine the project of inquiry. This study assumes there is value in interrogating young people's everyday lives in order to learn about the intersecting and disjunctive social and political areas in which they live. This interrogation needs to work as an intervention to constantly remind us that studying the media and media education (and, by extension, those who are educated) are dynamic fields that deserves regular visitation. In (re)visiting this field, many valuable things are learned: inquiries about the media, school/ing, education and pedagogy must account for the personal lives of students and methods must embrace questions of participants' trust in the researcher.

The questions of cultural studies grew from literary scholars who queried texts other than literature, situated those texts within the larger environment from which they were found (Hoggart 1957/1998; Leavis & Thompson 1933;

Williams 1958, 1961) and made space for studying youth cultures and their relationship with the convergence of popular, academic and labor cultures (Hall & Jefferson 1976; Hall & Whannell 1965; Hebdige 1979; McRobbie 1976; Willis 1977). Cultural studies examines the immediacy and locality of everyday life against the passage of time in a broad environment. By studying real people in their quotidian environments, we expose sedimentary layers that constitute our current moment in time. Through cultural studies we learn broad swatches of politics as well as precise moments of being in the world. We learn about power and control–who has it, who wants it, who subverts it–and how this frames our existence.

This study initially examines young people's stories about their knowledge of and experiences with media and media education, which ultimately reveals information about the larger culture in which the participants live. As I learned about education and New York City public schools, I wanted to know what young people knew (and how they knew it) about their experiences with media education and, in learning about lived experience, what their activities and choices revealed about their role in society. I adhere to Corrigan and Frith's (1976) assertion that young people should not just be studied because of their youthfulness. That is, I do not focus on "their adolescence, budding sexuality [or] individual uncertainties ... at the expense of their sociological characteristics, their situation in the structure of the social relations of capitalism" (p. 236). Instead, adolescence, sexuality, individual uncertainties, and a host of other situations important to the participants, are looked at as *part of* their sociological characteristics, wherein the 'structure of the social relations of capitalism' are revealed.

Sociological characteristics enfold the local and immediate environments where the participants live, mostly poverty-stricken and working-class neighborhoods of Manhattan, the Bronx, Queens and Brooklyn. All participants share various commuting lengths and difficulties to meet at their West Side high school. These young people are labeled 'inner city,' however there is little that is 'inner' about their lives and, as will be shown, is a label with which they are largely unfamiliar; they are, instead, pushed to the fringes of the city. Sociological characteristics also include, on a macro level, the broad and pervasive world in which the participants live that is systematically and institutionally organized. They live within the boundaries of American neoliberalism and thus, adhere to its orthodoxies, even when that adherence operates as subjugation. Society is written on the bodies of the participants: as teenagers within an American culture that values consumer-oriented white suburban privilege, stereotypes serve to belittle their lifestyles, behaviors and social and economic positions. Feminism provides a lens through which to examine alteration of the subjugation.

The participants are aware of certain oppressions they face, marked especially by their race/ethnicity, economics and geography. On the process of studying women through conversation, Gorelick (1996) contends:

> To some extent these hidden relationships can be discovered (and are discovered) by the oppressed themselves as they begin to interact, collectivize their experiences (for example, through consciousness-raising) and start to change their situation ... Direct experience has its limitations ... there are some hidden aspects of oppression that no amount of direct struggle will reveal (pp. 28-29).

I borrow and re-conceptualize this idea for teenagers of both sexes. They cannot always or thoroughly articulate the depths of oppression, but do sense it and are aware they are alienated. In many instances, they feel systematically incapable of changing their situations and are complacent to replicate the alienation within their oppressed environments. Even more prevalent, they are so ensconced in their own paradigms they do not see the 'hidden aspects of oppression.' As will be shown, they know they are punished by the physical construction of their school building, but do not extend this knowledge to the punishment they receive by the construction of their school experience. They know the media represents them poorly, but they do not see the financial benefit for others of this negative portrayal. What role does the researcher play when s/he can see that oppression in action? To hear the participants speak complacently about or reveal a lack of awareness of their oppressive circumstances was remarkably difficult, but as researcher, *telling* them of their oppression would do nothing to alter their experience. Their oppression is deeply multi-generational, it is part of the very fabric of their existence and no research can force awareness.

McRobbie (1982/1991) discusses the relationship between feminist researcher-researched, particularly the researcher's responsibility to be "aware of the exploitative or patronizing propensity" of being in a power position and work diligently to avoid abusing that power (p. 126). The stories told are not mine, despite my entanglement in the environment. As researcher/author, I bring these stories forth and have authority in their presentation, however, my word is not context- or content-free. There must be a critical examination of the space between researcher and data. Fine (1998) argues feminist scholars must engage in "working the hyphen" between Self-Other to discuss the negotiations between subject positions and subjects' awareness of their positions (p. 135). In addition, researcher/ed should examine those fissures *not* discussed: where is power found and how is it manifested in the research process? How is power challenged or reaffirmed? In that space between researcher/researched lie the 'knots' Fine discusses where questions are found that have yet to be asked and relationships that may bring new light to the social structure of society.

The feminist researcher studying everyday life must allow his/her own privilege and position to be secondary to that of the researched bodies. However, his/her privilege inevitably colors the site of data gathering. In Heldke's (1998) discussion of privileged women studying underprivileged or oppressed bodies, she advises feminist researchers to be 'traitors' to their own privilege. She explains, "Becoming a traitor means creatively thinking and acting through understandings developed by thinkers on the margins, not stopping at their assessments, but using them to shift one's understanding of oneself and one's relations" (pp. 92-93). The participants are 'thinkers on the margins' operating in a culture that works diligently to regularly reinforce those margins. They are funneled into and out of institutions whose public faces speak of benevolence but who, in actuality, reinforce their subjected positions. School is a primary example of this. To understand their experiences, I worked to become a traitor to my own privilege. If, in my mind, I was willing–eager, even–to do this, in the actual effort, I realized that I could not give up my privilege–the young people regularly reminded me of that– but I could work to be more aware of their environment and how choices were made and behavior enacted in that space. I worked to move beyond my own privilege, especially the knowledge that at the end of my tenure in the school, I would return to a comfortable home and academic institution whereas these young people lived permanently as subjected bodies inside oppressive environments.

The conceptual methodological convergence of critical cultural studies and feminism values the role of everyday life and young people's sociological characteristics as occurring within a broad, carefully organized system that dictates, especially to subjugated bodies, roles and responsibilities. Feminism and cultural studies work to make explicit these dictates by examining them through the words and stories of the subjugated bodies. In so doing, we learn and gain clarity on the political complexity of lived experience. The young people with whom I worked know the world is made of structures and institutions larger and more powerful than they, and often unwittingly adopted and continuously reinforce neoliberal orthodoxies. The participants believe it is their responsibility to make change, but for the most part, they believe change is impossible. They have been taught that official assistance reinforces power positions where benevolent powerful bodies provide aid but do not make space for equality or true integration. If this position is maintained, subjugation seamlessly replicates itself.

Research must be dialogic in order to work to counter the replication of subjugation. In the dialogic process, the researcher works to understand the positions of those researched (Freire 1970/2000). I cannot give up my privilege, but I can work to understand that it is constructed and fallible. 'Understanding,' however, does not happen automatically, despite assurances of a private, confidential site of research. Trust and trustworthiness must be developed over time. Participants who answer personal questions honestly–answers that could jeopardize them in some way–take a risk. Therefore, dialogic research must also prove to the participant that s/he and his/her stories are safe; trust and trustworthiness must be cultivated.

Trust, Truth and Knowing Participants

Individuals who participate in any research process are asked to participate in a paradoxical activity: to remain situated within their natural lives, but to focus, momentarily, on particular moments of that natural environment. To focus on these moments is to break from the natural, no matter how 'natural' the topic appears. The participants engage with and talk with each other about their media experiences everyday. However, they rarely speak formally about the media. It is 'normal' to go to school, however it is not necessarily 'normal' to talk formally about it. To take casual, daily topics and make them formal needs a strong foundation: participants must trust the researcher and the researcher must, in turn, trust that the participants' answers are true. There are both multiple ways to understand truth as well as multiple truths told, particularly by adolescents who experience rapid social, psychological and biological changes that influence shifting stories. As Murray (1999) explained in her observation of teenage girls' conversations in Internet chatrooms, while the 'truth' of their identities cannot be 'known,' the identities they construct must be believed. Without this belief, little research can be completed. In this study, 'truth' was found in multiple locations: in what they said, what they did not say, and the conversation of their body language and physical presence. Participants in group interviews had to balance their desire/resistance to reveal personal, vulnerable stories against the presence of other classmates. Participants in private interviews could not 'disappear' or avoid answering questions. Overall, participants work to give 'good' answers, which may mean paths of discussion take on certain flavors intending to please the interviewer. Because these participants are teenagers, some conversations and answers may be constructed to make them appear cooler and more in control than they actually feel. Some participants were bold and unaffected in group interviews, while more emotionally available in private interviews. Because of the possibility of violation, the participants in group interviews must cautiously and continuously gauge their own talk, especially about sensitive topics, such as sex, drugs, gang and crime involvement.

Many of the participants shared deeply personal stories that went beyond the initial scope of the interviews; I heard stories on drug dealing, pregnancy, prison sentences and physical/sexual abuse. Knowing the participants for well over a year before the interviews, I believe, established a bond that made them comfortable (or at least, less uncomfortable) sharing intimate, sometimes troubling information. Some participants told me deeply personal stories and I asked them if they felt more comfortable sharing these stories with me because of our relationship. I was also curious, when they told me of activities that were illegal, what made them trust me. Did the familiarity we had with each other prior to the interviews contribute to the depths of information they shared?

The participants with less troubling experiences (or those who were less willing to share troubling experiences) believed they could answer the questions from anyone but granted it was easier to get comfortable more quickly because they knew me. Further, the presence of a digital recorder made many of the participants feel 'weird' at first, but they acknowledged they mostly forgot about its presence. The mutual development of trust is a necessary tenet of qualitative methodology and I was curious as to both *why* and *how* the participants grew to trust me. Granted, I promised their participation would be kept confidential, that I would disguise their identities through constant use of their self-chosen code-names, alter identifying details and remove them from the larger project if, at any time, they felt uncomfortable. As an independent scholar, I was not conducting this research for any pecuniary gain and in no one's name or interest other than my own. Something beyond this rhetoric invited the participants to believe its veracity. I share the reasoning of Marlo, Joan, Lucy and Alvin, participants who shared deeply troubling tales with me and articulated why they were able to do so as a way to conceptualize how and why they grew to trust me.

Marlo: No Snitching

Marlo, a petite Latino of Dominican heritage, is a boy on the verge of destruction. In 2007-2008, he was in the 9th grade for a second time and he only attended school to satisfy the attendance requirements of his probation. If he does not drop out, he will most likely repeat the 9th grade a third time. Marlo is a known drug user and a mid-level drug dealer, selling Ecstasy to clubgoers on weekends. Marlo make enough money to support himself, but not enough to cause concern among authorities; he echoes the economic findings that street-level drug dealers earn about minimum wage throughout their careers (Levitt & Venkatesh 2000; Venkatesh & Levitt 2000). To paraphrase Bourgois's (1989) study of the late-1980s crack epidemic in East Harlem, Marlo is frantically trying to get his piece of the pie as fast as possible. When he comes to school he is almost always high and confirmed that he was high when we conducted our interview. Marlo often gets suspended; he curses at his teachers, instigates fights, comes to school high and sneaks out of school after being marked present. When he is in the building, he initiates complicated, sophisticated conversations with various staff members about race relations in America, the injustices of the prison system, the impact of absentee fathers, and the difference between street knowledge and book knowledge. He starts these conversations a way of avoiding class and does not articulate why he will not attend class other than to say that "It's boring." Marlo is a highly intelligent individual, however, he has no skills to transfer his intelligence to a classroom environment. For our interview, as soon as I turned on the digital recorder, he spoke monosyllabically and only appeared comfortable when we stopped talking about anything associated with school and started talking about drugs, a topic he initiated.

Marlo told me some highly detailed stories about his involvement in the drug trade; had I chosen to, I could have easily violated Marlo's trust and informed school authorities or the police about his activities. Arguably, no one would do anything–my tale would be hearsay at best–but I was curious why Marlo was not concerned about this. When I asked what made him believe that I would not tell the authorities he answered, "You just hope it don't happen." "You" in this case referred to me: if I told anyone and Marlo found out, I would suffer the consequences. 'Snitching' carries grave consequences; one's word is one's bond and must be held, irrespective of consequence.

Marlo let me know that my snitching on him, if discovered, would not be tolerated. When I said that he had shared with me a lot of dangerous information he responded, "Hell yeah I did." After some prodding he detailed his calculation that there would be no gain on my end for snitching. He measured the consequences against the people he knows and created a trajectory that if I snitched it would ultimately hurt me more than getting in trouble at school would hurt him. I did not take this as a threat to my safety but rather a coldly logical assertion of the facts: his drug dealing is not enticing enough for the police to follow up on and he is fully aware that school staff have no real-life authority over him outside of school. He makes a livable wage, has a great deal of independence and, in his estimation, has suffered no consequence serious enough to alter his behavior. He knows enough not to bring drugs to school to sell, though he has in the past. He explains, "I don't do nothing here. Last year, I was tryin' something, but I … I quit. You feel me? School, they fuck you up when you do things in school." He explains the difference between getting caught on the street and getting caught in school:

> It's not the same. It's not the same if you have a dime in your pocket in school than on the streets. In the streets, you have a dime in your pocket, the cops can't do much. Like, you could get locked up, you feel me, you could go for a day in central booking, you could be locked up over the weekend if it's a Friday, but when you in school, you get caught for something, they find you with weed, they crucify you. You gonna do time and it's gonna look ugly when the judge sees it.

Though teachers, counselors, principals, and probation officers are traditional and well-known authority figures, for someone like Marlo, they are empty archetypes: his success on the street and at keeping his dealing secret from his mother and various authorities deflates any perceived power over him. There is no way to legally or ethically corroborate Marlo's stories without violating the parameters of confidentiality, therefore it is my choice to believe the truth or falsity of his stories. I choose to believe the stories as truth because of the detail he provides, the consistency he maintained throughout the interview, and my multiple interactions with Marlo on other occasions. While Marlo's activities are wrong and illegal, in his environment, they are perceived as a legitimate means to survival and success. In his reality, school is something he must do until he is old enough to drop out or get a GED; it is not a means to a more secure income and given the evidence of his daily existence, there is no incentive for him to believe otherwise.

Joan: Privacy and 'Knowing Me'

Joan, unlike Marlo, is not explicitly involved in any illegal activities. However, she is a fiercely private young woman who lets few people into her life. She is in the 10th grade, a difficult year academically and socially: students are no longer coddled 9th graders; nor do they yet have to take the SATs, apply for college, or get ready for graduation, so they do not receive any special treatment or attention. These factors contribute to 10th grade as a forgotten year. Joan is capable of context-appropriate social behavior and communicates effectively, if superficially, with her peers and adults alike. She is motivated and smart enough to do well in school without taking up much space or being explicitly noticed or forgotten. Joan is a loner; she skips lunch because the cafeteria is too loud and hides in the girls' bathroom, drawing pictures, reading or listening to music on an iPod she sneaks in. She used to, in her estimation, run with the 'wrong crowd' until she got jumped and decided to change her life. An extremely fashionable young African-American woman, she lives with her mother, several siblings and an uncle in a dangerous, violence-ridden housing project in East Harlem. She has seen people shot before and is trying to avoid a 'dramatic' life.

When asked if she felt comfortable telling me some of her more difficult stories because we knew each other, she agreed. She would not be as forthcoming with a stranger. She explains:

> I wouldn't want a stranger to know me. You know, that would make me very uncomfortable. Like, for example, the guidance counselor, he's kind of like a stranger to me 'cause we never talk and one time he was tryin' to get to know me and talk with me and it was so hard for me. You know, I was just like, why is he tryin' to get to know me for?

The guidance counselor has a clear role in the school: he programs and schedules students in their classes and coordinates non-punitive disciplinary action. In Joan's estimation, these official capacities are a threat to her privacy, and she will be the one to determine who is allowed in. As will be shown throughout the data chapters, the participants express dis/trust of authority figures based on the quality of their interpersonal relationships and how they understand and make meaning of authoritative relationships. That Joan says 'I don't want a stranger to know me' marks a clear boundary between the trusted and the un-trusted: she will know, and possibly trust, people of her choosing; she will not trust someone simply because a label/title tells her to do so. Joan's words introduce a valuable discussion of semantics:

she says she does not want a stranger to know her, which is not simply about not knowing people but rather about unequal distribution of power and motivations. She believes the guidance counselor–representative of a position of authority–has ulterior motives. The struggle Joan faces is her desire to protect her privacy and to control the parameters of familiarity.

Lucy: Trust Through Dubious Behavior

Lucy, an 11th grader, is a young Puerto Rican woman who is perpetually in danger of failing her classes. She lives with her mom and little brother in a crime- and drug-ridden housing project in Brooklyn. Though she is a proud and public drug user, she insists she is trying to cut down because her girlfriend does not approve of drug use. She came out as a lesbian her sophomore year and has been in a tumultuous relationship for just over a year. Lucy spends most mornings getting high with her friends and shows up late to school. She believes she would be better off without school and does not make much of an effort to pass her classes. Lucy believes it is easier to be honest with me, especially about her drug use, because we know each other. She explains:

> I don't trust that many people. But since I've known you for a good while now, I can talk to you and, and obviously you said it's confidential, you're not gonna tell anybody. And I trust you. With someone else, I probably wouldn't have been that honest. 'Cause I don't know them.

Similar to Joan, Lucy's need to know someone contributes to her willingness to trust. Lucy's honesty with me stems from an incident where I unintentionally earned her trust.

About a year before my interview with Lucy, I found a notebook in my office with my name and contact information on the inside cover. This was not surprising; many students had my phone numbers or email. The notebook was a journal of drug experiences, written by Lucy, implicating her and many of her classmates in illegal activities. I returned the notebook to Lucy and we never spoke about the incident until our interview. When I asked her how it made her feel knowing that I had 'proof' of her behavior, she responded:

> At the moment, it's just like, oh God, she found my book. But then again, I don't know, I really didn't pay attention to it that much. I understand you were upset, 'cause your numbers were in there and, oh shit, that's crazy, but like I knew that you wasn't gonna open

your mouth. I had a feeling you wasn't. So I really didn't pay much attention. If it was someone else, like the principal, then I would have been very worried. Like, oh my god, *she*'s gonna do something real crazy with it! But then I never brung that book back to school!

At the time that Lucy was keeping the drug journal, she was not as public about her drug use. Like Marlo, anything I reported would have been hearsay and there was no incontrovertible proof the journal was 'fact.'

Lucy is a person who tested my role as confidante/ researcher/ authority and forced me to examine closely the parameters of feminist, qualitative research. To snitch on Lucy would re-affirm my authority, however, it would have shattered our relationship. To *not* snitch on her felt, in part, like I condoned her behavior and choices, which I did not. Experience told me that reporting the journal to school officials would lead nowhere constructive. I chose to take Lucy's 'side' in an effort to better understand her position.

Alvin: Confidence Born From Negativity

Alvin, an 11th-grade dark-skinned Latino boy who was discharged from school for several weeks while held in jail on robbery and assault charges, shared with me stories of his time in jail. As a 10th grader, Alvin was a loud kid who dressed in bright colors. After he began working with his brother–a neighborhood drug dealer–and got involved in a local gang and petty crimes, his behavior and appearance at school changed. After his experience in jail, Alvin dressed in subdued colors and grew more pensive and serious. Alvin tried hard to make change: from a distance, he respected his brother's behavior, but stopped working with him, broke ties with the gang and worked to stay out of trouble. Alvin had a restrictive probation and a probation officer who checked in regularly. Though Alvin wanted to do well in school, he often skipped class because of emotional difficulties he was having, especially depression and anxiety from his time in jail and the death of a close relative.

Like Marlo, Alvin shared with me some disturbing, dangerous stories. When Alvin told me about his involvement in the gang he made sure to ask me, after the interview, to be careful with that information, lest his former gang members read his criticism. Though it is unlikely the gang members will read this work or recognize Alvin in the pages, his desire to protect his and others' privacy led me to believe that he was telling me the truth. Like Marlo, he could have been lying or at least exaggerating, however, the dramatic changes in his physical presentation and his subdued behavior led me to believe there was little incentive to lie. When I asked him what made it okay to speak so frankly about his experiences, he answered:

> What makes it okay is basically I'm very confident, like I know what I'm saying because it's my life, nobody can tell me my life, nobody can tell me what I been through. I speak for myself. I speak for what I've been through. I speak the truth and I know what I'm saying so that if somebody has a question about it, I know how to answer it.

Alvin's insistence on the truth stems from his concern that he was arrested and convicted on charges beyond his involvement. He claims he was an accomplice, however, he believes his partner brokered a deal and foisted all the charges on him.

As neither judge nor jury, with no discernible power over Alvin's legal dilemmas, I asked him if he was the lead actor or the accomplice; he repeatedly insisted the robbery and assault were not his ideas and he admits to assisting in the incident. While it is plausible that Alvin was rationalizing his behavior and trying to convince both of us of his innocence, there was little to nothing I could do to advocate or punish Alvin. When I asked him if he felt like he could tell me this information because we knew each other, he answered, "It'll be difficult to talk to a stranger because they probably haven't been through what I've been through." I have not been through what Alvin has been through, but in his estimation because I did not judge I was deemed trustworthy. There is an inherent distrust of strangers–especially strangers who are also authority figures–that has developed over time for urban youth of color. Alvin told me the judge who presided over his case looked at him "like a black man," even though he is Latino, which speaks to deeply held racist beliefs. Alvin believes he was convicted, in part, because the judge thought he was black.

Authority Versus Friendship: Shallow Cover

A concern in this research is the possibility of authority issues between investigator/participant interfering with the quality of the data. Because I worked in their school, I was an authority figure, however, not a clearly defined one. I did know them and was a confidante to many. This gave each of us the responsibility to protect personal and sometimes intensely private information. In the participants' estimation, they felt more comfortable telling me their intimate stories because they knew me as a consistent presence in their daily lives.

Engaging in interviews with young people is embedded with ethical implications from the outset. Buckingham (2000) argues, "it is clearly naïve to believe that we can ever take the child's perspective–or that this perspective is something which will simply be revealed to us if we ask the right questions" (p. 117). Instead of trying to *take* their perspective, I want this research and my role in it to understand and highlight the *value* of young people's perspective. Fine and Sandstrom (1988) encourage the researcher to develop a harmonious relationship with participants, to "interact with them in the most trusted way possible–without having any explicit authority role" (p. 17). I was an authority figure within the confines of the school, but one without a clear title: I was not teacher, principal or disciplinarian. However, as a well-educated white woman in an environment made up primarily of young people of color, I was certainly the minority and it took time for trust to develop. Indeed, sometimes trust developed because I proved to them that I could hold on to and keep private information they deemed damning. I was able to develop a relationship outside the traditional boundaries of schooling without violating trust or responsibility. Furthermore, I was a consistent presence in their daily lives and whether the participants knew me well or not sometimes mattered less than the regularity of my routine and presence.

Fine and Sandstrom (1988) detail three different ways to explain the research process to youth participants: explicit, deep or shallow cover. Explicit cover provides the participants with a detailed explanation of the purpose of the research. Through explicit cover, I would divulge any and all information regarding the project. Despite the appealing honesty of explicit cover, there is no guarantee that the participants know enough about research to 'get it' even with a detailed explanation.

The polar opposite, deep cover, provides the participants with no explanation of the project and the participants are unaware they are being studied. While this method guarantees the privacy of the purpose and construct of the research, it violates some of the philosophical principles within which I work. It unfairly and incompletely weighs all the power within me to develop and maintain secrets and subversive explanations for my presence. Deep cover counters the feminist stance that intimately connects researcher to participant (Fine 1998; Gorelick 1996; Heldke 1998; McRobbie 1994, 1982/1991, 1976; Way 1998).

This research situates itself between the two poles and I draw on shallow cover to explain the research to the participants. I provided the participants with a partial explanation of the research and their role in it. I believe the participants deserved a fair explanation of the research and its constructs in order to accurately provide ongoing consent and continued participation. I gave them a "credible and meaningful explanation of [my] research intentions" in age- and context-appropriate language (Fine & Sandstrom 1988, p. 30). All participants knew I was interviewing other students and those who participated in group interviews knew specifically who some of the other participants were. All participants respected the privacy of others and did not inquire who else was participating. They knew that to fairly protect their privacy, I also had to protect others'.

Conclusion

My relationship with the participants before and after the interviews inevitably added a level of complexity to our interactions. To pretend otherwise would be foolish. However, I believe that complexity neither violated ethical boundaries nor compromised the research process. Indeed, I argue that knowing the participants contributed to the data gathering in significant ways that could not have happened had I not known the participants. All 21 participants were students with whom I was familiar though certainly I knew some better than others. I believe that if I were a stranger to the school–if I showed up 'just' to conduct research–I would have learned a lot, however, I would not have learned the depth or breadth that I did. If my relationship with the participants began and ended with the interviews, I would not have been able to fully understand their references, nor do I think they would have shared with me the intimate details that they did. I probably would have learned about their relationship with and understanding of the media and their experiences with media education, but I would not have seen the connections they made to the other areas of their learning and school experiences. I would have left the research site believing that media education was *not* a significant part of their education, but I do not believe I would have fully understood *why* or how the disconnect occurred.

My involvement in the participants' school, where I saw them on a regular, near-daily basis and my position as a white woman of privilege indelibly contributed to the data gathered for this research. In spite of my experience with qualitative research, I was nevertheless surprised by the depths of data I learned from the participants, especially their willingness to share deeply personal stories. The behavior and choices of Marlo, Joan, Lucy and Alvin are not without political consequences and it is the work of the researcher to understand the stories from the perspective of those telling them and then translate those stories responsibly to the page. Responsibility rests deeply–if precariously–in the risk taken to acknowledge the moment in history when the research is conducted and how those moments influence the stories told.

The next three chapters share, in the participants words, how they understand the media, media education, their school and their socio-political environments. Chapter Four examines closely the media class trajectory and the integration of media education into LSHS and argues that the opportunity to build a school focused on media education has been wasted: LSHS is a media school in idea only. Chapter Five explores how the participants understand their participation in the project of new school reform, examining their definitions and meaning making of the vocabulary that constructs new school reform and how the media theme is (not) integrated in their school. Chapter Six focuses on how the participants understand adolescence and education through media representations and their own experiences.

Notes

[1] The interviews were audiotaped with the participants' permission; after each interview, I listened to and transcribed the data material. With the help of my research assistant, Wendy Chen, I coded the interviews in multiple directions. The transcripts of the interviews were coded through Coffey and Atkinson's (1996) data complication guidelines and Lindlof's (1995) procedures for organization. In the initial reading of the transcripts, I looked for concrete information, such as their definitions of specific terms, declarative stories on their classroom, media and personal experiences, and construction of their individual stories. In further readings of the transcripts, I broke the conversations into broad categories as a method of organization.

[2] I conducted both group and private interviews. The group interviews took on the tone and flavor of conversations; the students who participated in group interviews were friends with each other and had a rapport that began long before they entered our interview space. In the group interviews, I provided some basic guidance and asked the questions, but tried to play a minor role. I was interested in how the conversations flowed between the participants and in observing how they engaged with each other. I listened for and documented when they interrupted each other, how they conversations went down avenues that I had not introduced, and observed how they interacted with each other. In the private interviews, I began with or repeated the questions from the group interviews. The private interviews were distinct from the group interviews because there were no conversational interruptions and I was able to follow through more directly on each individual's personal stories.

Chapter 4

"I Mean, in What High School *Don't* They Use Media?":

Questioning Media Integration at LSHS

Lamenting the absence of challenging media classes throughout his high school experience, Popcorn, a 12th-grade student of mixed African heritage says, "I mean, in what high school *don't* they use media?" Popcorn's lament illustrates that media education is not effectively integrated at LSHS and this chapter illustrates the absence of media studies, despite its theme designation. The chapter begins with a discussion of the shaky, disorganized development of media studies courses during LSHS's first four years and discusses reasons why media courses could not be successfully, consistently implemented. Inspired by Popcorn's words, this chapter shows how LSHS students do not critically understand the principles of media education. For the most part, they cannot define media education and believe that the inclusion of technology in their classrooms is evidence of the infusion of media studies. Participants discuss their experiences with, and what they know about, media literacy and video production and articulate how they believe media studies is integrated across their core courses.

In the spring of 2006, a staff member who was interested in organizing and providing structure to the media curriculum invited me to visit LSHS. In addition to developing some brief activities to help them close out the school year absent a significant number of teachers, I worked to scaffold a media studies curriculum, including media literacy and production courses, for the 2006-2007 school year, and to develop a set of courses based on development of skill and critical thinking. I worked to implement these curricular ideas and to organize the media studies, elective and non-core courses. My goal was to develop a 4-year media studies program where all students would take courses that would build their production and analytic skills and knowledge. I tried to follow closely the literature that had informed my knowledge and training in media education, but this proved wholly impossible. There were, to put it simply, too many obstacles.

With hindsight, I am confident in writing that I failed miserably at these tasks, not due to lack of effort or interest, but rather because of the near insurmountable obstacles faced by the school and the staff. This chapter explores the work done–and its failure–in media studies development. This chapter introduces the majority of the participants and frames the understanding of LSHS as a media school. I begin with an examination of what the media studies courses–or those courses loosely labeled as 'media studies'– looked like as LSHS grew. The primary focus of this chapter shares, in the participants' words, how they understand media studies at LSHS and critiques these understandings against contemporary efforts to include critical media literacy in schools. Students do not understand and are not able to critically articulate the basic fundamentals of media studies because media education is not part of their school experience in any significant way. Subsequent chapters will show that the absence of articulation includes their lack of awareness of the pedagogical rhetoric of new school reform, the negative social labels applied to them and the images and perceptions of adolescence and education. The experiences of the participants match, not challenge, their representation in the media and of that they are clearly aware. Their school– the site where stereotypes should be challenged–teaches them they are subservient, degenerate citizens.

Media Studies at LSHS

In spite of its designation as a media school, by the end of the 2007-2008 school year, media studies were conspicuously absent from LSHS's curriculum. In the first four years of the school's operation, the media studies curriculum had no consistency and followed no clear methodology or epistemology. LSHS began under the auspices that young people would use media as tools for social change, however there was no clear dissemination of this vision. Other than myself–admittedly not trained as a high school teacher, though sometimes forced to be one–there were no media scholars or media professionals on the full-time faculty or staff. The mixing or absence of skills by adults was a portent for the absence of critical articulation amongst the participants. Without a clear trajectory of their learning, it is difficult to expect their understanding and meaning making to be clear.

From 2004-2006, the specific 'media' classes were piecemeal at best, taught by faculty with arts and professional experience but no pedagogical training. The students took courses in aesthetics, dance or poetry. As a startup school, each year LSHS grew by about 100 students and each year the initial cohort was in classrooms with unfamiliar teachers who were always brand new to the students and often brand-new to the New York City Public

School system and teaching. The first graduating class of LSHS 'broke in' several teachers and was 'guinea pig' to several curricular ideas and Chapter Six will share their reflections on four years of new school reform.

In LSHS's initial year, 2004-2005, there were 100 students in the 9th grade, with a minimal faculty of full-time core teachers, part-time elective teachers and a small number of administrative staff. The single, failing school that initially occupied the entire building continued its process of being phased out as new, small schools moved into the space. Families of students in the initial cohort had a clear memory of the problems with the single large school: a revolving door of faculty, administration and especially principals; high drop out and low graduation rates; and a shooting, that ultimately served as the impetus to close the school. Parents, guardians and families were understandably hesitant to send their children into the building. LSHS occupied the entire basement of the building, but only needed a few classrooms. The idea was that with each new school year, the entire floor would ultimately be occupied. Students ate lunch together in an empty classroom rather than going to the cafeteria, which was shared by the other schools in the building. The entire student body and staff would go on near-weekly field trips and/or leave the school building to explore the neighborhood. The intimacy of the first year–where everyone, adult and student alike, was embarking on a new experiment–allowed for a great deal of flexibility. The connections between staff and students that were a desired part of small schools' development and new school reform were clearly evidenced in the first year of LSHS. The 12th grade students who participated in this study all look back at the first year as a time of both disorganization and excitement. The participants remember their teachers and staff as devoted to them, with good ideas and energy that, while far from organized, were perceived as radical and visionary.

In the 2004-2005 school year, there were no identifiable media studies courses. LSHS is managed in a top-down, authoritarian style where, when ideas are generated, they are given little thought to follow-through or practicality. The media studies classes were implemented in this way: when the principal or a staff member had an idea, or met a person whose art was valued, planning would be done to find a way to work the idea or person into the school's curriculum. This ultimately exposed the initial class to bits and pieces of lots of ideas, rather than a streamlined, cohesive curricula. All students were provided with disposable cameras as a way to document their personal process, but there was no technology more advanced than this and by

2008, the pictures had yet to be developed. The ideas and vision were very present-tense, focused on the moment rather than on the long-term impact on, development or needs of, the students. There was no clearly articulated goal in mind, the courses developed for the initial cohort were not thought of in terms of how they would prepare students for their progression through high school, preparation for college or, develop their understanding of media in all its variations, forms, content, representation or industries. Radical vision does not always translate to the appropriate number of expected credits, so the initial 9th-grade class finished their first year of high school with murky transcripts at best; credit accumulation was not part of the larger conversation. LSHS did not have a Regents waiver, so students needed regular and increased preparation for their state-mandated exams.

In LSHS's second year, 2005-2006, there were two grades of approximately 100 students each and new teachers for the 10th graders. With a 100% increase in students, there was still room, but less so, for the intimacy of the first year. The students now ate in the shared cafeteria with students from other schools and there were fewer field trips. Two computer labs were put together and a few digital video cameras were purchased. Students needed state test preparation, so teachers grew more concerned with the work being done inside their classrooms than in expanding their curricula outside of the classroom.

The media studies courses remained disorganized and part time at best, not least of which because the teachers hired for the media classes did not last the entire school year. There was a teacher of poetry who left about halfway through the school year. The person brought in to take over his classes changed them into journalism classes where the students put together one issue of a school newsletter. About halfway through the year, there was a loosely organized video production course taught by a video artist; this was not a skills-based or critical theory class, but rather a place for students to create videos without coherent goals or objectives. The work done by the students in this course revealed minimal production knowledge at best; videos were created with little to no narrative development, choppy editing and near absent audio. Within the umbrella of media courses was a dance class that also only lasted for part of the year when the teacher left; a new teacher was found, but he was unreliable and often absent. Unconfirmed reports and rumors were that the media/elective teachers left because of the verbally abusive and emotionally manipulative treatment by the principal and the absence of any workplace security. Because they were not licensed teachers and were hired as part-time or temporary workers, the elective and part-time teachers belonged to no union and had little incentive not to take better, full-time job offers. This was a well-known and well-discussed problem at LSHS, but because no one spoke out in any formal, public environment, the treatment of the part-time staff was never formally documented. While there is no confirmation of these rumors, I mention them because students were aware of them and participated in the rumors and that awareness undoubtedly impacted their trust in the school. While it might be expected that students will participate in rumors and gossip about their teachers, staff and each other, it might be less expected or accepted that teachers and staff participate in gossip and rumors *with* students. As will be shown throughout their stories, especially about interpersonal relationships with school staff, there is a great deal of shared personal and intimate information which, while it undoubtedly brings students and staff in closer emotional proximity and develops trust, also means that young people are privy to information that might not concern them. At the end of the 2005-2006 school year, almost all the full-time faculty and staff left, resulting in a near-100% staff turnover after the second year of the school.

In 2006-2007, LSHS grew by another 100 students and an almost entirely new faculty and staff. However, a fair number of students in the initial cohort had dropped out, transferred, or been held back, so the school still had fewer than 300 students. There were still several empty classrooms because the school was not at capacity, but the hallways were growing more crowded, it took a bit longer to learn (and remember) every student's name, and there was the distinct probability that one would not see or chat with every staff member throughout the day as more people entered the school. The building as well grew more crowded with a total of five schools occupying the six-story space. The single failing school was fully phased out, but family memories were still clear and detailed. The intimacy of the first year was clearly not part of the third year's agenda, though founding staff and students recalled those days with fondness. The 11th graders were concerned with the state tests, especially if they had not passed those taken in the 9th or 10th grade. The staff grew concerned with college preparation and making sure the students had the appropriate credits to graduate. The media and electives courses desperately needed organization.

In 2006-2007, the media and elective courses were structured into a formal 10-week rotation of classes so that students would take 4 media/elective courses throughout the school year. The electives courses included physical education, college preparation, Spanish and dance; the media courses included media literacy and video production. As in other years, not all teachers made it through the entire school year. The dance teacher left within the first few weeks of the school year. The college prep teacher doubled as the physical education teacher. In 2006-2007, the first efforts to introduce a foreign language class occurred and two people co-taught the course. The video production teacher from 2005-2006 decided two days before school began not to come back and the person hired at the last minute to replace her could only teach for one semester. His replacement, an independent filmmaker, had worked with LSHS students before on extracurricular projects, so he was a familiar face. The media literacy class had a different teacher or pair of co-teachers for each cycle of the school year, so students did not experience any consistency between classes. Every effort was made for every student to take media literacy or video production, though this did not always happen. There were no more school-wide field trips, though there were a fair number of grade-level and class field trips. Students ate lunch in the cafeteria, but at their own time, not shared with any other school.

By 2007-2008, LSHS was at full capacity: all four grades were registered and there were just under 400 students in the school. The building now housed seven separate schools with more than 3000 students entering and exiting through the same doors. The incoming 9th-grade class had just over 100 students. The 12th-grade class–the initial cohort–had shrunk from 100 students in the fall of 2004 to just over 50 by graduation in June of 2008. The difficulty in remembering names of so many students and staff was tempered by the excitement and energy of a full school and the first graduation. Even in September, the seniors were already excited and nervous for graduation and related celebrations. Some would be the first in their families to graduate from high school; almost all would be the first to contemplate or attend college.

With the increasing number of bodies also grew increased disciplinary problems: physical fights, truancy and interpersonal conflict were a regular part of the school day. Students were frustrated they could not bring in cell phones or iPods to school and developed complicated schemes to hide or smuggle their equipment. As will be detailed in Chapter Five, scanning and metal detectors did little to staunch the flow of contraband material and most staff grew weary of enforcing what seemed like pointless restrictions against cell phones (which got no reception in the basement school) or iPods (which students promised to keep off during class, but felt were necessary for long subway and bus commutes). The basement visibly stunned the 9th graders; the 10th and 11th graders were resigned to it; and the 12th graders were restless and eager to get out of it. The 12th graders grew increasingly restless as they fretted over their credit accumulation and began their college application process. The need for increased organization of the media/electives courses was palpable: this was perceived as the last chance for some students to take their necessary requirements and the first chance to see a full four years of courses at play. However, the desire for organization did not become a reality.

Once again, there was absence of teacher consistency throughout the year. The third dance teacher was dissatisfied and disappeared; he was replaced by an art teacher, thereby effectively ending the dance class. The principal believed that principles of media literacy were found in the core courses, so the media literacy class was dropped. There was a video production course for three-quarters of the year until the teacher resigned. While he tried to include elements of media analysis and self-reflection in the class, as a filmmaker himself, he focused mostly on production. Because it was so close to the end of the school year when he left, he was not replaced. The art teacher doubled his course load to teach both art and video production. In my estimation, the only 'official' media class in 2007-2008 was the video production course. All 12th graders took a photography class, however, in this and the video production course, there was no official scaffolding or development of skills. The 9th graders learned basic video production skills, but only the self-motivated, independent 12th graders were able to move beyond the basic level. While the quantity and quality of the video equipment had increased, when something broke, it was neither replaced nor repaired, so technology dwindled throughout the year.

The first graduating class of LSHS had little consistency or coherence in their media studies training and it was shaping up that the rest of the student body would experience the same inconsistency. There are several reasons for this inconsistency that connect LSHS to the larger challenges faced by urban schools and alternative curricula; the most conspicuous reasons are the high teacher turnover, lack of long-term planning, lack of formal media training for core course teachers and lack of pedagogical preparation for media and elective teachers (Domaille & Buckingham 2001; Kellner 2002; McLaren & Hammer; Moore 2008; Trend 1994). Despite being a media studies school, the attention and respect paid to the development of a media studies curriculum was minimal at best (Jenkins *et al.* 2006). The division between media/elective classes and core classes was palpable in multiple ways (Jenkins *et al.* 2006; Kellner 2002; Kellner & Share 2007). The media/elective teachers were part time; the core teachers' preparation period was 'covered' by the media/elective classes. In urban schools, there is often high teacher turnover; in LSHS media/elective classes there was often multiple teacher turnover within the school year. Because there is no licensure for alternative curricula, and as a way to keep the budget down, the media/elective teachers were not hired as teachers, but rather in administrative positions with legitimately vague job titles, a part of new school reform, that allows for flexibility in job description and expectation[1]. If students fail a certain number of core classes, they are held back and forced to repeat the grade. If students fail their media/elective courses, they are moved to the next grade and expected to make up the missing elective credits over the course of their time in high school.

In observations of the core classes and curricular scope and sequence, teachers intend to respect the media theme, but did not have any formal training in media studies. Many of the teachers included 'media' as part of their curricula through the use of technology rather than through a frame of critical inquiry within the subject. Professional Development workshops in the concepts of media education and media literacy, video production and editing were developed and offered at various times, but time was not allocated for execution. Teachers who needed to prepare students for state tests were less inclined to include media work in their curriculum. Newly licensed teachers with little to no teaching or classroom management experience were eager for and dedicated to alternative curricula, but first needed to become familiar with and confident in their classrooms (Cope & Kalantzis 2000; Kalantzis & Cope 2000; Grant & Murray 1999). The question that remains is how the students fared and made meaning within this environment and whether significant change can be built from the participants' stories.

The remainder of this chapter shares, in the participants' words, how they understand and make meaning from their media studies training. What will be shown is that the students do not have much formal critical knowledge of the media as incoming ninth graders and that their learning and critical knowledge does not develop as they move through high school. The inconsistencies they have experienced as students are reflected in the ways they discuss their media training.

Defining Media Education

Any student studying the media and participating in media education deserves a clear starting point. There are significant and important definitions of media education and if these definitions are not brought into the classroom, students will not move beyond their own colloquial understandings. It was my intent to integrate a critical democratic approach, which privileges students' pre-existing knowledge, teaches them to question ideas, encourages them to challenge authority figures and authoritative systems, and to be self-aware of how they know what they know (Bazalgette 1992; Buckingham 2003; Jenkins *et al.* 2006; Kellner & Share 2007; Moore 1991; Tyner 1998). Students have a great deal of knowledge about, and experience with, the media, however, this knowledge is largely colloquial (Jenkins *et al.* 2006; Moore 2008; Morrell 2008). They can be very critical of texts and demonstrate solid analyses, especially on positions of subjugation. However, they do not employ a formal vocabulary nor do they negotiate the differences between their opinions and critical inquiries and analyses. In personal, spontaneous conversations, they are succinct in their criticism, however, once the conversation moves to the classroom, they fall back on expected classroom behavior and remain largely silent or seemingly unmotivated. The participants reveal assumptions that their teachers are trained in and aware of formal approaches to the study of media and critical approaches to analysis and production of texts.

The students interviewed for this research have a range of understanding, articulating and defining media education. Arguably, students' definitions should grow in complexity and sophistication as they move through high school. The 9th graders entering in 2007 had no formal media literacy training prior to enrolling at LSHS. The 10th-12th graders have conceivably been exposed to formal media literacy, multiple courses in production and attempts at media education integration across the curriculum.

Monica, Tom, Jose and Marlo are all 9th graders, presumably the least versed in media education and define it thus:

> *Monica:* Um, learning about communication and the outside world, like anything new that you want to learn.
>
> *Tom:* Media education is you're learning about being on TV, all the media stuff, what you could learn possibly from this school.

110 *Media Education Goes to School*

> *Jose:* To have a study of our society.
>
> *Marlo:* Um ... media education ... media, like, the word media.

All these definitions are, arguably, 'correct.' They capture ideas of society, communication and 'the outside world.' They are unsophisticated, colloquial definitions, understandable for students with no training or exposure. There is no precise articulation or evidence of classroom-based information.

Their answers are reflective of their commitment to the strictures of school. Marlo, introduced in Chapter Three, a deeply disturbed young man and problematic student, provides a content-void definition. Monica is a cheerful, petite Latina girl of Mexican heritage, who lives with her parents in a working-class neighborhood in Queens. Monica comes to school every day, is almost always on time and attends all her classes. She has a gentle way about her that is a calming presence to some of her rowdier friends. Tom is a skinny African-American boy who lives with his mother in Harlem. He is an only child with no contact with his father. Tom is in school most every day; he has trouble concentrating and is often gently reprimanded by his teachers to pay attention. He has a bright smile and difficulty sitting still. Jose is a slight Latino of mixed Dominican and Colombian heritage. His sister, Nino, who also participated in this research, is a senior at LSHS. Jose is almost always smiling and possesses a great social ease with a variety of people, including classmates, his sister's friends, and most of the staff. As teenagers, Tom and Jose are immature and naïve, however, it is evident their maturity and ability to focus will grow rapidly and steadily. Monica, Tom and Jose want to impress their teachers and do good work; their focus and attention skills vary, but there is no doubt these individuals will move successfully through high school.

The 10th- and 11th- grade students have conceivably been exposed to media literacy and may be expected to have a more solid grasp of a definition. Tenth and 11th graders have greater experience with media classes and it should be expected that they are more thoroughly versed in definitions of media education. However, in hearing their definitions, it is clear they are not. Tenth graders J-Trout and Joan each explain media education as:

> *J-Trout:* TV. I mean, learning how to work a camera, but it doesn't take rocket science for a person to learn how to use a camera or a computer or something.
>
> *Joan:* Media, when I think of media, I think of everything that I feel has to deal with the

media. Um, computers, television, singing, dancing, art, um, so when I think of media, that's what I be lookin' forward to seeing.

J-Trout and Joan are both are capable of context-appropriate social behavior and communicate effectively with their peers and adults alike. Each is motivated and smart enough to do well in school without taking up much space or being explicitly noticed or forgotten. Both are also mostly loners. Joan, introduced in Chapter Three, has shown that she would rather be left alone. J-Trout is a young African-American man who lives in Harlem with his mother. He does not know his father and believes he and his mother are fine on their own. J-Trout is reputed to have deep, multigenerational gang connections, though he denied any of that to me[2]. J-Trout is deeply cynical of LSHS and believes that while education is important, this school is a waste of his time.

Eleventh grade Lucy, introduced in Chapter Three, does not have a sophisticated or complete definition of media education. She struggles with the following, "Media education. I don't know, I don't really have a definition for that." In contrast, both Genevieve and Alex are focused on their grades and academic success and work hard to please the adults they encounter. They desperately want to think the best about their school and work to answer questions 'correctly.' In conversation with each other, Genevieve and Alex, both 11th graders, discuss their understandings of media education:

> *Genevieve:* Just educating us on the different types of mediums. Like we talked in our English class. Our English teacher said that, you know, editorials come in different mediums like newspapers, um video, magazines, cartoons. So, just educating ourselves on that.
> *Alex:* I think it's to educate ourselves on different stereotypes, things that are stereotypical in this world.

Genevieve and Alex are arguably the brightest young women in the school. Genevieve, a heavyset African American who lives in Harlem with her overprotective grandmother, mother and older brother with a mental disability, works hard at school. She is incredibly smart and desperately wants to impress authority figures, to the point that it manifests as a deep insecurity when she feels she has disappointed people. Genevieve is not boastful about her intelligence and is friend to motivated and problem students equally. Contradicting the stereotypes of urban youth, especially low-income female youth of color (Brown 2005; O'Connor, Lewis & Mueller 2005), Genevieve is socially naïve: at 17, she has kissed one boy; is not allowed out on weekends; expresses no interest in drugs, alcohol or gang life.

In contrast, her friend Alex, a 17-year-old Latina who is equally as smart, carries the burden of an over-awareness of street- and life-knowledge. Alex is the primary caregiver to her older sister's two children as well as her own little sister and brother. Alex 'parents' her mother and older sister, who do not bear the responsibilities of their children. All seven of them, plus occasional boyfriends and non-family roommates live together in a housing project in the South Bronx. If Alex's mother is caught renting out rooms, they will be evicted from their apartment, although because the New York City Housing Authority is so overburdened, it is unlikely she will get caught. Alex has lived in homeless- and domestic-violence shelters and an ex-stepfather sexually molested her for almost 10 years; because her mother needed child support–which she believed would be rescinded if he was prosecuted–no adult ever pressed charges against the ex-stepfather. Alex is sexually active and has had multiple partners; she insists she has always used contraception because she has no interest in repeating her mother's or sister's behavior. Alex constantly works to construct a semblance of family and acts as caregiver to most of her friends. She seeks out damaged individuals with whom to be friends and works diligently to heal them. Because she maintains a straight-A average and is always in school, it is not recognized that Alex is in crisis and she receives no social services from the school. Both Genevieve and Alex adopt the neoliberal position that it is their responsibility to learn the material–both use the phrase 'to educate ourselves'–which limits the school or school systems' liability.

The most advanced definitions of media education presumably come from the 12th graders, who have ostensibly been through four years of media studies training. This, however, is not the reality:

> *Nine:* Um, media education I think it's like, um, everything that can communicate what's going on in the world, like what's happening with anything, like, um, anything that informs us basically, I don't know.

> *Nino:* I think we need it. We need to pay attention to the media. Even though they not very truthful most of the time, and sometimes they are, but we need to pay attention, we need to know how it works. It's like the media's the future, we need-a learn about technology. I think they need to put it in every school. So everyone knows like an idea of it. So they pay attention to it, you know.

Nine and Nino, two 12th-grade girls, could not be more different from each other in behavior or demeanor. Nine is a heavyset Latina who is equally extremely smart and uneasy. She, her mother and younger sister have significant financial difficulties and move a lot. Most recently, they lived with Nine's aunt and cousin in a 1-bedroom apartment in the Bronx. During that time, Nine, her mom and sister spent most of their waking hours in their car so as not to disturb life in the cramped apartment. Nine is a worrier and is often in complete disarray when a friend is unhappy in a class or having a bad day. She is fiercely private and protective of her mother; despite her intelligence, she may not attend college so as not to increase her mother's stress.

Nino is a petite Latina with long curly hair who always dresses in a multitude of extremely bright colors. Not much appears to upset Nino: she is almost always laughing, has a wide variety of friends and does well in her classes. Nino is interested in feminism and politics and spends most of her free time skateboarding with her friends. She is a devoted older sister to Jose, who she has enveloped into her social circle.

In conversation with each other, 12th graders Bruce, Peter and Popcorn[3] discuss their definitions:

> *Bruce:* That's a really broad topic.
> *Popcorn:* Yeah, it's a really broad topic.
> *Peter:* It could be commercials.
> *Popcorn:* It could go into anything.
> *Bruce:* Yeah, 'cause when you say 'media,' that could be from a magazine to like your favorite commercial.
> *Peter:* Newspaper.
> *Bruce:* So when you do media studies, film drops in there, magazines drop in there, it's like a whole bunch of stuff is under the category of media, so that's very broad.
> *Popcorn:* And how to like communicate-
> *Bruce:* -Yeah, communication-
> *Popcorn:* -With people. I think, I think that area should be in like every school. Like, they should just have a class for that, 'cause like, if you know how to communicate with people, I mean, 'cause a lot of people don't.
> *Bruce:* Yeah, 'cause ah, there is an art to communication, there's an art to everything. Like, yeah, like I said, media's very broad and, and everything falls under media, media's just how something is presented. So like that's why like media is so broad 'cause everything is presented, like. Like if I was a journalist and I'm presentin' an article to my boss to put in the newspaper or the magazine, I gotta be very presentable in like the topic I talk about.

Popcorn, Peter and Bruce are best friends. As the school year ended, they were increasingly unfocused and had difficulty concentrating or coming to school on time. Popcorn, first met in the Introduction, is an intense young man who lives with his mother and siblings in Harlem. He is a serious photographer and often walks around school with a camera around his neck. Popcorn is extremely bright and has a witty sense of humor, but internalizes the stress and pressure of school and feels he is a disappointment to himself and his teachers. Peter is a charming, light-hearted young African-American man with a slapstick sensibility who lives with his mother in Brooklyn. To see Peter crashing into a wall or stumbling down a flight of stairs because he was momentarily distracted is not out of the ordinary. Peter is a bright young man but has no ability to concentrate and does not measure the consequences of his actions. Similarly, Bruce, a tall, skinny young African-American man who lives in Brooklyn with his mother and sister, has not been to school on time even once. He is extremely funny and very bright, but cannot focus. Bruce wants to do many things with his life–become a journalist, a photographer, a writer, a filmmaker–but cannot sit still long enough to complete any task. Bruce is universally admired, but because no one can successfully or seriously discipline or reprimand him, he, too, does not measure the consequences of his actions.

These definitions do not grow in sophistication and do not reflect a formal knowledge of media education. No student interviewed was able to formally state principles of analysis, production, critical inquiry or multiple literacies (Bazalgette 1992; Buckingham 2003; Grahame 1991; Jenkins *et al.* 2006; Kellner & Share 2007; Tyner 1998). The absence of a coherent, developed definition is, presumably, the fault of LSHS for not providing a media literacy class with clear learning objectives and activities. However, LSHS operates within a larger environment whose interests increasingly focus on the test and simultaneously does not provide space or resources to equip teachers to teach this material. 'Blame' for failure is easily shifted across multiple locations and neoliberal ethos point to individuals as responsible for his/her own failures. The absence of definitions explores the tension between test-centered and student-centered education. Media education is not a 'test-ready' subject, but rather, draws liberally from student participation. Yet, teachers must be well versed in the guiding principles and concept in order to develop a critical, well-framed course. This demands a teacher trained in media studies who is comfortable drawing from student knowledge and cultivating a space for critical autonomy. Unfortunately, LSHS teachers have not had this training explicitly and the evidence of this absence of training is clear. The teachers draw from their own colloquial knowledge and bring this knowledge into the classroom. The absence of coherent, sophisticated definitions of media education is representative of the pedagogical difficulties within LSHS specifically, New York City schools broadly, and is a topic of concern among global media scholars (Domaille & Buckingham 2001; Moore 2008; Tornero 2008).

Video Production

For three-quarters of the 2007-2008 school year, video production was the one formal media class at LSHS. Context is vital to learning and the space and time where video production occurred included a series of obstacles. The video production teacher was highly skilled in production, but by his own admission, not in pedagogy. In May, he abruptly resigned and the art teacher took over the class, an imperfect, stopgap measure at best. Each class cycle only lasted 10 weeks, each meeting time under an hour, and many cycles were interrupted by holidays. Include the students' attendance problems and there was very little consistency throughout the school year. All students were expected to complete a video within 10 weeks and were, in theory, required to document their process with storyboards, production notes, or scripts. Overall, if a student completed a video, these preparatory aspects were overlooked. This illustrates a disregard of video production as a viable, complex subject worthy of more time and materials. At no time would students be expected to master traditional literacy without significant draft work; indeed, the revision process is built into curricula, across grades and subject matters. Yet in video production, it is acceptable to create one video, in one 'draft,' without application of formal production work, and be considered 'proficient.' As will be shown in Chapter Seven, this superficial approach to video production does not embrace the multiple, complex nuances of multiliteracies.

Most students who were interviewed express little beyond basic technical knowledge in talking about their video production class. Ninth grade Jose explains, "In video production, I learned how to film. And like, break time codes and like how to cut up the movie." Pyro, a 10th grader, explains video production as a class where "we get to make videos by using camcorders and cameras and using computers." Pyro is a baby-faced African American who lives with his mom, little brother and brand-new baby sister in Queens. Pyro has had minimal contact with his father and his mother and stepfather are currently getting divorced. For 17 years, his stepfather was in jail for murder and drug dealing, and from behind bars, supported Pyro and his brother. Pyro was a fair student in the 9th grade, but his grades and focus faltered in the 10th grade. He failed most of his classes and was regularly suspended. Pyro insists he has to be the man of the family and needs to take care of his mother and siblings, which is why he chooses not to focus on school. He says the new baby and the divorce do not bother him, but his self-sabotage in his schoolwork and attendance speak otherwise.

In the interviews, I encouraged the participants to talk about their work in video production, but this was not a substantive part of any conversation. For example, when I asked Nino her favorite class, she replied, "I could say media?" I said yes, however, she followed up by saying, "Well, since I was little, I always liked math. But I really like photography. I wish I could take that all year." Many participants expressed a desire to have 'more' or 'real' media classes. Popcorn, for example, chose after-school programs in photography and art because he felt the video production class did not challenge him. The absence of challenge is manifested through a minimal quantity of equipment to be shared by all students; a lot of time was spent waiting for cameras or computers. During time scheduled for production, there was not enough preparatory or process work for students to complete–or, students chose not to complete any preparation/process work–while awaiting equipment. Because the class was only 10 weeks long, there was little room for development or reflection within the cycle.

Integration Across the Curriculum

Media studies is not integrated across the curriculum. Instead, well-intentioned teachers use technology and videos to bolster their curricula while less adept or less flexible teachers make no attempt to include media in their curricula. Without a common foundation or collective agreement, media integration is predicated on teacher discretion and skill. For the most part, students believe they receive media training in their classes and are generally supportive of their teachers' work. If students get along with their teachers, they are willing to take instructional risks; without a personal connection, however, they retreat. This interpersonal trust–or its absence–forms the basis for many of the participants' relationships with faculty and staff, which will be discussed more specifically in Chapter Five.

On media inclusion, Nine defends the teachers' use of technology. She explains, "Yeah, we're a media-based school, so it's like in every class, we try to integrate the media, like we try to watch movies that will relate to the class, like in math class, we watched *A Beautiful Mind*[4]. That has to do with numbers, I guess." Watching movies is important and can be used to facilitate critical thinking and textual analysis skills, but it is not what makes a media-themed school unique. Eleventh grade Ivette sums up the inclusion of technology-as-media-education. In her estimation, media education is integrated in all her classes and she explains, "The way that we use media in our school is by typing, researching, using a Smart Board or the teacher uses a projector in order to tell us what he wants us to do, telling us what's right, what's wrong, you know, he uses the board, he writes on the board." Ivette, a 17-year-old Latina of Mexican descent is currently pregnant. When Ivette first found out she was pregnant, she and the baby's father ran away to Los Angeles, California, where they lived for three months. Ivette's parents did not know where she was or that she was pregnant; they ignored calls from the school regarding her lengthy absences. Ivette and Danny, the baby's father, were lonely in Los Angeles and missed her family. They told her parents about the pregnancy and agreed to come home to New York; Ivette's parents emancipated her and she has married Danny and lives with him in Queens. Ivette insists she will finish high school, college and graduate school to become a psychologist; however, missing three months of school and continued absences since she has returned put her in jeopardy to pass the 11th grade. By the time her baby is born, she will be 18 and there is talk of transferring her to a school for expectant and teenage mothers.

Genevieve, too, argues the media are worked into all the classes, especially in English. She explains:

> [In English] we break down the media, what we see everyday in newspapers, in magazines, and even on-line. We break that down and say what's your point of view on this? What's your interpretation of this piece? And how do you feel on it? What's the tone? And we start to see behind the layers of the media that things aren't what meet the eye. And we began to develop our own ideas.

Her use of the words 'interpretation' and 'layers of the media' are encouraging, as are the articulation of point of view and the assumed respect for pleasure associated with questions about feelings. However, Genevieve speaks only about this process of inquiry in her English class, a class dedicated to textual deconstruction, not in any other class. This also represents the continued burden put on English classes because of their focus on literary theory and deconstruction of texts, to absorb media studies into their fold (Buckingham 2003).

Nine is critical of the media inclusion, but believes her teachers do their best to include media studies. She explains:

> I think the teachers, when they plan their curriculum, they try to bring the media into it, and at times they do, but I don't think that the students can sometimes tell the difference between when we're making connections with our media studies and when we're not. Like, they just know it's a math class or it's an English class, they don't really notice the times that they integrate the media into it.

These answers reflect the students' respect for and trust in their teachers' expertise. No participant says their teacher does *not* integrate the media into classes, however, their answers show their understanding of media studies inclusion is varied, with shifting notions of responsibility. Ivette discusses the use of technology, especially computers, Smart Boards and projectors, as tools for learning and equates the *use* of technology with the *infusion* of media studies. Genevieve's list of questions provided by her English teacher reveals work done to uncover how students know what they know. These questions are not part of her other core or media classes. Nine's commentary about teacher planning and student awareness belies the overall trust in teacher awareness and authority. It is the student's responsibility to 'make connections' between the subject and the media infusion. Because students generally believe in the authority of their teachers and trust in the knowledge of their subject matter, it rests on the students to be responsible learners: to learn from technology, to articulate epistemological positions and to recognize the presence or absence of media studies connection. In this iteration, students inadvertently draw from the neoliberal orthodoxy that it is their own responsibility to learn about the media within the planned curricula.

Without a formal grounding in media education, the resulting curriculum gravitates toward an approach where the inclusion of 'media' is largely about the inclusion of technology. Students rarely have opportunities to discuss audiences, analysis and production topics within a critical media studies framework. They are invited to share their opinions, though in Nine's estimation, this might not happen with the knowledge that it is occurring in a media studies framework. The following shares how the participants articulate media studies integration in their core classes.

Social Studies

Pyro, 10th grade: We use the computers to do Social Studies projects, you can make a slide show for any event in history.

Genevieve, 11th grade: And history, we looked at different articles like in the past. I know we looked at this article from um, from around the 1800s, um early 1900s about the women's movement.

Popcorn, 12th grade: I mean, we look at news for political science, we look at newspapers about being on the debates.

Math

Pyro, 10th grade: In math, yesterday we were watching *My Super Sweet 16*[5] because we're on a budget project. So the assignment was to plan out a project for your Sweet 16, plan the ultimate birthday party. And you have to work on a certain budget.

Science

Jose, 9th grade: We were studying optical toys and that has to do with movement and that relates to media production.

Pyro, 10th grade: Science, we've looked at videos from like the Discovery Channel, *Planet Earth*[6]. We watched basic educational programming.

Genevieve, 11th grade: In health class we're talking about viruses and vaccines, so we read an article about this town affected by this virus and how certain mothers didn't want their child vaccinated because they heard from the media that it harmed more than helped. So we learn a lot about health in America through articles and movies and television, like *House*[7], you know there was an episode where there was this virus that spread through a maternity ward. So, we studied the skills that House and his staff applied to find the sources of that virus.

Popcorn, 12th grade: In science we read science articles, *New York Times*.

English

Pyro, 10th grade: In English we watched a couple of movies for certain assignments. Like the movie *Speak*[8] and we spoke about a current event that's somewhat like an epidemic, we talked about rape. We read a screenplay called *Fences*[9], which spoke on stereotypical stuff, like a black woman being the head of the family and everything.

Genevieve, 11th grade: In English we did editorials. Pick a social issue that affected us. The one that I picked, human trafficking, that's global. And the way I found out about it was from a movie on Lifetime, *Human Trafficking*[10]. And also looked up on the website, which is also a form of media.

Popcorn, 12th grade: In English, we watch movies and read movie reviews, you know just as another form of writing.

Media education at LSHS does not have a common definition or plan to integrate the theme across the curriculum. The use of computers, news articles, television shows, public health issues and films certainly enhance subject learning. However, these cannot be 'inserted' into a curriculum without corresponding work on their political implications. Moore (1991) details ways to include media across the curriculum and writes that one promise of media education is to "provide teachers of existing subjects with strategies for dealing anew with aspects of the media in their own teaching ... ideas for treating study texts as dynamic *producers of meaning* about history, geography, science or whatever" (p.173, italics in original). Without analysis of the texts–and meta-analysis on the inclusion of such texts in the classroom space–the development of critical autonomy is lacking. The inclusion of technologies and texts can be used to open doors and make approachable discussions of political economy, construction and power of institutions, systematic racism/sexism/classism, and the history and purpose of schooling, among other subjects. That is, they can be used to draw directly from student experience and situate that experience in time and space. Use of technologies and texts can help make unfamiliar material familiar. To encourage students' critical autonomy and to help guide them beyond oppression and away from replicating their subjugated social positions, the study and use of the media is a necessary component. Approaching unfamiliar material and possibly controversial topics through familiar material may provide students with a strong multidisciplinary foundation and provide them space to be active participants in their classrooms; this thought will be expanded over the next two chapters and will be discussed fully in Chapter Seven.

At LSHS, there is not a common community of learners with a coherent pedagogical approach to the study and inclusion of media. Media education *could* be successfully integrated into LSHS and as it is, is reflective of the larger environment: a massive overhaul of each class, the curricula of the school and the role of the school in the community is necessary. Broader than that, a massive overhaul of the urban school system–especially its continuous punishment of vulnerable students–remains necessary.

Conclusion

Popcorn illustrates that the use of media in his classes does not appear unique or extraordinary and his frustration was the inspiration for the title and framing of this chapter. Discussing the inclusion of watching movies or writing editorials or movie reviews, he retorts, "I mean, in what high school *don't* they use media? You know, like as a way of learning. I mean, every high school watches movies. Every high school uses the computer, so I don't really see a special thing about this high school." Popcorn taps into a key political problem in the attempt at media inclusion: What makes watching movies or using computers special? Popcorn is mostly disappointed by the undeserved reputation that the school is somehow unique because of its stated emphasis on self-expression. He argues, "I expect the school to like have a solid art class, but the only class we have that's like art-based, I would say, is film production. As far as intensity, it's not really intense, only if you're passionate about it." Popcorn struggles to explicate his frustration at the minimal access he feels he has to 'real' arts- and media-based curricula. Through his and his fellow participants' iterations, media education is not clearly defined with explicit goals and objectives. The definitions provided by students are superficial and do not grow in complexity throughout their high school tenure. The work done in the name of media studies, according to the participants, belies technology inclusion, especially in the use of videos, computers and the Internet. Popcorn reiterates the question of responsibility: does it lie within the system or the student? Is it the motivated student who wants to do the work, or the school system to make the work challenging? Popcorn observes that "we only have like one period a day that's media-based and most of the classes are not media based." He does believe it is possible to make the course work more complex and stronger, but is not sure himself how to go about it. "Most definitely it is possible to, you know, make media a stronger base [and] force in this school," he says. As a graduating senior, he believes his role in the school is finished and does not think decision-makers at the school would be interested in his critique.

The media are a major part of our culture and they are worthy of study. Though this is an overly obvious statement, it has not worked its way into secondary schools in a significant manner. Media education, or work done in its name, will have no lasting impact without significant changes within individual schools and across the school system. Specifically, to fulfill its media theme, LSHS needs a series of media courses with clear goals and objectives that increase in analytic and production complexity from 9th-12th grades. Students should have courses in media literacy and media production that provide them with solid definitions and foundations of study, especially in textual analysis, roles of audiences and producers, issues of ownership and control, and dissemination of information. Without formal and systematic media literacy training, students will not move beyond their own colloquial analyses. They will not be able to explicate *why* studying the media is important, how the media inform our daily choices, or how the media are intricately a part of and mutually influenced by the material studied in their core courses. These media classes should not operate in isolation; teachers of media should make intellectual and curricular connections with teachers of core subjects and all teachers should receive training and Professional Development courses in media education that are relevant and applicable to their subject matter.

The students who participated in this study, especially those who are highlighted in this chapter, show that there are serious gaps in media-specific classes and in the implementation of media studies across the curriculum. Upon graduation, students are not equipped with complex media analysis skills and have encountered an education in technology inclusion at best, not media education. At this stage, it is known what students do not know, are not learning and are not involved in. Media education will not alter the social or cultural capital of students, but it can provide the disruption that responds to the problematic test-as-education model and rattles the status quo. Chapters Five and Six spend more time inside school, exploring what students (do not) know about their experiences within new school reform and what they do know about the negative social labels and representations applied to them. Parsing out the data in these three ways–what they do not know about the media or media studies, what they do not know about new school reform or the social labels externally applied to them and how they understanding adolescence and education from the media and their own experiences – will illustrate how young people's social positions are negatively replicated by and within the very institution that is designed to protect and encourage their growth.

Notes

An early version of this chapter, titled 'Thinking inside the classroom: Notes from the field' appears in Tyner, K. (Ed.). (2009). *Media literacy: New agendas in communication* (pp. 76-97). New York: Taylor & Francis.

[1] There is licensure for foreign language and physical education teachers, and schools are expected to hire licensed teachers. At LSHS, the foreign language and gym teachers are not licensed in their subject matter.

[2] Young people who talk publicly about their gang connections are often labeled '8-4 gang members,' meaning their gang connections are tangential at best and they use their knowledge of gangs to show off during school. Students who are deeply involved in gangs know better than to talk about their involvement; gang involvement in school is grounds for suspension, transfers or expulsion and could ruin the deeply complicated workings of the gang. Gang members observe subtle announcements of gang affiliation, such as wearing certain colors or beads and communication via hand signs. J-Trout's denial could mean that he is in fact deeply involved and protecting himself and his fellow gang members; or it could mean that he is not involved at all.

[3] Their full chosen names are Peter Parker, Bruce Wayne and Popcorn Beverage (inspired by a pre-set button on a microwave). For brevity, I have shortened the names in text.

[4] *A Beautiful Mind*, the 2001 biographic film, chronicles the life and career of John Forbes Nash, Jr., schizophrenic mathematician and winner of the Nobel Prize for economics in 1994. Nash studied at Princeton and taught at MIT and was known for his antisocial tendencies and his work on Soviet code breaking (see imdb.com).

[5] *My Super Sweet 16* is an MTV reality show that details behind-the-scenes preparations for coming-of-age 16th birthday parties. Each episode documents one individual's party preparation, including (and highlighting) fights with parents, family members and friends. The final parties are extravagant, ostentatious displays of wealth and consumption (see mtv.com).

[6] *Planet Earth* is the Discovery Channel's 11-part series chronicling animal behaviors on land and in the sea and a variety of geography and topography (see http://dsc.discovery.com).

[7] *House* is the Fox Network's medical-mystery-drama show with an irrever-

ent, anti-social doctor, Gregory House, who solves medical mysteries. The show chronicles the working lives of a variety of doctors who tolerate the antics of House as he solves problems associated with infectious diseases. The show has won several awards and has been on the air for five seasons (see fox.com/house/showinfo).

[8] *Speak* is a 2004 film based on the novel of the same name about teenager Melinda Sordino who starts high school as a social outcast because she called the police during a summer party, where she was raped. As a result, she lives as a near mute. Melinda has troubled relationships with authorities, her family and her peers, but finds support in an arts teacher and school friend (see imdb.com).

[9] *Fences*, August Wilson's Pulitzer Prize winning play, tells the story of the Maxon family and the struggle for awareness of social and family change and African-American identity, set in the 1950s (see plays.about.com).

[10] *Human Trafficking* is the 2004 Lifetime film about women and children kidnapped and enslaved in sex-trafficking rings. The film tells the story of the women and children as well as the rookie immigration agent who works to rescue the women and children and punish the perpetrators (see mylifetime.com/on-tv/movies/human-trafficking/about).

Chapter 5

"It All Depends on the Person":

The Value of Small, Theme-Based Education for Underserved, Inner-City Youth

When asked about the value of attending small schools, Bruce, a 12th grade African American student answered, "It all depends on the person." This chapter uses his words to show there is no failsafe formula for 'success' within the public school system. Small schools are not better places because of their size and there is no causal proof that these schools will be more successful for struggling youth. This chapter discusses how the participants understand their school and its value as a small, theme-based school designed to reach out to underserved, inner city youth. The New York City Department of Education describes small schools as those which enroll about 500 students, "provide classes designed to ensure that all students meet high standards" and may have a theme "which enables students to connect what they learn in the classroom to the world beyond" (New York City Department of Education, *Choices*). Asking students how they define and comprehend 'small schools,' 'theme schools,' 'underserved,' 'inner city,' and how they feel in the physical space of their school, this chapter focuses on the changes within the Department of Education and how those changes are manifest within LSHS.

This chapter maps the participants' stories against the public language used to describe urban schools. LSHS students reveal they know very little about the components of new school reform or their participation within it. Chapter Four showed the participants are not learning the concepts of media education; Chapter Five explores the implications when students are unfamiliar with the constructs of their own schools and the external constructs of their own identities. How is the theme integrated, if at all, across the curriculum and how do the students articulate the value of media studies learning? What do the participants know of the labels applied to them and their schooling and how do they feel about the physical structure of their school? Through the participants' stories, I explore how ideas of radical pedagogy are mobilized to ultimately fail students and serve to replicate their already disenfranchised positions.

Definition and Value of Small Schools

There is a considerable disconnect between the language of new school reform and its implementation in schools. There is, further, a vast gulf between the language and students' awareness of the implementation of terminology. At LSHS, participants cannot provide comprehensive definitions of small schools, theme-based education, underserved or inner city. For the most part, their definitions of small schools are focused on the number of students rather than any pedagogical infusion. Ninth grade Monica understands small schools as made up of "A few students, like an easier environment to learn because you'll have more attention for yourself." This notion of 'a few students' is repeated by many of the participants across grades and the definitions do not necessarily develop in complexity. Eleventh grade Ivette explains, "Small schools, more education, more information, more communication between students and teachers. Knowing the students around you. You know, getting to know everybody around you." In the small environment, Ivette felt that she had a grudging approval and support of her pregnancy and marriage from most of her teachers and staff.

The participants consistently talk about fewer people and small classes and make regular correlation between small class size and quality of education. However, they do not speak authoritatively about the *how* that correlation occurs, nor can they speak on whether small schools are responsible for quality education. Overall, the participants embellish the definitions of small schools with discussion of valuable intimate connections between teacher and student and about interpersonal and emotional connections made with their classmates and with staff. They do not display knowledge of how or why smaller classes are necessary for increased learning and better educations.

The decision to construct and attend a school based on its small size illustrates a major push of new school reform: the idea that small schools are inherently better for student development. Small schools are not automatically better, but they do have certain advantages in providing a more intimate connection between staff and student and for many students, this could be beneficial to both their learning and their willingness to stay in school (Alonso *et al.* 2009; Goldstein 2004; Noguera 2004). In discussion of the positives and negatives of small schools, participants touch upon a connection between classroom learning and social pressures found in small schools.

"It All Depends on the Person" 127

In conversation with each other, 10th graders Pyro, CML and Ventura deconstruct their thoughts on the positives and negatives of small schools:

> *Pyro:* Small schools, you focus less on bein' popular and you focus more on the little bit of friends that are there. And it's also easier for you to learn. Small schools might be good, but there's too many kids in the world to do all small schools. Sometimes big schools are necessary.
> *CML:* I think of small schools, I think of a school that just started and is trying to move to a higher position.
> *Ventura:* I wouldn't really enjoy a small school 'cause it's just wack. It's a little bit of people. I like to associate with a lot of people. I'm very associative.
> *Pyro:* So you're saying you don't like it here? Would you rather be somewhere else?
> *Ventura:* Not that I don't like it here, it's just … It's also a new school.
> *Pyro:* Not all big schools is bad. Sometimes it's the kids that you have in it. In order to make a big school better, as if it was a small school, how about trying to get to know your students? Instead of your principal saying 'Hey boy, come here, hey girl, come here' –
> *Ventura:* - It's too much chaos in big schools -
> *Pyro:* - In small, expect to be called by your name. My principal knows everybody's name. I don't know how she does it, but she knows everybody's name. I appreciate it at times, but she makes hearing your own name sometimes sickening. And that's the thing about small schools: it's too much attention on yourself. 'Cause you don't have nobody else to take that attention off of you.

Pyro, CML and Ventura are deeply troubled students with a battery of social and behavioral issues evident in their poor class attendance, absent attention to school work, and ability to distract–and be distracted–quite easily[1]. Pyro, introduced in Chapter Four, participated in both a group interview with CML and Ventura and a private interview. In private, he shared more intimate details, especially about his relationship with his incarcerated ex-stepfather, currently divorcing his mother and the implications for care of his baby sister. With CML and Ventura, he presents a more guarded and defensive version of himself.

CML and Ventura are volatile students and a constant source of struggle for teachers and staff. CML is a mixed ethnicity white-Latino student who lives with his mother and stepfather in Manhattan and, contrary to the majority of his classmates, is economically stable. His father is in prison and CML visits him over the holidays; his behavior, before and after major holidays, takes a deep plunge. Always aggressive, he is more antagonistic and vulgar than usual before and after visits with his father. CML's mother is sexually provocative in appearance; CML resents his mother's self-presentation and becomes viscerally angry when friends comment on her looks. He believes friends hang out at his apartment because of his video game collection and to ogle his mother. His stepfather is a bully who pays little positive attention to CML, which he shrugs off as irrelevant, yet CML is a classic bully himself, picking on and antagonizing both students and staff he deems vulnerable.

Ventura is a petite Latino boy who lives with his mother in upper Manhattan. He is an avid skateboarder and soccer player with little to no interest in school. He spent the majority of the 2007-2008 school year getting suspended, often with CML, for various infractions. Near the end of the school year, he broke a glass windowpane in a classroom door and immediately upon return from a 2-week suspension, graffitied the outside of the school building, a criminal offense. He rarely spoke about his home life and during various suspensions, he would phone me to see what was happening at school and if anyone noticed his absences. Though all three boys claim on various occasions they do not care about much beyond partying, sex, drugs, alcohol or video games, this posturing–further exemplified in Chapter Six– does not feel authentic. Instead, they present as deeply troubled young men whose negative behavior alienates those who set out to help them.

Ventura's comment that small schools are 'wack' and Pyro's alternating admiration and frustration that the principal knows every student's name illustrates their deep desire to be lost in the system. While they cannot articulate the pedagogical value of a small school, they do recognize that their destructive behavior does not go unnoticed. In a rare moment of self reflection, CML told me he vows every morning before school to 'stay good,' but when something sets him off, he 'lets loose' and cannot control his anger, even though he knows he will get in trouble. As 10th graders, these young men are in the middle of high school; CML's comment that small schools are trying to get better is reflective of his own position as a student in the middle of a tumultuous developmental period.

Equally concerned with the social aspects of small school, but in a more affable tone, 12th graders Popcorn and Bruce speak about the needs of students in small schools:

> *Popcorn:* It is good in the educational aspect because you get to learn more, it's more like family based. But not in the social aspect, like larger schools tend to be, you get to like know more people and if you know more people, you'll probably get more different experiences, in that sense. But in the small school setting, you'll get more experiences because you know these people. And they would probably be more meaningful.
> *Bruce:* I could take the other side of the coin, on the social issue, 'cause in a small school, like the one we attend, you know everybody. You know everybody's face, but if you go

to a big school that has thousands of kids, you get lost in schools that big. In a small school, which keeps it in a small community, I think it betters your social life 'cause you know how to talk to people.
Popcorn: It helps you develop your identity.
Bruce: I consider myself a social butterfly. Like, I could go to a place where there's thousands of kids and befriend like one-fourth of them in a week. I'm very talkative and very friendly.

In the two discussions shared here, students who are friends with each other express their own unique needs and awareness of others' needs. Bruce and Popcorn's conversation is different in tone and aggression from Pyro, CML and Ventura's. Pyro, CML and Ventura are in trouble more often than not; Ventura, especially, is unable to contain his frustrations or compose his behavior. That he wants to attend a larger school–where he can be lost–is not surprising. Pyro interrogates Ventura's apparent misunderstanding of what type of school he attends and does not recognize that Ventura may feign ignorance as a way of disappearing. Popcorn and Bruce have greater strength of character as individuals and awareness of each other as developing human beings. They debate the value of socializing in a small or large environment and reveal their awareness of each other's strengths and needs. Both Popcorn and Bruce participated in group and private interviews and were equally open with intimate details in each setting, revealing the level of trust they have for each other. Popcorn and Bruce disagree consistently about who is responsible for the struggles and disorganization within their school–Popcorn blames the system while Bruce blames the individual–but they have a mutual respect and admiration for each other's abilities and methods of expression.

This awareness of interpersonal connections garners student approval of small schools. Eleventh graders Stacy, Genevieve and Rain discuss the importance of classroom size and personal attention from teachers:

Stacy: If you have a big class of like 40 kids, you're not gonna recognize their names. Their names are just a piece of paper to you. You can't match that name to a face. Here, everybody knows your name. Everybody knows who you are as a student. I think it's more personal, you get more work done. At least you know that the teacher cares about you. At least to know your name and what kind of person you are.
Genevieve: In this setting, they know when you skip class. Our advisors, they check in every day. So, it's not just how you are as a student, but also as a person. And also, they look into your personal background, like your family, your history, not just the history of your grades, but your work ethics. So, they really dig deep.
Rain: It's more easier for students to learn in an environment that's small. Because if

you're in a big school environment, it's really hard to, you know, concentrate. The teacher is going ahead and not paying attention to you. Some people, they need that attention 'cause if you don't have that attention that you need to succeed, you can't really succeed. You'll go through class just sittin' there, like, 'Why am I here?' That's why I think it's better to have a small setting.

Genevieve and Alex, introduced in Chapter Four, participated in a group interview with Stacy and Rain; Genevieve also participated in a private interview. Stacy is an African-American young woman who lives with her mother and little brother in Manhattan. She has no contact with her father, who was physically abusive to her mother. She can be a bully, interrupting and overtaking conversations if she perceives she is not getting enough attention. Rain is a petite, shy African-American young woman who lives with her mother and brother in Manhattan. Rain initially appears easily bullied, especially by Stacy, who interrupted her regularly and consistently in conversation. However, throughout the conversation, Rain is unfazed by Stacy's bullying, talking through her or waiting until an outburst subsides to continue speaking. Rain presents a calm, collected self whose confidence in speaking increases throughout the conversation. As will be shown in Chapter Eight, Rain has an acute understanding of her geography and how external changes from private enterprise will significantly harm local populations.

The lofty expectation of small schools–personal attention, intimate relationships between students and staff, social cohesion between students and less volatility among social groups–does not always translate to the work done in a classroom. The theme, and its integration, needs greater examination.

Definition and Value of Theme-based Schools

Less concrete than their understandings of small schools are students' definitions of theme-based education. For the most part, participants were unable to precisely define theme-based schooling. Some students define theme schools as being 'about something' and are able to list various topics, but do not make connections between theme education and integrated learning, or, in some cases, that they themselves go to a theme-based school. In conversation, Pyro, CML and Ventura reveal they do not know what theme-school means:

"It All Depends on the Person" 131

> *Pyro:* A school with a certain theme?
> *CML:* I've never heard of theme school–
> *Pyro:* -Yeah, me neither–
> *Ventura:* -Me either.
> *Pyro:* But the title sounds pretty self-explanatory.

Despite the brevity of this interaction–barely a few words each per sentence–the fact that the boys are not aware of what theme-based education reveals itself to be a source of frustration and cause for defensiveness in their tone. It is easier to group together in a chorus of 'I don't know' than admit they may be confused by the concept[2].

It is young men like Pyro, CML and Ventura that small schools and theme-based education rhetorically claim to reach: troubled students who would easily–and eagerly–fall through the cracks in a large comprehensive school. At LSHS, 10th-grade classes run more smoothly when one, if not all three, of these students are absent. They are smart young men who make destructive choices and, inevitably, lose their support systems[3].

In a conversation that belies a similar minimal lack of awareness, but whose tone is much more friendly, Popcorn and Bruce dance around the idea of what a theme school might look like and what its value may be:

> *Popcorn:* A school based off a specific theme that most likely a majority of people would be interested in.
> *Bruce:* I think of a theme school, I dunno, probably specialized to the point where you're going to school for one particular reason. You go to a high school, specifically for film, then right then and there, you're making a decision that you want to be a filmmaker. A theme school's like–especially at the high school level–I think it's kind of drastic for a student to pick a school that has one theme. Especially a theme like film.

When Bruce says 'it's kind of drastic for a student to pick a school that has one theme,' he displays a conservative politics. These young men *do* attend a theme school, yet somehow appear unaware of it in this conversation. They have somehow chosen to distance themselves personally from the question and instead, try to approach it from the outside, imagining what a theme school might be like. Theme schools do not demand that students determine a career path at the start of grade nine; that Bruce had adopted this belief reveals two disconcerting flaws in the rhetoric of new school reform. First, students are not explicitly aware of the construction of their own schools. Second, vocational education has not been eradicated, but rather, has been given a radical label that covers a more insidious form of tracking that filters students to separate schools rather than separate routes within school, making assumptions of student worthiness. Only now students are 'tracked' into schools separate from one another rather than separate classes within the same school. Small, theme-based schools do not recruit the city's brightest, most intellectually competitive students (for that, there are the historically strong application/audition-based selective schools that, incidentally, have multi-thousand enrollment numbers) but rather, vulnerable students who struggle to stay on track.

In a similarly friendly tone, Stacy, Alex and Genevieve bounce ideas off each other to determine the definition of theme schools. These young women are highly focused, to the point of anxiety, on their education and schoolwork. All three are intelligent young women who want to do well in school because school is something they like, but also to prepare for their futures: these young women desperately want to leave New York City and volatile home lives permanently, starting with college. However, in their conversation they talk about professional skills acquisition, which reveals more about preparation for labor than preparation for intellectual advancement:

> *Stacy:* A school based on a certain thing. The arts. Theater. A school that really specializes in a particular theme of the world. Like, music, drama, drawing. Like our school's based on media. Like I think it's all just based on a certain thing that a lot of kids would like to have a profession in.
> *Alex:* I think it's related on a certain topic, a certain idea that comes to mind.
> *Genevieve:* Women and business. They're creating an atmosphere where they teach you certain skills on that certain topic.
> *Alex:* To kind of keep kids more interested in actually continuing going to school. Yeah, it will definitely be helpful, I think, doing things like that. It keeps kids interested. Even if they eventually don't want to go into that profession, they still have that skill and they also have the skills they learned throughout high school in reading, math.

All three young women work hard to please their teachers, to complete their schoolwork early and to care for the more troubled students in their school. Both Alex and Genevieve continuously look to cultivate family amongst their classmates. When Alex says that theme schools 'keep kids interested' in attending school, she intimates her friends who, without her prodding, she believes will drop out.

Across these definitions, theme schools are equated to vocational or technical schools: they teach a specific set of skills that will contribute to job- and labor-readiness. The irony, however, is that with the dismantling of the large, comprehensive schools that formally tracked students in academic or job-readiness threads, so too was the language of vocational education dismantled. Its spirit, however, lives on in understandings of theme-based education. While the language of new school reform defies academic or labor-preparation tracking, Bruce's concern that high school represents career decision making time, Genevieve's observation on the teaching of skills in a certain topic, and Alex's assertion that skill sets are labor's foundation illustrates that the essence of vocational training remains at the core of language and learning of these students. The rhetoric of new school reform does not undo the layers of social learning that operate invisibly and yet concretely reveals where these young people belong.

Participants cannot necessarily articulate *why* theme schools are valuable or important. The participants have come to accept on some level the rhetoric they are given: theme schools are a valuable part of new school reform. Ultimately, what is revealed is that themes do not really matter to the students for a variety of reasons. Tenth grade J-Trout astutely points out that themes do not always–if ever–have an impact on schools. He observes, "Schools that have themes? They don't really follow the themes a lot. I'm not gonna lie, it wouldn't matter to me if we had a theme or not. That's the reason why kids are here, for media, but if it was a school that didn't have a theme, I think it still would have the same impact that it does now." In J-Trout's estimation, that impact amounts to mostly nothing and what reputedly makes the school 'special' is a waste of his time and the theme simply does not matter to his education.

Integration of Theme

The participants are not necessarily clear, or are not able to clearly articulate, the definition or implementation of theme-based study. Furthermore, several participants are unclear how to discuss the theme of their own school. In separate interviews, 12th-grade Bruce and 11th-grade Ivette each work to explain how the media theme is integrated across their school. Each explanation results in a manifestation of integration that has little to do with media education:

> *Bruce:* My principal said she wants it a community and self-expression is big with her. So like, your image, the way you look, your actions, what you do, how you write, self-expression is big. So, the theme is individuality and being an individual in a joined community.

Ivette: It's basically, like, being part of everything. Like if there's a performance in school, try to be part of it. You know, try to help out. You don't have to be in the performance, just help out with the curtains, the lights or anything, it's like group work. We have to, we all have to join in, chip in with anything we can. That's basically what it means.

While media education indeed incorporates notions of self-expression, community and collective work, this is not what makes media education unique or special, nor is it the theoretical underpinning of media studies. Developing self-expression skills, community building and collective work should be implemented across all high school curricula, irrespective of theme. Community building and collective work counter neoliberal ethos and can help make high school a force for social change. However, it does not make a school's theme unique. These are basic skills that pedagogues, parents and communities at large might reasonably expect all citizens to possess. That no participant discusses the analysis of texts, the role of production or the development of critical inquiry shows that these concepts are not worked into the school. Media industries are not used as a way to frame learning, to examine or critically assess social and political locations or to develop tools for social change.

When participants do discuss aspects of the media in their classes, it is mostly through the inclusion of technology. Tenth grade Pyro, 11th-grade Genevieve and 12th graders Nine and Nino all say that yes, the media are integrated into their classes. However, when examining their responses, it is clear that it is technology, not the concepts of media education, used in class:

Pyro: We have specific media classes where we get to make videos by using camcorders and cameras and using computers. And how our academic classes relate to them is we use these computers to do projects.

Genevieve: They teach us media is all around us. And it's a big influence on the way we think and the ideas we present in class. By writing an editorial, getting my voice out into the media, it helps get my opinions on it. And hopefully it will influence someone else, like media influenced me.

Nine: We're a media-based school, so it's like in every class, we try to integrate the media, like we try to watch movies that will relate to the class.

Nino: Our school is media-based. We do classes that have media influences, like photography, film. We have college stuff, but that's not really media. In Spanish class we watch movies and we have to translate them. And we read Spanish newspapers and stuff. And learn about other countries and what they've been through.

Using cameras and computers to do projects, learning from Web sites and watching films are all part of media education, but not independent pieces that constitute the unique qualities of media education or are reflected in the concepts of media education (Buckingham 2003). Genevieve seems to implicitly understand the tenets of media education, but does not explicitly articulate them. She refers to her role as a media maker and the responsibility inherent in expressing herself, but struggles with her articulation of that knowledge. Loosely echoing Popcorn's frustration from Chapter Four, in the 21st century it is difficult to imagine a school that does *not* incorporate technology into its classrooms. The inclusion of technology–especially computers with high-speed Internet connections–is presented as the successful public face of reformed urban education. High-speed Internet access and computers in classrooms are showcased as evidence that class divides have disintegrated: now poor students have the same technology as privileged students. Yet, having the same technologies does not unequivocally translate to having the same quality education.

The pieces that do constitute new school reform for underserved youth do not actually result in concrete pedagogical advancements. In a specific focus on media learning, participants cannot articulate the fundamentals of media studies and yet it is meant to be a major part of their high school experience. At LSHS, technology inclusion masks the absence of critical media learning. The school system that focuses on ways to mobilize the *image* of learning rather than focus on avenues that *improve* actual learning further perpetuates the superficial notion of success.

Understandings of Labels: Underserved and Inner City

While many of the participants acknowledge they are poor, that their families struggle with money and live absent financial security, most of the people they know are in similar circumstances, so they do not express this struggle as different or deficient from their peers. There is little outward explicit shame or embarrassment about their poverty; some students have more or less money, some students get free or reduced lunches, some students are eligible for free breakfast, some students live in public housing, but whatever the circumstances, all students struggle. All students live, whether in private or public housing, on the fringes of the city's dilapidated neighborhoods, yet on their journey to school, they traverse the city's wealthiest neighborhoods and share the subway, bus and sidewalk with some of the city's most gifted arts' students and professionals. *These* neighborhoods and students are the ones who are different, but in their difference, represent the socially dominant position against which the participants are negatively compared. These young people have internalized the hegemonic arrangement of social divisions that 'common sense' prevails and their oppression is accepted (Freire 1970/2000). Through this acceptance, they unwittingly perpetuate their own oppression and advance neoliberal beliefs in the individual's responsibility for success or failure. As will be shown, they know on a certain level they are punished for their identities: their school has metal detectors while the school across the street does not. However, they do not link that frustration to broader ideologies of oppression. Overall, they are not cogently aware they are labeled 'underserved,' 'inner city' youth or that these labels have shuffled them onto a particular educational track.

Underserved

Most participants do not specifically define 'underserved' as connected to education or to their own educational experiences specifically. Some participants, such as Nino who states, "Underserved? I don't know," acknowledge they not only do not know what the word means, but also that they have never heard it before. Jose and Ivette understand underserved to be the antithesis of equal, "unjust, unequal," and "like not treated equally." For Marlo, Joan, Monica and Nine, to be underserved is to be "not given enough," "like nothing, basically," and "you don't get all the attention you need." CML, Ventura and Pyro agree that underserved is an absence of material goods, low school supplies and "not getting what you need to be getting." There is no self-reflection in any participant's commentary; the participants do not see themselves as underserved or otherwise treated unequally. They do not make connections between the antithesis of equality or the absence of material goods as something they experience. They most certainly do not connect their life experiences with either the way the New York City Department of Education views them or the way left-leaning scholars argue on their behalf (Anyon 1997; McLaren 1999; McLaren & Kincheloe 2007; Steinberg & Kincheloe 2004b; Macedo & Steinberg 2007; Weis & Fine 2005).

Peter, Bruce and Popcorn connect 'underserved' directly to schools, but not to their school. Instead, they focus on the representation of Principal Joe Clark and the high school he oversaw in the 1989 film *Lean on Me*[4]:

Peter: Improper funding. Schools not getting what they need. I remember sophomore year we had to write an essay about forgotten schools and we watched *Lean on Me*. And, maybe *Lean on Me* was an exaggerated movie, but in that movie, there was a hundred kids on a stage who got kicked out of the school because they didn't want to be there and they didn't care to be there.
Popcorn: You know why? Because the school was a bad environment. It sucked when you got there, you got yelled at, it was dirty.
Bruce: - The teacher got decked in the eye -
Peter: - How a school end up like that? The teachers don't do it.
Popcorn: Through underserving the students!
Peter: And eventually the students are gonna take that and mess the school up.
Bruce: School's already messed up.
Peter: So you feel that if this school was like that you would take what you're offered and be a wild kid?
Popcorn: Yeah, yeah I would be pretty angry, yeah. If this school was like the school in *Lean on Me*, I probably would be angry. I wouldn't be the well-mannered person I am today. I would be quiet, but if somebody stepped up to me, I would probably deck 'em. Just 'cause it's that jungle, wild-like environment.

What is interesting about this discussion, coming from 12th-grade students who attend a media-themed school, is that, other than Peter's comment that the film might be 'exaggerated,' there is no discussion of the representation of authority and control in the film, or the sanctioning of violence in the brutally heroic presentation of Principal Joe Clark who put his school on lockdown, ruled with a baseball bat and dismissed disruptive students to improve statistics. They do not discuss the assignment of a 'forgotten school' or whether there might be connections between the assignment and their own school. Instead, the boys accept the film and its presentation as truth and they move on to debate whose responsibility it was to let a school reach such a depraved level:

Bruce: I don't think you can say 'I have a proper student,' 'cause what does it mean to have a proper student?
Peter: A student who's gonna be attentive, who's an actual learner, wants to be there. 'Cause, again, the students do make the school. Yes, the teachers and the money, but, you can't have a good school without students actually putting their heart into what they do. What if there's a kid that can't be served? That doesn't want to be served?
Bruce: Then he shouldn't be here.
Popcorn: But most kids want to be served.

In the discussion of *Lean on Me*, Popcorn and Bruce continue to stake their claim, while Peter vacillates, unclear who is responsible. Popcorn reiterates

138 *Media Education Goes to School*

his belief in the responsibility of the system when he says the school represented in the film was a 'bad environment.' Bruce continues his belief that it is the individual when he claims disruptive students should be removed. Peter is conflicted; he initiates the example of *Lean on Me*, with the observation of 'improper funding,' but also discusses students making poor decisions and suffering the consequences. They unknowingly enter into the classical structure/agency debate, though do not make the links between their debate, frustration and personal experiences.

Stacy, Alex, Rain and Genevieve are the only ones to immediately connect 'underserved' with their own educational experiences:

> *Stacy:* We're definitely underserved. Like when you're not getting what you need. You're getting under what you need, you're not even getting average. You're getting what's below the average.
> *Alex:* I wouldn't even think any of us really deserve just plain old average. We could get so much more if we actually worked hard, but then again, it won't work that way.
> *Genevieve:* There's dried blood on the walls by the water fountain. And like gum and candy bar wrappers, tissues. It's disgusting.
> *Stacy:* It's disgusting. And they leave their garbage on the floor. I want to know what their rooms look like.
> *Rain:* Their homes probably look the same way the school look.
> *Genevieve:* That's why they trash it.
> *Stacy:* But I'm saying, you hate the school so much, why don't you change it instead of addin' to the crap that you're doin'?
> *Alex:* It's not that they hate *this* school. It's that they hate *school.* They don't need a reason for it.

In describing their own school and its physical failings, the young women acknowledge that they experience the ramifications of an underserved educational experience. Yet their disgust is not novel; many reports of urban schooling discuss physical disrepair (Alonso *et al.* 2009; Anyon 1997; Kozol 2000; Steinberg & Kincheloe 2004b). I have described the physical surroundings of LSHS, so I, too, am a participant in showcasing the grim realities of urban schools. When these descriptions are nothing new and continuously horrific, why are they so prevalent? What, if anything, new is learned? I have two thoughts on this. One, descriptions are horrific and continuous because they must be in order to make change; until they can be written about in the past tense, the descriptions must continue. Two, descriptions are horrific and continuous because they must be in order to make sense of them. How is it possible that the descriptions of Berube and Gittell (1969), Anyon (1997),

Kozol (2000), Alonso *et al.* (2009) and this text have not changed in 40 years? This reveals that something is seriously the matter with the way and under what physical conditions urban students are treated.

Alex's comment that students could get more 'if we actually worked hard' and her immediate resignation that 'it won't work that way,' reveal her internalization of neoliberal beliefs. Her and her classmates' job is to work hard(er) but that job does not matter. These young women know that school is part of a larger environment where destruction is acceptable, evidenced through their claims that those who disrespect the school also disrespect their homes. 'Plain old average' is an aspiration, which reveals these young women know their surroundings are well below average. Alex's cold, but probably true, assertion that those who destroy the school hate *school*, not their specific school, effectively ends their conversation, but it introduces much more than it concludes. What leads young people to so much anger that they destroy a place where, in theory, they spend most of their day? When decades of urban school descriptions are explored, it is clear that the hatred runs deep and is implicitly sanctioned in the absence of explicit social and physical change.

Inner City

For as long as there have been concerns with the betterment of the poor, there have been labels applied that mark 'them' as deficient. In the primary source documents gathered by Berube and Gittell (1969) to discuss the Ocean Hill-Brownsville strikes, labels such as 'ghetto child' and 'slum child' are used interchangeably and without obvious malice; these were the socially acceptable names of the time used to refer to the urban poor. When Freire (1970/2000) critiques the inadequate education the poor receive, he unabashedly uses the term 'oppressed' and makes clear the abusive relationship between the oppressors and the oppressed. In Macedo's (2000) introduction, he writes of the bravery displayed by Freire in his clear, unforgiving language: those in power positions are not treated gently or made to feel better for their circumstances.

Today, we do not talk of the slum child unless speaking specifically about less developed countries (a metaphor for those people/geographic areas that have not fully embraced capitalism) and 'ghetto' has been reclaimed as a fashion statement, a commodity, a term of praise (which further clarifies power positions by granting those with less social capital ownership over what was once a term of derision). Absent 'slum' and 'ghetto,' there remains 'inner city.' This gentle term puts a safe distance between young people and their families whose communities are in significant need of maintenance and repair and those whose intellectual and capital efforts are aimed at healing–but not integrating–these young people and their families. These young people are subject to yet another rhetorical term perpetuating their oppression: the inner city, despite it nominal centrality, is in fact on the fringes as the impoverished are continuously pushed to the edges and regularly expected to expand and grow communities in increasingly limited and shrinking space. Through gentrification and continued increase in real estate premiums, the poor are pushed further from the center and must lay claim to geographic margins in addition to their already social and economic marginality.

None of the participants think they live in the inner city, even those that describe their housing and communities as dangerous, gang-, crime- or drug-infested. Ivette believes she lives in the inner city because she is not on the most well-known Queens subway line, "'Cause when people say 'Queens,' people think it's like, on the 7 train. And I live on the A train. Where I live, it's like, 20, 25 minutes away from like the *real* Queens, which is Roosevelt and Jackson Heights. So I think I do live in the inner city, due to that." Ivette makes no mention of income, housing style or geography, but instead, connects 'inner' to the neighborhood in inner Queens, applying the term literally. Jose, Lucy and J-Trout all define inner city as "New York City." Admittedly, what these young people know of New York City is an isolated, increasingly segregated division within the five boroughs, however, that they make no distinction between geographic areas of the city reveals an absence of understanding of labels applied to their living situation. Nino and Monica both describe the inner city as "different than the suburbs," but again, make no clear distinctions within the city confines. As Alex and Genevieve discuss, the inner city is a bustling, busy place:

> *Genevieve:* The neighborhoods. Being inside the city, interacting with different people within your setting, within your environment. I mean, in this school we have kids from Queens and the Bronx and Brooklyn or wherever.
> *Alex:* When I think of inner city, I think of, kind of craziness, it's a rush. You're always on the run, you never have time to appreciate little things. If you've lived in New York City your whole entire life, when you think of inner city, you think, okay, it's the city. It's New York. Whatever.

Genevieve's use of 'inside the city' connects inner city to its literal meaning, similar to Ivette's belief. In Alex's observation that 'if you've lived in New York City your whole entire life,' inner city equals New York City in its entirety. However, these young women live on the fringes, not the inside, and in their absence of understanding, provide evidence for the increased segregation in the city.

Bruce and Popcorn, in a debate with each other, point out that inner city is an externally applied label attached to poor urban kids and the schools they attend. Applying such a label separates urban from suburban kids and those who apply the labels do not realize that all kids face similar concerns, irrespective of labeling:

> *Popcorn:* I think the reason why they call it 'inner city schools' simply because it's in the city and that's basically it. It's no diff–it probably might be less funded than a suburban school. Other than that, the kids face the same problems of identity. They face the same problems of discovering yourself.
> *Bruce:* It is the same thing, but if someone said, 'what would you rather go to, an inner-city school or a suburban school,' the inner city is a label. You gonna think, minorities, rowdy kids and stuff, so that's why I said it's a label that's put on. And yes, every school has these problems with like teen pregnancy, identity, finding yourself, people going through crisis in high school. But like, when you say 'inner city,' you think about those rowdy black kids that you don't want to be next to.
> *Popcorn:* When you think of a suburban school, you probably won't think of bad kids, you might just think of *kids*.
> *Bruce:* Yeah, white preppy kids.
> *Popcorn:* You know, and their typical teenage problems. But in an inner city school, you don't think about the inner city students in that aspect of them facing teenage problems, you just think of them as being bad and outspoken-
> *Bruce:* - And primarily minority-
> *Popcorn:* -Yeah. And just ignorant and they're not getting a good education and they resort to crime to get what they want. It is basically a label and I mean, unfortunately, some people do fit into that label. And it doesn't mean that kids from suburban schools, they don't fit into that label, you just don't hear about it as much. Because the main focus is on inner city kids.

Similar to Stacy, Rain, Alex and Genevieve's understanding of underserved schools, Bruce and Popcorn understand inner city, and make a direct link to school, via negative examples. Bruce mentions 'rowdy black kids' and 'primarily minority,' using a term that refers to black and Latino populations who, across the city and especially in Popcorn and Bruce's school and community are quantifiably the majority. Popcorn once again cautions against the power of the institution in labeling and expecting certain behavior of young people. In Popcorn's estimation, *all* kids 'face the same problems of identity,' especially self-discovery. The tragic difference, of course, is that young people struggling with identity and self-discovery with invisible social privilege are supported in that search while 'rowdy black kids' are punished. Though only a few participants are aware of the social and contextual impact of the labels 'underserved' and 'inner city' all of them live within the reality of these labels, which has a multigenerational past, is deeply embedded in understandings of the urban, and will not be easily undone.

Concerns Within School: Interpersonal and Architectural Relationships

Undoing and reformulating this reality is a necessary step to change the operation of urban schools and students experiences within; the participants articulate clearly their frustrations and struggles with school and their words can serve as an entrypoint for change. Marlo speaks for many of the participants when he says, "I feel trapped" by school. Joan further elaborates, "This school has no windows. When you're looking to see a sunny day, you don't. You don't know if it's snowing, raining. You don't know what's going on outside 'til you go outside. You know, it's kind of like trapped in." Although LSHS students are allowed to take video and still cameras home from school to work on class projects, the SSA officers who process the students through the scanning and metal detectors upon entry do not distinguish between the more than 3000 students and cannot be expected to know which schools students attend; various LSHS staff wait upon entry to collect equipment from security personnel. Participants have two broad concerns with their school: interpersonal relationships with faculty and staff, which reveals their ability to trust or reject authority and the forced scanning and metal detector entry to school, which is a major source of frustration and anxiety.

Interpersonal Relationships

When participants critique specific aspects of their school, it is often about personalities and individual teachers. That young people complain about their teachers is not surprising or unexpected; these complaints reveal concerns about what they value or perceive is lacking in adult authority figures and their own desires for schooling. All 9th-grade participants shared a similar dislike for one particular class because they felt the teacher had little to no control over the class. Despite a vocal desire for freedom and frustrations with feeling trapped, students are more critical about the absence of control:

Jose: It's not so much the subject, it's more the teacher. Like, we get off task so much because [the teacher] is always yelling at students, he calls on someone, this leads to that, and we like never really get to a lesson.

Monica: I sometimes don't understand the work. My teacher has a tough time explaining it.

Tom: The teacher's okay, but I don't feel like I'm learning anything. I don't feel like I'm learning as much as I do in the other classes. The teacher talks too much and we always get off subject. Like, he'll be about to start the lesson and somebody will say something and he'll get all the way off subject about that thing. And we seem to never learn what we supposed to learn.

Jose, Monica and Tom are hard-working students who have no significant disciplinary problems. Their frustration with this one class reveals a desire to learn upended by a disorganized teacher and willfully disruptive class. When students cannot make a focused connection to their coursework, their willingness to do work is undone.

Many of the participants felt they could not trust their principal, claiming that she behaved inappropriately and knew too much about their personal lives. That students express discontent with the principal is expected: as the most visible authority figure, a principal both sets and represents the ethos of any school. As adolescents test out various identity positions and stake personal claims, authority figures occupy clear battlegrounds, ostensibly with explicit boundaries. The participants who complain about their principal express a discontent with *personal*, not *authoritative* aspects of leadership. Participants who critiqued the principal believed she treated and manipulated them personally, not professionally.

Lucy, who has gotten in a significant amount of trouble because of cutting school and not doing her schoolwork, believes the principal has a vendetta against her. The principal knows about Lucy's drug use, which she believes is used against her to increase the severity of her punishments when she inevitably gets caught. Directing her anger at the principal, Lucy explains, "The thing with her is that if you get in trouble, she takes it on a personal level. She includes things that shouldn't be included. Like she starts talking about your family and how you're disrespecting your family." While it is true that Lucy should not be cutting school, missing homework or doing drugs, she, correspondingly, is offered no social services within the school; admittedly, if these were offered, Lucy would most likely decline. That the response to her negative behaviors is to increase suspensions does not address the foundations of Lucy's self-abusive behavior. Instead, Lucy feels encouraged, on a certain level, to *increase* her negative behavior because it provides her with a guaranteed day off. She explains, "She doesn't understand that by suspending me, it's giving me a break." Lucy tells a story about getting caught smoking on school property with another student; she received a 4-day suspension while the other student only got a 1-day suspension. Lucy believes the disproportionate punishment was because "She doesn't like me. She took it to a personal level."

Lucy does not see that her punishments may be more severe because she has been caught a significant number of times and the consequences increase with each infraction. Nevertheless, her behavior and its consequences deserve further exploration. Lucy's behavior echoes Brown's (2005) discussion of differences among working-class and middle-class girls. To paraphrase, Lucy knows her presence in school is disruptive; she knows how to behave badly *well* and, more importantly, bad behavior is expected of her. What does it mean when students believe the principal treats them as personal problems? This erases what should be a clear behavioral boundary: adult/child, administrator/student. The title of 'principal' carries with it a great variety of complex and contradictory responsibilities, however, when a principal is abusive of students, as many of the participants feel she is, a confusing environment is cultivated. Principals set the tone of any school and if the tone is one of personal badgering, to whom is a badgered student to turn for help? This, in turn, cultivates a symbolic violence of fear and distrust amongst students, furthering their distrust of authority figures and of school as safe places.

In a similar story, Popcorn, generally a well-behaved student who is well liked and admired by faculty and staff, feels the principal intentionally hurt him over a misunderstood event. He tells the story of being caught with a cigarette and the principal telling his teachers she caught him smoking marijuana. Popcorn is not a smoker, but "like a normal teenager," he experimented, and:

> she caught me and one thing led to another and the next day in school, she told everyone. People were coming up to me all day, 'Popcorn, you smoke weed? How you let [the principal] catch you smoking weed?' I'm like, I don't do that! Why would the principal – and this is like a professional environment, school – why would she go around telling everyone about something that didn't even happen? I just found that really childish. I felt sabotaged.

Popcorn works hard for the respect he has earned as an artist, photographer and filmmaker; he would not intentionally jeopardize that reputation. "'Cause it did ruin my reputation for like a day, like a lot of faculty members that I respected kind of lost respect for me until I explained it to them. It definitely threw a wrench into the factory of my being. I definitely stopped the flow of Popcorn for the day, you know."

What is problematic is that Popcorn spent a day telling teachers and staff he did not smoke marijuana. As a student, he felt it was his responsibility to clean up the rumor, generated by the principal. What links these stories of distrust and disappointment is the highly personal information the principal possesses about the students and the power she wields through the possession of such information. One of the things small schools are promoted for is the ability to foster intimate relationships between students and staff; what needs further rumination is how these relationships can be manipulated. While the anonymity of large schools is not desired, the ease with which students and staff engage in rumor mongering *together* seems less likely. When dealing with fragile populations whose lives are marked by inconsistencies, schools can and should be a place of consistency. When the individuals who run their schools are inconsistent bodies, the students' tumultuous experiences are replicated, not eradicated.

Safety Measures

While many participants spoke critically about individuals, by far the biggest source of ire was the scanning, metal detectors and closed-circuit cameras that monitored students' every activity. Participants knew that scanning and metal detectors were in their school because of past violent incidents and were meant to protect them, however, almost all the participants felt these safety measures were a violation of their innocence and constructed them as criminals. Tom says:

> I really don't like the scanning. I know what happened, the incident that happened in the school that made the scanners come. Somebody got shot. I still don't like the scanning. I don't think that kids should be searched and they look through your stuff. I can't get mad at them for putting the scanners in 'cause somebody got shot in school, so, well, it's okay. But I just don't like it.

Joan believes scanning is a personal violation and the knowledge that the kids who attend the school across the street do not have to go through scanning engenders embarrassment. "It's very uncomfortable considering the fact that in the morning we have to go through scanning, it's like we're entering some major court building. And it's just school." Tom's acquiescence, revealed when he says 'I can't get mad,' and Joan's feeling of violation paint a deflated image of contemporary urban schools.

Scanning and metal detectors also give the school structure an inarguable power. J-Trout comments that the closed circuit cameras are like "eyes on you all the time" and makes the observation that "it's like that in the street. So, it's really no difference except someone can rewind what you just did and say what you did was wrong." There is a power within the walls of a school monitored by closed circuit cameras: time can be stopped, rewound, and perpetually replayed. This makes schools, on a certain level, more powerful than the street, which cannot stop time. Marlo knows if someone (like him) even looks like they *might* be doing something, this leads to trouble, which is why he knows better than to sell drugs in school. "They got you on camera, not even actually doin' something, but lookin' like you makin' some moves. They just see how you move. And they catch you, you feel me, school – you don't do things in school. There's people that do it, but that's stupid." The presence of cameras, scanning and metal detectors have not encouraged Marlo to stop selling drugs, but rather, have taught him to sell drugs *elsewhere*.

There are clear power boundaries in the scanning and metal detection entry to the building. No faculty or staff of any school must go through scanning. Guests to the building must go through scanning, but are permitted to keep electronic devices and do not have their bags or clothing searched. Therefore while adults are perceived innocent, students are presumed guilty every morning as their school days begin. All 3000 students from the different schools enter the building through the same doors, must take off any metal items, have their bags searched and are frisked; many participants talk about having to leave home earlier than necessary in order to avoid the long lines at scanning. For students with already long commutes and those with family responsibilities, such as transporting younger siblings to school, scanning makes the morning routine increasingly stressful. If there is ever a malfunction with the machines, the students are held responsible if they are late to class. The metal detectors were installed as a permanent fixture after the school shooting and were never removed when the failing school was phased out. Therefore, the small schools suffered the consequences of the previous school's problems. Scanning, however, is far from flawless and in a self-

"It All Depends on the Person" 147

initiated part of their conversation, Alex, Rain and Stacy argue against the effectiveness and safety of scanning:

> *Alex:* Scanning's crazy!
> *Rain:* I hate scanning.
> *Stacy:* It makes you feel like you're a criminal.
> *Rain:* I hate scanning. 'Cause it's a waste of my time, I feel. In the morning, coming to school and walking here, you see a long line, its makes you extra angry. In the morning time when I come to the school and it's a long line, I'm like, oh no, people gonna have to move!
> *Stacy:* Yeah, 'cause then they hold you.
> *Rain:* Because somebody do something, you know, and it gets me heated. And now, when you get scanned, you gotta get scanned twice. It's just a big hassle. I hate it.
> *Allison:* Why do you think this school has scanning?
> *Rain:* Because of the history that had, the people who was here before us, the things that they did, so we're paying for their actions.
> *Alex:* And their mistakes. Which is actually something that happens all the time. Like I know kids who went to this school a good 5-6 years ago and they were like, it's a mess. They had the pool and everything open and now all that's shut down. The place used to get lockdown like every day. And it was crazy. And scanning is probably another big reason why kids don't like coming to school. Or kids come to school really late. They just don't want to deal with it.

Scanning dually inspires anger and apathy. Rain says it makes her angry to see the long lines and Alex concludes that it is because of scanning that students 'don't like coming to school.' As discussed in Chapter Two, the safety measure, ostensibly designed to protect students, does no such thing (Advancement Project 2005; Miller 1996; Noguera 2000, 2004; Rivera *et al.* 2009). Rather, scanning is an identifiable source of anger, hatred and frustration. If students show up to school significantly late, they enter through a different door where there is only one scanner, so entry is even further delayed. The young women also explain that when students come in late, the security guards are less likely to pay attention to school bags or go through pockets. If students want to bring in forbidden items or weapons, they know which doors do not have cameras or permanently stationed security guards and will stash their stuff in garbage cans on the sidewalk or other hidden locations to be gathered later. The young women describe in detail the way students get material inside school, including hiding razors in mouths, clipping iPods inside belt buckles and employing girls to bring in weapons, knowing there will not be full-body searches. Stacy observes, "It's not hard to get around the system." Alex, who comes to school almost an hour early to avoid the lines at scanning, knows students who enter the building and then meet people at an unmonitored back door "and they have their cell phones and they have their iPods and they bring in people and they let them out." Rain posits, "That's why my question is whether scanning is worth the hassle," when students are still getting stuff in, adding that if someone really wanted to do something, "they could just kill everyone in the scanning area."

These are well-behaved young women who do not bring weapons or contraband into school. The question that must be asked of this exchange is if these rule-abiding students are aware of all the tricks to bring in weapons or perceived weapons, what exactly is the point of scanning? Beyond the rather disturbing image that schools are safer because they are like jails, scanning does not seem to address the root cause of violence or why young people might feel the need to bring weaponry into their school. Furthermore, metal detectors, searches and cameras sanction a city- and state-supported violence that marks clear lines of authority and power over the students.

Conclusion

In discussing the worth of a small school, Bruce acknowledges that different students have different ways of approaching school. Comparing himself, a self-proclaimed social butterfly, to his best friend Popcorn, he states, "Popcorn is very shy, he's a very like, stay-to-himself kind of guy, so it all depends on the person." Bruce's comment that it 'depends on the person,' the inspiration for the title and framing of this chapter, is important to consider further. No single school system is guaranteed to work for all students. Individual students possess a complexity of individual needs, which undoubtedly alter and develop throughout their high school tenure. Small, theme-based schools with innovative vision are not separate from the traditional, bureaucratic system of public education. Small schools ultimately process a large number of students and these vast numbers result in a continued factory system, albeit a greater quantity of smaller factories with egalitarian labels.

The participants' stories shared here reveal they are not explicitly aware of the parameters of new school reform or their participation in it. They are unable to critically define or construct the value of small, theme-based education and, for the most part, are unaware *they* are the underserved, inner city youth for whom new school reform is designed. They rely primarily on the interpersonal qualities of attending a small school, rather than articulation of pedagogical value connecting small schools with rigorous education. They judge their trust of school based largely on the interpersonal connection made and are universally frustrated by the presumed daily guilt exemplified by scanning and metal detectors. Despite the language of alternative pedagogy, schools remain conservative and traditional, thereby further alienating socially and economically disenfranchised students.

This need not be the case. With clear goals and objectives and transparent implementation, the language of new school reform can become the material reality of small, theme-based schools. If the radical attempt to integrate alternative curricula is a robust part of the conversation, then further research needs to be done on how to make the necessary changes manifest. Students' stories should be the foundation of inquiry into what kind of school will make youth feel safe, supported and accountable and foster a robust environment of learning. Students' experiences should explore what kind of structure will welcome students as scholars, not prisoners, and engender pride, not destructive desires. Unhealthy, unclear interpersonal relationships should be explored to create safe, healthy relationship where young people can learn that those in positions of authority can be trusted. Overall, what needs to be explored further and with greater attention is how education can serve to undo, not perpetuate, oppression.

Chapter Six further tackles the question of social inequalities, exploring how young people understand 'adolescence' and 'education' through media representations and their own experiences. How do their experiences and their media knowledge weave together to form their worldview? Though they cannot articulate the labels attached to them, they have an intuitive worldview that reveals a deep knowledge of their oppressed circumstances.

Notes

[1] For most interviews, I worked to not interrupt students' class times. I tried to conduct all interviews before or after school or during lunch. However, knowing Pyro, CML and Ventura's behavioral problems in class, I asked one of their teachers if I could take them out of class for one period; the teacher thanked me for the opportunity to actually teach her class because, absent these boys, she could focus on the students interested in school.

[2] During the group interview, the boys seemed most at ease when they could 'show off' their knowledge of drugs, sex and partying. However, each one came to me individually after the group interview and said they had more to say if there was the opportunity for a private interview.

[3] There were a few weeks after our group interview when, if any of them acted out, got in trouble, or needed quiet time, they would ask to be with me. In some way, our interview developed a bond of trust between us. However, over a short period of time, the bond of trust disintegrated: I learned that both CML and Ventura were lying to me about their activities and were trying to hide in my office because I was the last adult staff member who would support their antics.

[4] *Lean on Me* is the 1989 film based on the true story of Principal Joe Clark who takes over a failing New Jersey high school and, with unorthodox methods, including patrolling the halls with a bullhorn and baseball bat, locking the doors from the inside and dismissing students who appear uninterested in attending class, works to remedy the school (see imdb.com).

Chapter 6

"That's What They Want and a Lot of Kids Follow It":

Representations and Understandings of Adolescence and Education

Discussing stereotypes applied to young people, Alex debates the labels attached to suburban kids–rambunctious, energetic–versus urban kids–criminals, gang members–and concludes that adults and the media are invested in the maintenance of stereotypes as a way of categorizing young people, explaining, "That's what they want and a lot of kids follow it." Despite the language of new school reform where education promotes and provides space for interventions to make change in their lives, schools are not separate from the environments in which they are found. Schools that are created to reach out to struggling young people rely on deep-rooted stereotypes and labels as a way to categorize their constituents. Using these labels as inspiration for change replicates the students' negative environments. When they are constantly reminded they need the structure and expertise of school to make them better people and able to move beyond their current situations, young people are left with little alternative than the belief that, at the present moment, they and their families are damaged.

This chapter shows the participants are quite clear about the (re)presentation of young people who look like them and how they are supposed to act. The participants, as shown in Chapters Four and Five, are not fully aware of the social labels applied to them by those who claim to have their best interests in mind, and do not experience the full breadth of media education. Therefore, even when they see flawed and damaging representations of people who look like them in the media, they do not have the vocabulary to articulate a problem with this beyond their own dissatisfaction. Chapters Four and Five focus on what the participants do not know and how they are restricted from this knowledge production. Chapter Six focuses on what they do know, rooted mostly in intuition, self-experience and emotional intelligence. Their experiences with school and understandings of media representations do not challenge, but rather reinforce, their understandings of everyday life.

Echoing Bruce, Peter and Popcorn's conversation about *Lean on Me*, there is little to no critical analysis of what they see in the media. Media representations are either true because they have shared in similar experiences or false because the representations are unfair. School and the purpose of education are similarly understood: if their experiences are shared, school and education are valid; if they believe school and education rejects them and their choices, they, in turn, believe school is an unnecessary endeavor, a waste of their time. The media's representation of urban youth and urban schools is unequivocally negative, yet it is shown primarily as behavioral, not systemic. McCarthy *et al.* (2005) write, "The mass media's story of inner-city black and Latino people pays short shrift to the stunning decline of opportunity and social services in the urban center," including significant declines in the quality of schooling, employment, community connection and financial support (p. 127). With their oppressive treatment, schools reinforce these feelings and provided few concrete options to break out of their negative circumstances. In subtle and explicit ways, the participants learn they are less important and less valuable to society than their socially and politically advantaged peers.

Chapter Five showed that the participants were not fully aware of the labels imposed on them that carefully frame them as deficient bodies in need of salvation from the dominant members of society with greater social and cultural capital. Participants are less aware of how those labels, ideologies and representations impact their school and experience of schooling. They are aware of expectations and burdens attached to their age and gender and for the most part, both boys and girls agreed that adolescence is more difficult for girls than for boys, especially because of pressures on sexual identity, behavior and responsibility. This chapter shares the discussions by participants about how they believe they are viewed by society and their feelings about this. They speak clearly about media presentations of adolescence and education and make connections to the construction of their school and its endemic problems.

Arguably, because they attend a school ostensibly focused on media education, they should be more aware of the media's construction of teenagers, however as was shown in Chapter Four, their knowledge of the concepts of media education is not formally articulated and media education is not infused across their curriculum or evidenced strongly or consistently in specific classes. Yet, they possess an intuitive, emotional knowledge and ability to understand when they are being dismissed or insulted by the media. These negative representations of adolescence and education are shared by the participants' negative self-perception and what is expected of their age, gender, geography and role as students. This chapter also shares the reflections of the 12th-grade participants, the school's first graduating class who have, in theory, experienced four years of media studies learning and provide empirical evidence of the changes to the school system. This chapter explores what young people know about the images and presentations of adolescence and education within the media, how these messages reflect or contradict their own experiences, how they are 'supposed' to behave according to the rules of their gender, age, geography and skin color and how these lessons are replicated in their understandings of the purpose of education.

Being a Teenager: Media Representations and Personal Experiences

The participants' self and social awareness are connected to their media knowledge, where most texts construct them as degenerate and instead of learning to critically assess those messages, they are taught to succumb to them. If media education is to be integrated across curricula, both 'media' and 'education' need greater clarity as independent terms and interconnected institutions.

Media Representations: Adolescence

When asked about their definitions of what it means to be a teenager, without prodding, many participants immediately connected their own experiences to the media's representation both of teenagers and of school. In many instances, they spoke generally about 'the media' or 'them,' making no clear distinction between medium, content, actors, producers or writers. Though they do not speak about specific media or texts, 12th-grade Nino, 11th-grade Rain and 10th-grade Joan believe 'the media' portray teenagers and geography in a limited, negative way that do not match their experiences. Nino bristles at the media's presentation of teenagers as badly behaved and teenage circumstances as entirely negative, feeling that she lives relatively free from negative experiences:

> There's like this movie-persona of teenagers like they have the worst lives and everything. You know, they go through like the worst things. I don't really go through anything that bad. Like, I never been like, raped; they do that on shows, like, every child gets raped or something. They go through hard break ups with boyfriends and stuff, you know, or some of them are like sluts or something. I don't go through that.

Nino believes her life is both pretty easy and rather typical and while not much angers or upsets her, she is frustrated that the media appear to need to make teenagers either criminals or victims. Rain believes the media's portrayal of teenagers is too limited. She says, "The media portray all teenagers have sex. And portray that's all we think about." She defends herself and her friends against this limited view, "We think about other things, like for instance getting into college. Especially at this age, being 16 and in the 11th grade. Thinking about what colleges you want to go to, what you're gonna do in your life, are you gonna work, are you gonna become a person who's gonna be out there, doing things, other than just sitting home and relaxing." The labels attached to subjected bodies anger Joan. "I feel like they label everybody–black, white, Puerto Rican, whatever race you are–and that pop culture, they kind of like have this label for them. In this way that they're supposed to look. And I see a lot of females trying to follow the trend today, so it's like, it's so fake to me." She intimates the media encourage self-loathing among women who follow the trends set forth by popular culture images.

The limited presentation of teenagers as victims, self perpetuating stereotypes or sexually provocative individuals with dramatic one-dimensional experiences do not represent for Nino, Rain or Joan their complex, multi-dimensional experiences. However, these representations do fit the "poignantly sordid fantasies of inner city degeneracy and moral decrepitude" discussed in McCarthy *et al.* (2005, p. 117). Popular media support white middle-class values as normal and anything else as deficient. Never mind that Nino, in her estimation, has never been unduly victimized, that Rain thinks about college and career, or that Joan resists popular culture labeling, the fantasy of their deficiency suffices.

Many participants do feel that their lives are remarkably difficult and are disappointed that the media unfairly portray their complex difficulties one-dimensionally. Eleventh grade Lucy believes the media's treatment of the projects make them look worse than the actual experience of living in them:

> My projects are right there in how they talk about the projects. There's been gunshots, there are drugs all over the place and it's just fucked up. But sometimes they overdo it. 'Cause people think of the projects as 'Ew, you live in the projects.' It's not that bad. It really isn't. Because you can go into my apartment and it really doesn't look like a project apartment 'cause my mom keeps it nice.

She does not specify medium, but 'they' may refer to news reports of crime in the projects. As McCarthy *et al.* (2005) observe, "you watch network evening news and you can predict when black and brown bodies will enter and when they will exit" (p. 127). There is no doubt that housing projects are difficult places to live, in part because of crime, drugs and gang infestation, but also the regular reminder that private families need public assistance to live in increasingly dilapidated areas. No matter how much individual families care for their home and family's well-being, the persistent message is they are subjected bodies, readily available for public condemnation. No one outside the projects ever speaks positively about them and their negative representation is multigenerational and multigeographic; growing up in that space certainly has an impact on one's self-perception.

Some participants speak about specific films or television shows to explain the representations of adolescence and their experiences. Ninth grade Marlo connects his life and drug dealing experiences to *The Wire*[1], the HBO series about the drug trade in Baltimore, Maryland. He explains:

> *The Wire* is hot 'cause like I done seen mad things like that happen. I've never been to Baltimore, but it's a lot like where I'm at, what I'm up to. In life, mad crazy things happen, like you don't know what could happen from now. You don't know what could happen, you goin' to the store! You don't know what could happen, ah, let's say if you're dealing drugs. You don't know what could happen if you give that person something and they kill you for it.

Marlo connects his experiences with drug dealing to the presentation of drug dealing in Baltimore; it matters not that he has neither been to Baltimore nor that the show is fiction and that the scenarios depicted, though highly realistic and drawn from real-life stories, are scripted and performed by actors. For Marlo, the realistic representation of drug dealing and its inherent risk is similar to his experiences and renders his judgment of the show as 'hot' and realistic in its portrayal of the 'mad crazy things' that can happen.

Participants also speak specifically about rap music and the cultivation of identity within the lyrics and videos. Some participants are angered by contemporary rap music's construction of femininity and image cultivation while others feel rap music and artists are the only honest members of the mass media. Twelfth grade Nine and 10th-grade Joan both find rap music and rap videos problematic, especially in their treatment of women and hypermasculinity. Nine explains, "You also have to deal with like videos and everything, making girls seem like something they're not. Like they're disrespected often. They're called a lot of vulgar names that they get adapted to and they get called bitches and 'hos and all of that. And after a while you hear them referring to each other like that as well." Joan chastises rap music:

> I don't think [rap songs] are real. It's something that these people put out, it's like an image, that they put out so other people will be interested in them. You know, so it's like, 'Yeah, I been through this, I got shot in my face.' You hear the boys like, 'You gangsta!' Everybody put out an image, you know, whether it's fake hair, hair weave, rappin', being' ghetto, it's just an image that we have.

Both Nine and Joan speak of the rap music identity as commodity. To self-reference as bitch, 'ho or gangsta is to make an identity purchase that, while rooted in oppression or hatred, is now romanticized. Joan has seen someone shot and does not find rap's romanticization of gun violence and power displays appropriate. Both young women question the value of the image and its power to construct gendered expectations.

In contrast to Nine and Joan, 10th-grade J-Trout and 11th-grade Lucy both believe rap music represents the truth. J-Trout explains:

> Lil Wayne[2], Jim Jones[3], Max B.[4], they rap about the truth. They rap about things that kids in society go through and it's not like they're degrading some things. Like they say the truth, they say what's going on in society as a teenager and how you feel like you're the best at something, you say it, and if you have an explanation, you say it.

Lucy contradicts Joan's belief in false image of rap in her belief that rap artists, especially Lil Wayne, speak truth to their drug experiences, which she feels connects her to the rap artists. Lucy explains:

> 'Cause me being a pothead, there's a lot of potheads that are rappers. So when they talk about it, it's just, oh shit, like oh my God, I know what he's talking about! They talk about being broke and living in the projects and all that, so I could relate. And I know what they've gone through 'cause I'm goin' through it right now. My favorite rapper is Lil Wayne and all he does is smoke, smoke, smoke. He was caught with a lot of bud, so there's proof right there it's real.

For J-Trout and Lucy, rap music is not about the construction of an image, but about speaking the truth to experiences, being real and, more importantly, being heard, supported, and indeed, encouraged to continue such behavior. However, there is a delicate balance between speaking the truth and profiting from the ghetto and gangsta commodity. Lil Wayne, Jim Jones and Max B. are artists known for their drug, gang, gun and criminal enterprises on which they have clearly capitalized in terms of popular appeal (Grace 2009; Reid & Rodriguez 2009; *Rolling Stone*). As bodies performing firmly entrenched in the culture industries, their corporate, mainstream labels capitalize financially. Yet when drug dealing, drug doing, and criminal behaviors are part of popular culture, those whose lives *truly* follow this path themselves become a source of entertainment. That Lil Wayne has been caught with drugs, Max B. prosecuted on manslaughter charges and Jim Jones arrested on assault charges, marks them as actual violators of the law, yet they profit from these violations in ways that J-Trout or Lucy never will. Despite–or because of–their criminal provocations and gang connections, these artists are popular culture icons within, not subversive of, mainstream media: their experiences and behavior may very well be *real*, but are also highly profitable. What J-Trout and Lucy do not discuss is the adherence to capital accumulation these artists participate in as part of the corporate media institution.

Participants whose likenesses are punished desire greater accuracy in media representations. Eleventh grade Genevieve, a self-described heavy-set African American girl, notes there are minimal positive roles for large women, especially larger women of color, in the media. She explains:

> I am a thick person, physically. If there's any portrayal of that, it's usually bad. You know, even if I am healthy, on sight people will think, 'oh, she's obese, so she's unhealthy.' Which might be true, but not everyone that looks like me is unhealthy. You have actresses like Nikki Blonsky[5] and Queen Latifah[6] and you have comedic actresses like Mo'nique[7] that are sending out positive messages just to love ourselves. You know, movies like *Norbit*[8] have a giant woman being aggressive and mean and cruel and that sends out a negative message about the larger-size population. That doesn't portray us right. We're human, we're just like everyone else, we just like to eat a little more. Just because you're a size 2 doesn't mean you're healthy. I think there should be a more positive outlook on larger people than there is right now. Because they're just so focused on slender women with long hair and blue eyes and they're probably Caucasian or Asian. You know, have some African American actresses out there representing us big women!

Genevieve echoes O'Connor *et al.*'s (2005) discussion of black women's self-perception of beauty who "revealed that physical indices of femininity required women to be light in complexion, have fine and long hair and be 'thick' (neither fat nor skinny) in body" (p. 169). Genevieve, her mother and maternal grandmother are all large women who admittedly enjoy unhealthy food and do not exercise. Genevieve knows she will never be a 'size 2'; she is aware both of her genes and the choices she makes. However, the media representation of people like her is more often insulting and degrading. When she speaks about Nikki Blonsky, Queen Latifah and Mo'nique, these women represent the scant number of Hollywood professionals who are both overweight/obese *and* successful in positive and affirming roles. When Genevieve brings up the 'aggressive and mean and cruel' large woman in the 2007 film *Norbit*, she does not discuss that this character is in fact Eddie Murphy in drag and fat suit. While Genevieve is disturbed by the representation of obesity and its link to nasty behavior, she does not articulate the multiple levels of insult that a fat, angry black woman is portrayed by a thin black man for comedic effect.

Media Representations: School

Several of the participants discuss media representation of school, especially the distinction between urban and suburban schools. Ninth grade Monica explains:

> Sometimes they talk about how a school day would be or they have shows about schools, saying like this is like what an average school would do and look like and act like. Like *Saved by the Bell*[9], that's a good show of something that would happen naturally 'cause it talks about how, oh, sometimes you're late for school, sometimes you forgot to do your homework, and you have fights with your teachers or classmates. That's like a regular day that would happen here.

Monica is generous with her description that the Southern California suburban high school in *Saved by the Bell* is 'like a regular day that would happen here.' The antics of the teen cast–suburban, middle class, mostly white–are the stuff of humor where problems are solved within each episode. When Monica describes the school day as 'regular' she does not reveal an ignorance of the reality of her own school, but rather multiple understandings of 'regular.' This echoes Popcorn and Bruce's debate from Chapter Five regarding inner-city school and the labels attached to them. Popcorn asserted that all kids struggle with identity development and self-discovery, which does make LSHS's student experiences similar to the representations of students in *Saved by the Bell*. Yet urban youth are punished for their search for self and identity development project.

Lucy and Nine are more critical of the media's presentation of urban schools. Lucy explains:

> In the media, when they look at an urban school, it's just, they don't think we're getting anywhere, we're just a whole bunch of kids that slack off and we don't really care. And our classes are chaotic. That's what they see. Sometimes it's not like that 'cause there's a

lot of very, very talented and smart students in this school. So the media, they're assholes sometimes.

Nine further discusses:

> It's either like in a school, everybody pays attention and everybody does the work and everybody's like the same, they do everything the same, they're like the greatest students, which doesn't happen. Or then you have the school where everybody misbehaves and there's like one smart person that everybody teases because they're actually doing their work.

Both young women observe there is an unyielding, inflexible binary within the media representations of schools: urban students go nowhere, misbehave, and are disruptive, while other students and other schools are perfect. Further, both young women are frustrated that the media do not recognize the talent or intelligence of urban students, unless, as Nine points out, they are 'the smart person that everyone teases.' What the young women do not discuss is perpetuation of subjugation within media representations; it is not just that urban schools are presented as chaotic or that one singular student does the work, but that the savior who ultimately controls the chaos or rewards the student is usually white.

Twelfth grade Popcorn sketches a rough media history, distinguishing between an era of filmmaking that celebrates suburban adolescents and an era of filmmaking that punishes urban adolescents. He does not clarify when these eras occurred, their motivations or any specific titles, but nevertheless, paints a very clear picture of Hollywood's impression of adolescents, their problems and their saviors. Overall, in his estimation, Hollywood constructs adolescence as a dark, problematic time, but urban youth receive no positive representation:

> They made a lot of movies about high school teens and a lot of television shows about people in school. It's never, you know, pleasant. It's always like this dark theme that's portrayed, like the worst of the worst, you know. There was an era of movies about suburban high schoolers that dealt with problems at home or whatnot, somebody got pregnant, then it centered around the jocks or whatnot. And people just had sex and went to the movies and had fun. Then there was another era where they chose to show how inner city high schoolers act and it would just usually be, somebody's already pregnant, or probably having a second baby. Or somebody's on drugs, the kids in the class don't want to learn. Then some teacher miraculously comes and saves them.

Popcorn weaves a story about a teacher called upon to stop fights, disentangle the smartest kid in school from a gang or prevent him/her from committing a crime. Popcorn claims this teacher is always white and the saved student is always black or Latino. This narrative bothers Popcorn. "I've never experienced that. Ever! Okay? These films, I mean look, the problems that they try to get across are reality for some people. But it's just the way they do it, it's just based on general stereotypes." Popcorn admonishes the media for treating young people's real problems–struggles with sex and its consequences, relations between authorities and students inside schools, involvement in gangs or with crime and development of trust–as entertainments fodder with quick, neat solutions. Based on their personal experiences, the participants do not experience quick, neat solutions to their problems.

Personal Experiences: Adolescence

Many of the participants speak about understandings of adolescence based on their own personal experiences, frustrations and expertise. Some of the participants do not appear to have many concerns and provide general discussions of adolescence:

> *Tom*: Smoking weed or doing drugs, 'cause that's what a lot of teenagers do. But I don't smoke 'cause I can't smoke 'cause I play basketball.
>
> *Marlo*: It's the shit, but … you know, mad crazy things could happen.
>
> *Monica*: I think about parties and going out and then studying.

Ivette, who believes her pregnancy moves her closer to being an adult and farther from the struggles of adolescence, believes that early adolescence is difficult, but that things are easier now:

> It's very stressful, especially in the beginning years, like, 13, 14, middle school years. Middle school is very stressful. Like everybody's talking about you, you know, criticizing you on what you wear, what you don't wear. How you wear your hair, how you don't wear your hair. How you talk, how you walk, how you act. Now high school, like, you could open yourself more, but there's still people that talk about you. But now, in high school, you feel more strong and more self-esteem and you know, your esteem is not as low as it was in the beginning years of being a teenager.

Ivette speaks positively about her experiences, however, she has had significant difficulties with her peers, including fights that have led to suspensions. Taking her pregnancy and marriage seriously, it is possible she is trying to re-imagine herself as an adult and she challenges Edin's (2000) research that found low-income mothers choose not to marry because marriage entails "far more risk than rewards" (p. 28). There is also the grim possibility that Ivette's pregnancy was intentional and represented her participation in a competition with a classmate. On multiple occasions, Ivette fought with a classmate who had a 2-year-old daughter and was pregnant with her second child by a different father. The last fight the girls had occurred right before Ivette ran away to Los Angeles and the rumors among the faculty and classmates was that the girls were fighting over their attempt to get pregnant first.

Tenth grade Joan believes understandings of adolescence are mostly negative and make connections between bad experiences and geography, especially her first hand knowledge from living in bad neighborhood. Joan explains:

> Mostly ... it's not good. Being a teenager, that's when you start exploring, like you know, kind of come into adulthood. Especially if you live in like a really bad place. I mean, I've seen somebody get shot before. So, I don't think it could get any worse than that. She was 64 so it's like, why would you kill someone so old? It's really crazy where I live, but my mom will always say at least we try to make it at least peaceful in our home. Because outside, in society that we live in, is crazy.

Joan's discussion of the implications of 'exploration' echoes Popcorn's concerns with identity development and self-discovery. Joan believes there is little room for exploration in dangerous neighborhoods where bad things happen to defenseless senior citizens. The 'crazy' society that is Joan's neighborhood abuts some of the wealthiest blocks on Manhattan and the division between neighborhoods is palpable.

Eleventh grade Lucy connects adolescence with ethnicity, especially the direct link between Spanish ethnicity and poverty:

> *Lucy:* Me being Spanish, when I hear 'teenager,' I think of a Spanish teenager. And I'm pretty sure that most teenagers who are Spanish, it sucks for them, too, because they're Spanish. It's not like whites, a white boy teenager, white girl teenager, they get it different. Their life is different. Like, financially. I'm Spanish and I'm broke. It sucks, not having money. And for a white person, a white girl or boy, it's just different. They're up there, they get money.
> *Allison:* All Spanish people are poor?
> *Lucy:* Well, all the Spanish people I know are poor.
> *Allison:* Do you know any wealthy Spanish people?

Lucy: Besides famous people, no. Everything is money. You can't get anything without money.

In Lucy's estimation, famous Latino/a people have somehow gotten lucky and escaped poverty, but within her environment and community, all the Latino/a people she knows–primarily her Puerto Rican neighbors and her fellow classmates–are stricken by poverty. Lucy does not articulate any systemic knowledge of the construction of Latino/a poverty, but rather has internalized the racism intimately connected to the culture of poverty: she and her family are poor because they are Latino/a and white people are not poor because they are white.

The participants are well versed and experienced in many stereotypes associated with urban living, including sex, drugs, police and gangs. Their ability to talk about these categories does not necessarily mean they have direct, personal experience, but rather, that they live within these experiences, so even when they are personally absent direct knowledge, they perceive its influence. Similar to Rain, Alex, Genevieve and Stacy's knowledge of how to sneak in contraband material, young people can know something without needing to directly experience it. However, direct experience adds a layer of knowledge that confirms their positions and "proves" their intuition. J-Trout understands adolescence to be about "Sex. Drugs. Gangs. And police. I think in high school, you start experimenting with things, and our surroundings, from where I'm from, it's gang infested, it's highly drug infested, and police everywhere, so I mean, that's what you're raised by, so that's what you're gonna see as you grow up. There's danger in anything you experiment. There's a cause and effect in anything you do." Sex, drugs, gangs and police are all manifestations of power, with serious consequences. While experimentation and exploration may be endemic to adolescence, J-Trout cautions against naïve, blind exploration. Briefly, J-Trout lists his direct experience, "Gangs: no. Police: not really. Drugs: no. Sex: yes." He feels he his cautious with his experimentation, has seen too many consequences to need to explore much on his own and knows that his behavior is regularly watched because he is a black man in New York City.

In conversation with each other, 10th graders Pyro, CML and Ventura posture about the ease and frivolity of adolescence:

Pyro: For the most part, it's okay. It's not so much fun. Puberty, being forced to grow up. The parties, girls, you know, livin' life is fun.
CML: Well, I think being a teenager's great. You get to get in trouble, you don't get as

much trouble as you would. Now is like the best time to experiment with girls, alcohol, drugs, parties. Your teenage years are like the best years that you can have, is what I think.
Ventura: Yeah, I agree with CML. For the most part. You just gotta have fun, enjoy yourself, 'cause when you get older, it's gonna get hard.
Pyro: 'Cause life sucks.

There is a distinct line between adolescence and adulthood: one is fun, the other is work. Both CML and Ventura will forestall that entry as long as possible, but Pyro feels he needs to 'become a man' sooner rather than later. Furthermore, these young men are not so frivolous in private conversation. In private, personal conversations, each is more open and vulnerable about their experiences. His mother's sexuality, his stepfather's bullying and his father's imprisonment bother CML while Pyro is regularly bothered by his perceived need to become the man of his household now that his stepfather and mother are divorcing. The *idea* of a frivolous, fun, consequence-free adolescence is enticing, but the reality of it is much less likely.

Being a Boy, Being a Girl

Both the male and female participants believed being a boy was much easier than being a girl. Overall, the boys appreciate being boys largely because of the ease. Tom fully admits, "I don't think I could make it as a girl, so I love being a boy. Being a girl, the pressure and the pain. It's way easier to be a boy because you don't have to have a kid. That's how I think of it. Or pressure to have sex and all that kind of stuff." Pregnancy, childbirth, and it may be assumed, childcare are the women's sole responsibility. As the child of a single mother, this is Tom's understanding of gender and family relationships. Free-spirited Bruce does not believe that he could live the life he does as a girl. He explains:

> To be a boy in this world you get a lot of leeway when it comes to sports, social life, pretty much everything. If you think about it, if a girl talks to a bunch of guys, she's you know, subjected to being called a ho or very flirtatious. But if a guy talks to a bunch of girls, he's like Mr. Cool, so it's not really level. 'Cause if I was a girl, I would be like a big flirt and people would probably assume that I, you know, get around. I can like jump off a table and do like a karate kick and they'll just say I'm either immature or I'm just being a boy. But if a female was to jump off a table, then she's unlady-like, she's rude, she has no manners.

Bruce is accustomed to being called immature, behavior he readily acknowl-

164 *Media Education Goes to School*

edges as true. However, as he observes, no one blames or stigmatizes his immaturity or social skills *because of* his gender. The role of sexuality and sexual behavior is a major distinction between boys and girls with the perception that boys have much greater sexual freedom than girls. J-Trout explains, "We'll be judged, but not as bad as a female will be judged. Like a male can have sex with as many females as he wants. But if a female does it, she's a 'ho, so we have a little bit more power in society."

CML, Ventura and Pyro once again posture a masculine role:

CML: Be masculine, tough.
Pyro: Head of the household. You gotta be the man. Wear the pants in the house.
CML: Right now being a boy to me means going out, playin' sports, going out with girls-
Pyro: - Not crying. It's a no-no.
CML: Yeah, not crying's a big thing.
Pyro: Taking pain.
CML: Having fun. Being idiots while you still can.
Ventura: For me, being a boy is like, being a boy is like, what he said, playing sports, being active. Most of it, people like, see boys to be masculine, like masculinity is a big part of it.
Pyro: Being a boy gives you an excuse to be dumb. Like the saying 'boys will be boys.' You ain't never hear nobody say 'girls will be girls.' That's just how it is. Because boys are brought up to live life and then think about your regrets. Learn from your mistakes. But most people don't even think about the mistakes they can make before they do the action that is the mistake in the first place. It's like, act first, repercussions later, basically.

In their discussion, the boys reveal their concerns and fears: no crying, being the man of the household, taking pain without complaint, being masculine, moving on from mistakes. Playing sports, experimenting with girls, being active, dumb and getting away with it only last so long. CML, Pyro and Ventura ask for "permission to fail," continuously engaging in a pattern of aggression and avoidance so they are forgotten or actively rejected by authority figures (Ladson-Billings 2002, p. 110).

As boys grow up, they are generally allowed to do more and behave more independently, which certainly carries greater responsibilities, but the immediate freedom is enticing. Jose speaks for many of the boys when he explains, "I'm getting more possibilities. Like I could go outside more, I could go to different places." However, being a boy is not entirely easy, especially for young men of color; sexual, geographic and behavioral freedom does not translate to unencumbered ease for boys. J-Trout believes boys have difficult relationships with developing masculine identities. "We get judged more on like, we're thugs, or we're gonna be jailbirds as soon as we get out of school or something. People watch you and you don't even know. People watch you grow up and you don't think about it, but they're telling their friends they know how you're gonna grow up to be." In J-Trout's estimation, masculine identity development is carefully monitored. Eleventh grade Alvin feels he has been mistreated by the legal system and believes he went to jail, in part, because of a racist judge. Alvin explains, "Being a boy is a big responsibility. Especially being a black man. Not necessarily black, but my skin color. Because the government puts you down. If you get arrested, for whatever reason, you see a judge. Not all judges are fair." Alvin believes the judge at his arraignment 'saw [him] as black' and gave him a stricter jail term than he would have gotten if the judge realized he was Latino or, certainly, if he was white.

Girls agree that being a boy is easier and compare themselves and their difficulties against the perceived ease of being a boy. In school, girls have to work harder to get the attention of the teachers and in the neighborhood, girls have to work harder to protect their reputations. Ninth grade Monica does not yet have many freedoms or privileges outside her home. She's allowed to spend time in her neighborhood, a safe, working-class area of Queens, but cannot roam freely as she believes a boy might. She does not see too many major differences between boys and girls, but does believe that as she gets older, boys will have more privileges "I don't know," she explains, "there's not much difference between a girl and a boy except, I don't know why but, guys sometimes get more privileges. It's just like, if a girl, let's say, they start letting her out after, like at 15, maybe a guy, they start letting him out a little bit earlier. And they get to do more things, like they don't have as many rules as a girl does. It could be maybe because, I don't know, the parents think they could trust them more or something." Joan believes that boys have more social opportunities than girls, unless girls want to make bad or negative choices. "It's not fair," she explains, "like, you don't get as many opportunities to me, I feel like you don't get as many opportunities as guys get. Like guys are able to say and do things that we're not really able to say and do. For example, my younger brother, he's 15, he's able to come in like at 12. And if I come in at 12, I get yelled at. So, it's like really hard being a girl. It's like sometimes I wish I was a boy. You know?" Both Monica and Joan see that younger boys have more privileges than older girls. That Monica sees it as 'trust' may not be accurate: parents and guardians may believe boys pose less risk or are less vulnerable for long-term trouble or consequences. The participants' awareness of privilege fall along traditional, expected gender lines: boys are public, active bodies while girls are domestic, docile bodies.

Nine and Nino, both in the 12th grade articulate those different privileges and freedoms from their direct experiences, especially in terms of classroom behavior and social expectations. Nine laments, "It puts a lot of pressure because I think that a lot of girls, especially in school, take school more seriously than guys, so it's like you have a lot of competition to keep your grades up and then you also have to learn how to cook, clean the house, do chores that sometimes guys don't have to do." Nino explains further:

> It's harder to be a girl than a boy. Boys usually get like an easier life, kind of. Like the girls, they always get put down, sometimes in classes, the boys they get to whatever they want, a girl does it and, you know, they get in trouble. That's what I've seen since I was little. Usually girls aren't seen as the smartest kids, but you know, I'm pretty smart. I see the boys usually act out, the girls usually sit down and actually listen. So we gotta step our game up so we show that we're better than the boys. It's just how society was built, like men are better than women. Men are smarter, stronger than women. But it's not like that. There's always gonna be a woman that's smarter than a man. But you can't have that in society 'cause it means the men are weaker and you can't have that in the society.

In Nine and Nino's estimation, girls must stay closer to home not only to stay away from perceived trouble but also to assist with domestic chores. Even as Nino works to stake her claim as a smart young woman capable of intellectual advancement, she knows that no matter how strong she is, the ideology of masculinity will not disappear. She can be a smart young woman, but she cannot undo masculine dominance. Girls continue to live within the parameters of private, passive domesticity, separate from the active, public realm of boys (McRobbie 1976; Willis 1977) despite their individual intellectual or physical abilities.

The reputation that girls can get as sexually inappropriate does not follow strict hetero-normative lines. Lucy explains that as a lesbian, she has to work doubly hard for self-respect:

> I have to have self-respect, of course, because I'm a girl. But being as how I'm a lesbian, it's like, people see me different. Like um, they see me as a guy. They say, 'You shoulda had a penis.' 'Cause like the way I am and the way I dress. But, I still have to respect myself, of course, and like, be a girl. Even with the way I look. I don't wear tight, tight jeans the way girls do. I wear, not too baggy, but like right in between. Big shirts, a hat and I

don't like girly clothes at all. So, I dress like a guy. You would see, if I had my hoodie on, you look at me from the back, you'll be like, 'that's a guy,' until you see my face.

Lucy feels she has to protect herself as a girl and stake her position as a lesbian: she is not a guy and does not want to be a guy. She does not dress femininely or wear makeup, but she is still a girl and wants to be known and respected as a female and a lesbian.

Girls' behavior is supposed to be proper and demure and significant multigenerational work is done to maintain these strict expectations. Genevieve explains, "In my family, girls are supposed to be proper. You're supposed to stay in the–not in the kitchen necessarily–but you're supposed to have knowledge of cooking, talking to women your age or addressing older women as 'ma'am' and you know, doing things for them." She lives with her mother and grandmother, both of whom are stubbornly resistant to sending her to college because of their fears of letting her out on her own and the possibility that she might not succeed. Genevieve's grandmother did not have the opportunity to attend college; Genevieve's mother attended college for one semester but could not balance the coursework with her full-time job, caring for Genevieve, her grandmother and her adult brother with a mental disability. Genevieve believes that, in her mother's mind, college equals a direct route to failure, not success.

'Multigenerational work' can mean a lot of things; in Genevieve's family, it is about protecting Genevieve from perceived dangers. In Alex's family, it is her own dogged determination not to follow the path of her mother and sister. Both her mother and sister had multiple children by different, abusive men while still teenagers and Alex refuses to follow that path. However, she feels that it is what is expected of her, especially when she is in public with her younger siblings or nieces:

> *Alex:* Babies. In my family for like the last three generations, nobody has like, finished like high school or college. And I'm the first one that hasn't had kids yet. And I think my mom thinks that hell's gonna freeze over. It's you know, it's kids and having families and not finishing high school, that's what they all think. That's what they all think.
> *Allison:* Who's 'they'?
> *Alex:* Everyone. Well, everyone my family comes in contact with. They look at everyone and they assume–people assume that my niece is my daughter. I walk down the street with my 4-year-old niece and it's 'is that your little girl?' No, it's not.

Though she resents being thought of as a teen mother, she is the primary caregiver for her younger brother and sister and her two nieces, while also maintaining an after-school job and a straight-A average.

Personal Experiences: Education

Though all participants agree that education is important, they do not necessarily feel it is important in their own lives. Concepts of 'education' and 'school' are valuable, but many of the participants feel they can and will succeed without the bother or restrictions of school. As shown in Chapter Five, they are not aware of the labels applied to their schooling, but they have personal reasons why they trust or distrust education.

Purpose of Education

The 9th graders are the most circumspect about the purpose of education, knowing that it is good, but having just begun high school, college feels a distant four years away. Instead, college and full-time employment are ideas:

> *Jose:* Like, when I think of education, I think of getting out, like, going to college, like becoming something. That's what education means to me.
>
> *Monica:* An opportunity to learn new things and um, to try to change your, um, to go higher in life, in society, and be able to express yourself like more better. Like maybe I could get a better career.
>
> *Tom:* Education's what everybody needs to succeed in life.

Jose's sister Nino, in the 12th grade, is preparing for college, so it is a pertinent subject for him. Monica's father works in a restaurant and her mother does not work, so when she says she could get a 'better career,' she refers directly to her parents' desire for her to have more stable employment. Tom knows education is valuable, even if he has yet to experience its value. Marlo, who is repeating the 9th grade and, because of his regular absences, consistent suspensions, and lack of interest in completing school work, appears destined to repeat the 9th grade a third time. The thought that this might happen does not give him the motivation to work harder, but rather to take the remainder of the school year off. He also believes that it is largely beyond his control; it is not about the work that he completes but rather about the school's desire to promote him just to get rid of him. He explains, "I'll pass. Maybe. If my teachers get tired of me–it's up to my teachers. You know how

New York City is, like, tends to skip kids who aren't doin' nothin' just so, you feel me, it could look good on a school." Though he does not articulate the style or focus of his school, he knows how best to maneuver his way through the system in order to be pushed through. Marlo touches on social promotion, a controversial practice no longer part of the official conversation; young people are now gently guided to other options. The Department of Education directs New York City residents under the age of 21 who are behind in credits or contemplating dropping out not to "assume that earning your high school diploma or GED is out of reach" (New York City Department of Education, *Other ways to graduate*). Students are guided to multiple options and encouraged to become a Facebook fan of the Department of Education's "NYC Multiple Pathways to Graduation." The GED or alternative routes to graduation provide students with legitimate closure while simultaneously shifting school graduation, retention and promotion numbers.

By the middle of high school, 'education' is understood as more specific, both in its purpose as well as resentment for it. Lucy does not feel she needs to graduate high school to be successful and claims she only goes to school because her mother makes her. She defends friends who did not graduate who she perceives are successful, "Like I know a lot of people that didn't graduate and is getting money like crazy. But the only reason why I come is because my mom is making me. If it was up to me, I wouldn't come." Parental pressure is a good excuse: Lucy can claim to be fully disinterested in school but still attend because of her mother's rules. She does acknowledge that broadly, education will lead more directly and clearly to a functional, successful life. "Education means money. 'Cause obviously if you get an education, if you graduate from high school, go to college, you make a lot of money. That's what education is to me." Yet, based on her understanding of Latino/a poverty, she will inevitably make enough money to survive, but not get rich because of her ethnicity. Therefore, school is less important for her possibilities of success.

By the 12th grade, college is a daily conversation, one that feels most assuredly poignant for this graduating class because they are the first. By the 12th grade, there is a much more nuanced, complex understanding of education as something that happens both in and outside a classroom. Nino explains:

> I think of learning. I mean you can always learn from something else and you don't have to come to school and learn it, but it's just that school is just the best way for you to learn

it 'cause they give it to you, like, all in one. When, when you like not in school, you get it like separate pieces. You don't know if it's true, you get it like word of mouth. And you learn how to observe stuff. And you learn to take things on your own.

Education and media education scholars argue that education does not happen solely in classrooms and young people's life and media experiences are valuable additions to the curriculum. Nino echoes Kellner and Share (2007), Jenkins *et al.* (2006) and Moore's (2008) call for formal media studies when she points out that outside of school 'you get like separate pieces' and 'word of mouth.' School is a site for social change, if social change is beneficial to all, irrespective of race, class, gender or geography, if the goal and steps toward it are taken seriously.

Alvin, who was dismissed from school while in jail, believes education will help change his circumstances. "Education is a big word to me. Basically, I see education as power and power as education." He tells the story of a friend who was in jail, but is doing well now with a job and a family. Alvin connects this success out of struggle directly to education because no one can take away education:

> We talkin' the other day, he was tellin' me that education is power you know, 'cause once you have education, nobody can mess with you, you could do whatever you want to do. And with that, with education, knowledge, that's what keeps people away from you, people will look up to you because you know more. You got experience, you know what you're talking about, you could hit people with the facts and, you know, that'll just get you higher.

Education helps shift external perceptions on intelligence, imbalances of power and has the power to undo negative life circumstances. This is indeed a great deal of power that echoes the belief in education immediately following *Brown* and the Civil Rights Amendment.

Reflections From the First Graduating Class

The graduating participants have a variety of opinions on their experiences over their four years of high school. And as students who have experienced the full spectrum of new school reform, their empirical evidence is important to consider when measuring the impact of changes in the school system. Their perspectives range from mostly positive to highly critical and present a range of political awareness.

Nino is the most positive about the experience of being a first graduating senior. She explains:

> It feels great. We're always the ones to be remembered. We have to leave our footprint here so everybody has to follow us. I was telling my brother that he needs to follow our footsteps, but like, make them better. Like so it could cover our footprints. So they could be remembered as much as us. I think that's something important. I can always tell somebody, 'Oh, I was the first graduating class of this school.' So, if the school gets like really good, I'll be like, yeah, I was the first one.

Nino speaks of the importance of memory and legacy. She leaves memory and stories for her little brother to build upon. As she completed her senior year, she was focused on fun and adventure. However, in capturing memory and legacy so evocatively, Nino does not talk about pedagogical aspects of her schooling.

In a different realm, Nine is more concerned with what she missed by attending a small, start-up high school. Nine appreciates the closeness of the people in LSHS but feels that as a first graduate, she and her classmates missed out on activities and opportunities that ultimately make schools strong:

> We're the first graduating seniors. There's a lot things that we don't get since we're the first one to graduate. We don't have advanced placement classes; we don't have extracurricular activities. But I like it because you know everybody, you know your teachers, everybody's there to help you.

The discretionary dollars of small schools are based on the number of students; while principals may choose to spend those dollars however they choose, they are not in infinite supply. Advanced placement classes and extracurricular activities demand more teachers and increased staff, which cost a fair amount of money. LSHS's pedagogy is inclusionary, which means that teachers teach advanced and struggling students in the same class; there is only one subject teacher per grade. While significantly advanced or seriously struggling students can be moved to classes above or below their grade level, there are not multiple courses within grade levels. That Nine attributes this absence of choice to the newness of the school is understandable; she believes that, given time, the school will get itself organized and be able to hire more teachers. This, however, is not the case; it would take an administration with different pedagogical beliefs to implement advanced placement classes or extracurricular activities.

Bruce is ambivalent about his experience as a member of the first graduating class. He has been told repeatedly how special he is to be a first graduate, but that feeling has not hit him yet. He comments, however, on the quantity of students that did not make it with their cohort to senior year, either because they dropped out, were held back, or transferred to other schools:

> I don't know, I guess there's supposed to be a special feeling but it hasn't hit me yet. Right now, in this state of mind I'm in, it just feels like any regular graduation. It hasn't dawned on me how special this is. It's just, we went from 100 students, and now we're in senior year and there's about 60 students in my class and about ... maybe about 50 ... no, maybe like 45 come to school on a consistent basis.

There is a note of melancholy in Bruce's reflection, especially because he has calculated that almost 50% of the students he entered the 9th grade with will not graduate with him. Bruce believes that the students who left school, and those 10 or 15 who do not attend school regularly, have done so on their own volition, revealing again his belief in the responsibility of the individual. He unwittingly adopts the neoliberal ethos that constructs disenfranchised populations as responsible for their own problems.

Popcorn comments on the quantity of students who have left as well, but does not believe it was up to those students as individuals:

> We started out with 100 students and now it's just 60. So, you know, a lot of people came and went. We were basically the lab rats that will make this school great one day. I definitely think that we should be credited and rewarded for that. The school did get better from 9th grade to now. We were here from the beginning and we saw the progress from being totally unstructured and having a little bit of structure and a little bit more and so on and so forth. I think we did help build the school. They tried so many different policies and so many different ways to make the school unique that failed. We had different teachers, some great, some awful, some extremely great that left because they weren't used to the school and how it was just so unstructured. I think that affected a lot of kids, I mean, that affected me.

That Popcorn refers to himself and his classmates as 'lab rats' shows that he has a different concept of personal responsibility than Bruce does. Popcorn believes that the reason why so many kids left, got held back or dropped out was because of the massive disorganization in the development of the school. This disorganization and the inevitably messy qualities that correspond with development left many students shaken by the experience. As first-year students, each year they faced new, untrained teachers; more often than not, these teachers would leave after just one year. Therefore, those students who did make it through high school in four years did so with precious little consistency.

Popcorn sees himself and his classmates as lab rats largely because they were: the 'tests' done in the name of new school reform were done on the students. In the study of education there is no rational, antiseptic control group, no way to eliminate any other influence, or thoroughly measure causation. The laboratory is the real life and real environments of these young people and there is no way to eliminate the multitude of environmental forces at stake in their worlds. The students who are able to reflect on a full four years of small, theme-based education share the importance of memory, legacy, willingness to take risks and contribution, but do not articulate how their school fits into the larger system or contributes to the steps they must take as college students, laborers and citizens.

Conclusion

Alex, who lives in a dilapidated, crime-ridden housing project in the South Bronx, spent a summer at an exclusive, academic boarding school, her only experience outside of New York City. The experience gave her a different perspective on both her own geography and the ways adolescents are perceived in different geographic areas. She comments:

> I think it's mostly just city-type, 'cause if you go other places, kids aren't labeled as evil, they're more labeled as, you know, rambunctious, they just run around a lot. But I think teenagers in general in the city are labeled that way because that's the way they are portrayed us and we just end up falling in that same pattern, we just never break out of it. We just feel like that's what they want and a lot of kids follow it.

Young people are responsible for their own behavior and Alex has resigned herself to this responsibility. She believes it is easier for most to acquiesce to expectations than change them. While she vows never to repeat the behavior of her mother or sister, in using the first person plural, 'we just end up falling in the same pattern, we just never break out of it, we just feel like,' she connects herself to other, oppressed urban youth externally negatively labeled.

This chapter has illustrated how the participants interpret their everyday lives as understood through school and the media and highlights knowledge produced from their own experiences as teenagers and students. They know the media construct them and people who look like them negatively, but they cannot articulate why or how this construction builds. When they like or make connections with certain media texts, they believe the representations to be true. They appreciate that their stories are told–and are popular–yet do not connect that popularity with capital accumulation or industry power. When media representations are harmful or one-dimensional, participants reject them, but without critical appraisal. Many of the participants have experienced significant social and economic difficulties, but still see adolescence as a time of experimentation and exploration. For these young people, exploration and experimentation often have serious consequences and the freedom perceived as endemic to adolescence ends earlier when they face 'adult' responsibilities while still teenagers. The participants internalize their and their peers' experiences as natural and expected: the experiences are part of their communities and through generations of their families.

Their school has done little to effectively undo or make external these beliefs; that the participants see them as normal and natural is replicated in their school and its unfolding. As shown in Chapter Five, the participants are unaware of the labels attached to them and this chapter has shown the process of their acceptance. Their school is part of the larger system of schooling, a site where, historically, low-income urban families saw potential for significant change. The tumult of the 1960s shook this faith. However, the participants see change as possible through education. Their faith and belief should be encouraged through actual, systemic change. Chapter Seven returns to a focus on media education, exploring what is missing specifically and what steps can be taken to start making change. The participants' hopes and frustrations are the foundation for enacting change.

Notes

[1] HBO's critically acclaimed *The Wire* chronicled the politics, economics and social realities of the Baltimore, Maryland drug trade. The show ran for five seasons and drew from the series creators and writers David Simon and Ed Burns, who based much of the show on their experiences. Simon worked for the *Baltimore Sun* and Burns was a Baltimore police officer who became a public school teacher (see hbo.com/thewire/about/).

[2] Lil Wayne is a rap star and actor from Louisiana who has released several acclaimed rap albums. His freestyle is known for confident boasts about his skill as the best rap artist and he is personally known to be a regular and public drug user (see starpulse.com/music/lil_wayne/biography).

[3] Jim Jones is a rap star best known for 2006's biggest rap single 'We Fly High (Ballin').' Born in the Bronx and raised in Harlem, Jones raps about his life on the streets of New York City. He is currently involved in a docu-drama production of his biography, including his shift from street hustle to legal work (see jimjonesofficial.com/biography).

[4] Max B. is a rap artist from Harlem who works with Jim Jones. He has been imprisoned on robbery and drug possession charges and faces murder and robbery charges. Max is known for his mix-tape releases and work with many hip-hop artists (see last.fm/music/Max+B/+wiki).

[5] Nikki Blonsky is an actress known for her performance as Tracy Turnblad in the 2007 film *Hairspray*. An overweight actress, Blonsky has stated she wants more affirming roles for plus-sized actresses (see imdb.com).

[6] Queen Latifah is an actress who has been in movies and television shows, is a Cover Girl spokeswoman, a hip-hop artist and producer. She was first known for her public derision of the largely male-focused, misogynist hip-hop industry (see imdb.com).

[7] Mo'nique is a comic actress best known for her role as a single mother attending college with her daughter on the UPN comedy *The Parkers*. Mo'nique promotes her role as a full-figured woman, advocating on behalf of plus-sized women (see starpulse.com/Actresses/Mo'nique/Biography).

[8] *Norbit* is the 2007 film starring Eddie Murphy in multiple roles. The film tells the story of Norbit, a black orphan raised by a Chinese family connived into marrying an obese woman, Rasputia, while longing for his childhood friend, Kate (see imdb.com).

[9] *Saved by the Bell* was a syndicated sit-com about a group of Southern Cali-

fornia high school students, including trouble maker and group leader Zach; AC, the jock; nerd and comic foil, Screech; Kelly, the cheerleader; fashion-focused Lisa; and Jessie, the straight-A feminist. The show chronicled their adventures in high school and college (see imdb.com).

Chapter 7

Integrating Media Education:
What Is Missing, What Is Needed

I concluded Chapter Four writing that the data was organized in a way to show what the participants do not know about media studies, that they are not receiving media education, what they do not know about new school reform or their role in it, and how they do understand and make meaning of adolescence and education through media representations and their own experiences. The participants have shown they are missing significant skills in critical inquiry, yet have a thorough colloquial, intuitive knowledge of their experiences as located within their larger environments. I believe that media education can help shift their intuitive knowledge to critical analysis and, more broadly, can illustrate the shifts that are needed to heal the broader urban school system.

The goal of this chapter is to explore further some of the pieces missing in understandings of media and urban education. Undoubtedly, a grim picture has thus far been painted, but this need not be an entirely pessimistic text. There are two major questions unanswered in the text thus far. One, how does the contemporary literature on critical literacy and multiple literacies help advance understandings of critical media literacy? Two, how do the participants' stories show what can be–what needs to be–done to advance critical media education in the secondary school classroom? To end the text at this point would succumb to pessimism and assume that both media and urban education are doomed to failure because, as currently envisioned, they do not work. Is it time to capitulate to failure and allow the urban public school system to fall into a state of disrepair so devastating that it takes another disastrous shift, along the lines of Ocean Hill-Brownsville, to make change? In the country that produces and exports the most media, is media education doomed to fail because of the disparate ties between education, alternative pedagogies, and multiple school systems?

I think not. I share ways to integrate media studies into schools, however, I fully acknowledge any potential integration I write about is temporary, a stopgap measure at best. Long-term, institutional changes are needed to make significant progress. The conundrum, I believe, is that the structural problems of schools are not fixed because there is little concrete agreement as to what they are; scholars know there are problems, but are not entirely clear on what the actual structural problems are or where they reside. Mayor Bloomberg's efforts at centralized control, increased small school development and strict security measures have *not* tackled systemic structural problems. Three broad, long-term changes are needed to support integration of media education into public schools: a thorough expansion of the comprehension and use of the term 'literacy'; the development of formal teacher training in media education; and a focus on skills assessment and research into what is learned in a media education curriculum. To enable the successful implementation of these three changes, a radical shift in the organization, structure and implementation of urban schooling is needed.

This chapter explores what a radical pedagogical shift might look like by drawing from the literature on critical and multiple literacies, on the need for teacher training and research and assessment in media education. I refer to the participants' stories to construct what might be possible in media and urban education. Where Noguera (2000) argues in favor of listening to young people talk about their understandings of violence and safety in order to improve school safety and Alonso *et al.* (2009) draw from young people's stories on their negative experiences in public schools in order to make a case for bettering the urban school system, I draw from the participants' stories about their media and urban education to make a direct case for media education inclusion and a corresponding need for thorough exploration of the structural flaws within urban schooling.

Radical Change Needed

I wholeheartedly agree with Jenkins *et al.* (2006) that media education courses should not be a curricular 'add-on.' As a curricular add-on or elective course, media education is vulnerable to budget cuts and its reputation as an extracurricular, and therefore superfluous, subject is cemented. As evidenced by LSHS, when media courses are 'added on' they are easily excised or, possibly worse, sloppily integrated, reflecting larger problems of urban schooling, including high teacher turnover and inconsistent lessons. Media education across the curriculum is necessary; this can neither be denied nor a conversation saved for a later date. Just as it is inconceivable that young people would go through school without courses in math, science, social studies or English, it should be equally inconceivable to complete school without media studies. Media education should not be about protecting young people from the evils of the media; there are far greater (and genuine) evils in the world and young people rightly reject any attempt to curb their interests (Bragg 2001; Buckingham 2001; Domaille & Buckingham 2001; Kellner & Share 2007). Alternately, media education should not celebrate (blindly) young people's use of media (Buckingham 2008), especially with social networking and user-generated content as popular as they are at present. However, we do need to acknowledge the world is changing, there is increased development of, and in many cases, access to, greater quantity of media. Facebook, Twitter, My Space, YouTube and any manner of currently popular social networking or user-generated content sites may or may not be passing trends, but it is clear that the ways in which we are introduced to, come to understand, and make meaning from the world has changed and will continue to change to encompass more digital and mobile media at faster speeds. There are and continue to be significant shifts in our social interactions and how we learn about the world. The digital divide–whether it is a divide of access and class (Gandy 2002; Kellner 2002) or a divide between public and private usage (Buckingham 2007)–will undoubtedly yawn larger unless significant change is made. Media education can ignite that change.

Media education should begin in primary education. In their personal lives, high school students are already media 'experts,' both in their own private usage as well as to what they have been exposed and chosen to participate in throughout most of their lives. If media education begins in primary school, by high school, media-literate students will be responsibly trained, critical scholars who truly are experts, which will undoubtedly make them better prepared for entry into labor or university. That being said, my experience, research and work are at the high school level, so this discussion focuses on secondary school. A valid site for future research is inquiry into the integration of media education at the primary school level.

A perceived obstacle to incorporating media education across the curriculum is keeping up with the rapid changes in technology. Economically struggling urban schools that cannot afford the latest technologies further enlarges the gulf between urban and (successful) suburban schools. Teaching the most up-to-date, up-to-the-minute media or technology is not necessary; rather, young people deserve to learn critical inquiry and analysis through study of content and representation, production and technology, institution and structure, audience and ideology. Furthermore, the struggle to teach the most up-to-the-minute technologies is an exercise in dissatisfaction: at this point in time, texts and lessons cannot keep up with the rapid changes. Perpetuating the struggle is a clear route to dissatisfaction; however, it need not be an insurmountable obstacle. The latest trend and 'classic' media can be taught successfully from a foundation of conceptual, analytical and practical approaches. The specific texts, technologies and media studied will undoubtedly change–as will young people's interests in specific content or technologies–but what remains is a foundation for learning that is flexible. Social networking and user-generated content are forms of social interaction, which cut across all media and technology. Media education can critically embrace current changes in technology and see them within their context; media education can and should contribute to the radical change needed within the broader education environment.

Necessary Paradigm Shifts

While the nation's school systems need massive reorganization and a radical paradigm shift away from standardized testing and neoliberal philosophies, small steps can and should be made to encourage immediate change. My experience in one particular New York City urban public school, part of the latest effort at school reform, clearly shows what is *not* working. Participants show they do not learn the concepts of media education in particular classes or across the curriculum. They are not critically aware of, or are not able to articulate, the labels externally applied to them and their schooling. They are aware of negative media representations of adolescents and education, but do not speak thoroughly or critically about their awareness. That could help point scholars in a direction of what might work. Their absence of critical articulation is largely because they have not been provided a genuine learning opportunity; they have not been provided a genuine learning opportunity because their teachers have not, either. The gaps are conspicuous; how can those gaps be filled in and students supported in their learning in the process? A responsible media education, included across the curriculum into core courses can contribute small, valuable changes. Pieces of contemporary media and media studies need to be better understood in order to begin to make change, especially to undo neoliberal tendencies, including knowledge of social media and technology, awareness of teacher-student hierarchies and inter-discipline and self-reflection.

Social Media

Public and popular commentary on social networking and user-generated content refer to these media as 'social media' (Brockman 2009; Weinberger

2009). This name is awkwardly redundant: what media are *not* social? To engage with any medium is to engage with the social world; to watch television, or a film, to read a book, to listen to music, to surf the Web, write or receive an email, log on to Facebook, YouTube or MySpace, to Tweet, is to engage in a social activity. Admittedly, some media are more social than others, but all our media and all our media engagements are social. Media education can and should embrace that social element. 'Social' media can be used for mobilizing and organizing social change. Currently, new 'social' media are threatening, in part, because they mark a divide between generations. This divide is reminiscent of technological divides in the past, yet somehow always manages to feel 'brand new.' The behavior we engage with these media are not so radically different that they cannot be better explored and understood. In so doing, media education can help undo neoliberalism's focus on the individual and private accomplishment. If media and their construction within corporate and independent environments are transparent, young people as audiences, producers and scholars can possess a more thorough understanding of the often-mysterious corporate elements of media institutions. Knowing the corporate organization of Facebook, YouTube, MySpace and Twitter does not have to undo the pleasure young people get as audiences of, distributors of, or producers on these sites, but rather shows their role as (unpaid) laborers within the system. The proliferation of these social media illustrate they are *personally* social: many schools and school systems block websites deemed inappropriate within the walls of school, thereby creating a further divide between 'personal' and 'professional' use.

Technology

The inclusion of technology is exciting, but can be vacuous and ineffective if technology for technology's sake is the primary draw. Teachers and schools need not rely on or feel a desperate need for the latest technology in order to make media education 'work.' If access to technology remains a divide, then remove the obstacle: focus less on access within school and more on understanding the position of technology within society. While technology is enticing and inviting, I believe there are ways to bring in media studies without needing much electronic technology. Indeed, because schools and school systems must often block certain sites or technologies, young people may not be impressed with the technology offered within their classrooms when it is possible they have more advanced and, if so, certainly greater access, at home. Technologies now common and familiar in classrooms can be used as gateways to learning. The Internet can be a site to develop research and analysis skills, showing students how to evaluate the quality of data found on websites. The Internet need not be the excitement, but rather how the Internet can be used and data understood. Technology need not be overwhelming or intimidating if teachers and schools trust their expertise and use the technologies to bolster their own knowledge and strengthen their teaching beyond specific subjects. If the goal is to get students to think independently, to ask and answer research questions, and produce work that provides evidence of their learning and mastery of data, technology need not be fancy or 'overdone' to enable this. However, as shown by the participants' stories on media studies inclusion, technology cannot substitute the teacher's role.

Teacher-student Hierarchy

Media education can further disrupt strengthening the neoliberal training ground by fostering democratic classroom space. Media education disrupts the traditional teacher-student hierarchy and in so doing can embrace a social and intellectual re-imagining. Students come to school with a great deal of raw media knowledge and cultivated media pleasure. They learn quickly to stash that knowledge and pleasure outside the classroom or, they know that it cannot be accessed. Media education can serve to make the classroom a more inviting, less penalizing place by acknowledging young people's knowledge and pleasure. Kellner and Share (2007) write:

> Teaching critical media literacy should be a participatory, collaborative project. Watching television shows or films together could promote productive discussions between teachers and students ... with an emphasis on eliciting student views, producing a variety of interpretations of media texts, and teaching basic principles of hermeneutics and criticism (p. 17).

Embracing this idea, teachers and students can both work together while also creating a mutually respected place for personal, private interests. Students and teachers deserve their 'private' media usage: what is appropriate for an adult or a student in the privacy of his/her own home might not be appropriate for classroom discussion and students can learn valuable lessons about boundaries, respect and privacy not by keeping their media use secret, but by learning what is appropriate where and when.

Disrupting the teacher-student hierarchy carries with it the risk of creating an overly personal environment. As shown through the participants, authorities at LSHS know a great deal about students' personal lives and students participate in rumors *with* faculty and staff. Disrupting the teacher-student hierarchy, therefore needs constant attention; it should not be a pendulum that shifts from blind authority to false equality, but rather a space cultivated where young people practice their expert knowledge and work to share with and learn from teacher expertise.

Inter-discipline and Self-reflection

Clarification of social media, re-imagined use of technology and re-imagined hierarchies are not wholly independent topics of concern and what media education can and should provide is an acknowledgment of and adherence to the interdisciplinary qualities of study, the interdependence of various subjects and the need for self-reflection to make the process of learning both active and multidimensional. The skills learned in a media education curriculum can and should be transferable; critical analysis of television or film does not need to be isolated from critical analysis of election results, environmental changes or English literature. Questions drawn from media education are not the sole property of media studies: In the age of the 24-hour news cycle, is there increased value placed on the latest 'results'? What is the value of time? What is the relationship between a question asked and the answer received? Who owns information? These are not concerns specific to media studies, but rather ways to approach any subject relevant to the shifts in how information is accessed, analyzed, produced and distributed.

Media education can be the catalyst to re-imagine teaching and learning. One major hindrance that urban youth face when entering school is the absence of the invisible social privilege tethered to social and cultural capital. They do not necessarily possess the confidence to approach unfamiliar material with the knowledge that they can succeed because they have learned in other places that intellectual success is not theirs to possess. Re-imagining pedagogy, especially the education of underserved populations, to start with the familiar can help build that necessary confidence to tackle the unfamiliar and thereby make change and contribute more equally in school and society. In their video production class, LSHS students made a video, then moved on to a different, unrelated class. There was no room made or enforced for self-reflection or the process of development and the videos made did not cut across or embrace multiple disciplines or concerns.

Space should also be built for the process of self-reflection where students must review and analyze their own work and their own experience in the process of developing knowledge. In this way, their personal interests, likes and dislikes are not punished but rather are critically examined: what 'belongs' in school and what does not? How does group work and collaboration influence the process and development of a project? Self-reflection is an independent, individual activity that connects the individual to the larger group and thereby helps undo the neoliberal tendency toward hyper-individuality and individual improvement at the cost of others. If we continue to treat oppressed and underserved populations in the same basic way, making only superficial cosmetic changes, we will continue to have a dangerously divided society that is viewed and views itself as disconnected. Acknowledging and valuing the interdisciplinary quality of media studies, with a focus on accessing the unfamiliar via the familiar and emphasizing the importance of self-reflection can help shift perspectives. It then becomes plausible to believe, and act on the belief, that if we treat young people as responsible, intellectually capable individuals who can blend their skills and expertise with others in a highly functioning community, they will, in turn, act as responsible, intellectually capable members of a highly functioning community.

Notes on Paradigm Shifts in Classrooms

Problems can be solved and obstacles that initially appear insurmountable are overcome with a shift in perspective, through looking at a problem in a new way. Based on my work at LSHS, I believe the way to solve the problems in school and within the larger system of schools occurs in two places: change must originate within the classroom and influence a radical reorganization of the structure of urban education. These notes focus specifically on change that can occur in the classroom; Chapter Eight will focus on changes needed in the structure of urban education and the larger urban environment. My suggestions are not the only way to include media studies into the curriculum, and I am indebted to Moore (1991) who envisioned this inclusion almost 20 years ago. These suggestions are based on my experience with the troubled, incomplete and inaccurate inclusion of media education at LSHS, the participants' own inability to articulate their knowledge of the media with any critical vocabulary and Buckingham's (2003) concepts of media education. I willfully bypass very real concerns with testing schedules, school bureaucracy, time/space concerns, faculty access, teacher expertise, credit accumulation, copyright adherence and all the important realities of the school day. I believe these are all absolutely necessary challenges to work through in the development of any curriculum, however, the plan here is to share thoughts and potential that can be built upon and debated. It is easy to point out there are problems in school and much more difficult to change those problems. These are not 'final' thoughts, but rather blissfully early imaginings on what changes can be made.

Media Literacy and Media Production

Media education should be infused across the curriculum and the leader in a radical shift in pedagogy, however, I also believe that students deserve particular media classes to introduce and advance their media vocabulary and provide consistent practice in analysis and production. All students should begin their study of the media with a media literacy course where they learn basic, fundamental critical vocabulary and ways to apply that vocabulary in analysis of various media. Students should work with content and texts with which they are familiar as well as be exposed to media unfamiliar to them and not part of their routine. Confronting unfamiliar texts provides the opportunity to expand awareness and exposes students to media outside their concept of the mainstream. To bolster their media literacy skills, young people deserve the opportunity to explore 'other' media. Students and teachers should work consistently and continuously question what they encounter and reflect on their role as audiences and learners. The 'right' answer or 'solution' should not be the emphasis, but rather the process of and willingness to engage in inquiry, analysis and reflection. This course should draw from a variety of accessible media, both familiar and unfamiliar to study the concepts of media analysis within and across texts. Looked at through the concepts of media education (Buckingham 2003) will peel back the institutional layers, making clear the structure and organization of media. To disrupt the teacher-student hierarchy, teachers and students will work together on the study of the chosen texts, especially in inquiry into who is targeted and who is rejected by the specific text/medium. Irrespective of quality or enticement of high-end technology, much work can be done with production, such as script writing, production planning and storyboarding across a variety of media to develop production skills and awareness.

If the goal is to be analytically competent upon graduation, then students should begin their high school career with media literacy, ideally in their first year. The one year there was a media literacy class at LSHS, it was inconsistent in its intent, the multiple teachers over the course of the school year had varying ideas of what and how to teach and students did not make connections with their other classes or their own experiences with the media. A foundational media literacy course should survey the broad media landscape while more advanced courses could focus on specific media and/or draw on students' particular interests. Specific courses in film, TV or music analysis, game or Web design and journalism (in various forms), for example, could prepare students for both university study and provide valuable skills for labor and employment. Critical inquiry, analysis and self-reflection are not the sole property of media literacy, but rather are transferable skills across all subject matters. A foundational course in media literacy can be the space where students learn about the media and by engaging in complex activities and through familiar content, can gain the skills (and confidence) to approach unfamiliar, daunting information.

Furthermore, to take ownership and control of their knowledge development through production work, students can see their own intellectual and practical development. While many young people are clearly 'experts' in their own personal media production, this work might be independent and certainly informal. At LSHS, self-motivated students interested in art, video, music or Web production did so on their own, possibly using the school's equipment, but were not formally fostered or supported in their development. Popcorn explains he searched outside school for media and arts programs because his interests were not addressed within school. Providing students with formal, scaffolded production work may further emphasize the interdisciplinary quality of study across subjects as well as provide a more nuanced connection between their own personal work and their more formal schoolwork.

Production courses can provide a space for the basic building blocks of any production work, including working in groups, collaboration, development of a project from its nascent ideas to a final text, respect for deadlines, revision and draft work. Even 'simple,' low-technology productions can be highly complex processes when skills are built upon with a final project, whose goals, deadlines and form are clearly demarcated. Just as the foundational media literacy course would survey a broad landscape of analysis and invite production as part of its process, a foundational production course would open space for more advanced work. Students could begin with still photography and video work, which could develop into topic-specific courses such as photojournalism, PSA production, documentary filmmaking and game or Web development, for example. Again, production emphasizes the interdisciplinary and collaborative qualities inherent to media studies: to develop a project requires multiple skills and levels of expertise that can be found in a group; it requires inquiry, analysis and self-reflection as well as practical, physical work. Any successful production, irrespective of medium, requires at the very least, writing, an understanding of time and its management, skills to communicate with other individuals, gathering and manipulation of data, and the ability to construct a clear message. These are skills and proficiencies students need in all their courses, which means the study of the media can and will be both about itself as well as about the larger process of learning, which is reflected in the current inclusion of media inquiry across the curriculum.

English and Social Sciences

Because of their emphasis on analysis and deconstruction of texts, English and Social Science courses are generally considered the 'easiest' place to include media studies. This is both valuable and risky. The value rests in the flexibility and adaptability of these subjects: critical inquiry and textual analysis are part of their pedagogy. Therefore, 'adding in' the study of the media–even to an already developed curriculum–is relatively easy. This is where the risk rests: in that ease. Because the study of the media is easily 'added in' the implication is that its study is not necessary and when the curriculum gets busy, the study of the media can easily be excised from the courses. The stories told in English and the social sciences need not be disparate from the stories told in TV, movies, music, or disconnected from the stories constructed on social networking and user generated websites. Infusing the study of the media into English and social sciences does not undo what they already cover, but rather, encourages their coverage to be more holistic.

Math and Hard Sciences

Math and hard sciences might not seem like places where the study of the media could easily fit in, but these courses emphasize the concepts of media studies in their work. We learn about the world through the media, correspondingly many of us learn about the impact and action of math and science through the media: our acceptance or rejection of statistics, polling numbers, election results, unemployment numbers, and housing costs all come to us through the media and via persons deemed experts in a certain field. Our understanding of the environment, biology (especially of species other than our own), the Earth, its movement and relationship to other planets are often learned through television, specially produced documentaries, newspapers or magazines. These media take a specific perspective and have a particular purpose and under the guise of 'entertainment' or 'information' provide us with a great deal of data (if not knowledge) about mathematics and various sciences.

Without making significant changes to the expected learning outcomes of math or science courses, exploring these subjects through a media studies perspective invites critical inquiry and analysis. A slickly produced documentary or streaming updates of election results are enticing and engaging, but what do we learn? Can these flashy texts be used to help make math and science more multidimensional? How do multi-national corporations work to convince audiences they are socially responsible through their public use of media? The risk here is in teaching *through* media, using the media that emphasize math or science as the lesson rather than teaching the construction of data and knowledge production within a particular form.

Electives: Arts, Foreign Languages and Physical Education

In a pedagogical environment that favors testing and 'basic' studies, electives courses, including but not limited to the arts, foreign language and health/physical education courses, reside in a precarious place. Perpetually in danger of being cut from schools, when electives courses are offered, they feel like a special reward rather than a comprehensive, multiperspectival curriculum. The concepts of media studies can frame and contribute to electives courses. Foreign language and physical education courses emphasize the value of self-reflection, especially in the struggle to achieve and master new skills. Arts courses develop representation and production skills, thereby providing a more nuanced, complex home for aesthetic development and appreciation. Foreign languages make the construction of power visible by exploring who possesses the construction of the language and whose dialect and grammar is respected in labor and education. Physical education teaches young people the value of their bodies in ability and health through exploration of the representation of the fit and aesthetic body in the media. All electives course 'prove' the importance of interdisciplinary study when looked at through media studies concepts.

To make these 'simple' changes to classrooms, subjects and schools, teachers and administrators need to work together to make their school a cohesive unit rather than a series of separate, disconnected classes. This is where small schools have a built-in advantage: strictly in terms of size, it is easier for faculty and staff to work together. Admittedly, these changes are far from simple; they require a significant amount of support and encouragement from administrators, and undoubtedly a great deal of extra work from teachers. Lessons must be learned from past endeavors into alternative curricula, teaching methods and school development. The literature shows that, when given the opportunity, space and encouragement to make dramatic, radical change, teachers and administrators are able to do so, but those changes are not self-sustaining and when individual teachers or schools as a whole re-focus their priorities, the special attention given to alternative or interdisciplinary curricula is dropped (Carlson 2004; Tyner-Mullings 2008). As the participants in this study have shown, the study of the media is not thoroughly applied in their school. I do believe that change is possible, that it must begin in the classroom and that individual schools can make significant individual changes, however, for changes to be self-sustaining and to matter outside the originating classroom, the system of pedagogy and the structure of education need to significantly change as well. To begin that process, changes in understandings and manifestations of literacy, teacher training and research and evaluation need to occur.

What is necessary is a radical paradigm shift of primary and secondary school, but that paradigm shift must be cautiously and carefully detailed. Schools need to be re-imagined as democratic and multicultural environments that both resist and counter neoliberal influence; let schools, not private enterprise, be the model for social change. As has been shown through Harvey (2005), Klein (2007) and Giroux (2008), paradigm shifts can take many forms, not necessarily socially just ones. To make media education a successful part of the curriculum, the current and future paradigm shift must move away from neoliberal orthodoxies, embrace work that betters communities in their entirety rather than work that betters those already privileged, and must focus not on private enterprise or capital accumulation from otherwise public institutions, but on a remembrance of the intent and purpose of public education: to foster critical thought and active citizenship in all citizens of the nation. Kellner (2002) writes, "Education, at its best, provides the symbolic and cultural capital that empowers people to survive and prosper in an increasingly complex and changing world and the resources to produce a more cooperative, democratic, egalitarian and just society" (p. 99). If education remains in its current state of organization, the divide will soon be uncrossable, which leaves two wholly unacceptable options: increased anger with little constructive action or resigned complacency and grudging complacence to neoliberal philosophy.

This text does not solve the problems of the current state of urban education. One text, one project, one example of media education struggles and the connections to the larger urban public school system cannot make significant change in the system. I find myself regularly frustrated by and skeptical of stories of singular, successful change within one school for three reasons. One, pilot changes are often successful *because* they are small and intensely focused. CPESS was successful because of the tenacity of the administrative staff; the school's success dwindled absent this staff and other schools could not replicate the success (Dillon 1995; Tyner-Mullings 2008). Can pilot reform be made larger, to reach more schools, while maintaining the initial intense focus? When schools Chancellors Joseph Fernandez, in the 1980s, and Harold Levy, in the 1990s, experimented with small schools, they were successful because the experiment itself was small (Celis 1994; Ravitch 1974/2000). Bloomberg, however, opened *many* small schools, in rapid succession, *without* focus. Two, single school success stories reside often *within* the walls of the school, with no corresponding look at the communities in which the school resides (Levine 2002; Silva & Mackin 2002). Anyon (1997) cautions we must explore schools from *within* as inextricably a part of their communities. Three, who determines the formula for 'success'? In a school system under mayoral control, there will be little to no bad news from City Hall regarding the school system. If students shuffled into GED programs are considered high school graduates, graduation numbers inevitably rise. These things, however, do not make *school* successful, but rather, makes public relations and mathematical manipulation successful.

This text, and this chapter in particular, are intended as a step forward, an exploration of a significant problem and an initial examination of a new route toward making change in the system. Educators already agree that media literacy education must happen and that the urban school system needs healing.

These are huge projects. How can they be accomplished? What need happen along the way to foster their success?

Grossberg (1994) proposes a "pedagogy of articulation and risk" to fundamentally alter schooling and education. This pedagogy "is a contextual practice which is willing to take the risk of making connections, drawing lines, mapping articulations, between different domains, discourses, and practices, to see what will work, both theoretically and politically" (p. 18). A pedagogy of articulation and risk does not map out ahead of time the perfect plan or determined outcome, but rather endeavors a critical, contextual way to understand and make meaning of material. This pedagogy works to undo the teacher-student hierarchy and its unfounded assumptions that teachers possess all knowledge (and, in turn, that students are empty vessels). Importantly:

> It is a pedagogy which aims not to predefine its outcome (even in terms of some imagined value of emancipation or democracy) but to empower its students to begin to reconstruct their world in new ways, and to rearticulate their future in unimagined and perhaps even unimaginable ways (p. 18).

A pedagogy of articulation and risk begins to shed the hatred and myopic vision of neoliberalism and embraces the changes in technology and information gathering without falling prey to passing trends.

Expanding Meanings of "Literacy"

Critical Literacy

As discussed in Chapter One, the current approach to media education in the United States is named 'critical media literacy' and several scholars have adopted this term and work to define and contextualize its meanings (Furness 2007; Kellner 2002; Kellner & Share 2007; Mashburn & Weaver 2007; McLaren & Hammer 2007; Steinberg & Kincheloe 2004a; Torres & Mercado 2008). Critical media literacy works against acceptance/rejection dichotomies, moves firmly away from both protective and celebratory positions, and works toward acknowledging the multiple and mutual influences between audience and text. What is clear, thus far, in the term critical media literacy is 'critical' and 'media.' What is meant by literacy, especially these days with changing global technologies?

Literacy is going through taxonomic changes. Simply put, 'literacy' is the ability to decipher the meanings of letters into words, but there is nothing 'simple' about literacy. In an age where digital and mobile media have a rapid rate of adoption, 'literacy' must work to change and update its definitions to appropriately encompass multiple ways to approach these technologies (Tyner 1998). Traditional literacy is understood as intellectually active, but physically passive, whereas these days we must understand literacy as both intellectually and physically active. Literacy cannot be understood in isolation from other skills. To be literate is to possess power, to engage in a complex set of social practices, to understand language in action; literacy is historically conditional and opens us up to understanding past and current manifestations of power. Literacy invites us into a world of knowledge and power with a strict entry code. A vital piece of the discussion on literacy is what it means to be literate and how literacy lives in society. To be literate is to move beyond the ability to decode data, it is also a piece of being a functional member of society. Literacy and its infusion in society is part of the development of society; literacy does not exist outside or independent of culture. As shown in Chapter Two, America grew up with a foundational belief in compulsory schooling where literacy training was always a part of the curriculum. Literacy is not a-technological; the tools of literacy are very much technologies. The ability to read and write also includes the ability to ask questions, critique the status quo and demand change.

Reading and writing invite us to question and through asking questions, we become active members of a society, not passive recipients of data. When we critique society we no longer allow ourselves to be complicit in presumed or externally determined right/wrong or in/appropriate behavior. Reading and writing are skills of mainstream society and appear in normative education environments and dominant culture defines and delimits acceptable literacy. There is nothing 'natural' about literacy or the process of becoming literate. Literacy is very much learned behavior and as such, there is a distinct hierarchy: those who are literate possess the tools to inform/teach others and therefore control *what* and *when* will be taught. Literacy is a practical thing, an early and necessary stop on the journey through education, information, employment, citizenship and comprehension. Yet literacy is also and possibly more importantly, anything but practical: there is no one singular place where knowledge belongs.

Irrespective of definition, 'literacy' and all it encompasses involve a highly valuable set of skills. Being literate is more than 'simply' knowing how to read and write; being literate opens doors that will otherwise stay firmly, unequivocally closed. There are special concerns with young people of color whose literacy gaps put them at continued social and economic disadvantage. Mastering "dominant literacies" opens doors to university and ultimately higher paying jobs while rejection of or exclusion from these dominant literacies include increased unemployment, imprisonment, and teen pregnancy rates, especially among urban populations (Morrell 2008, pp. 2-3). These dominant literacies represent the actual, practical skills of learning to read and write as well as the invisible social and cultural capital possessed by those who control the ethos of literacy.

Dominant literacies, while broad in positive influence, are narrow in ideological scope: They are generally associated with white, middle-class values, not with embracing multicultural, multiclass values. Dominant literacies therefore set up who belongs and deserves to be rewarded and who does not belong and deserves punishment. Those who are 'left out' of–or actively excluded from–literacy are left out of a set of skills that are necessary for modern survival. More importantly, those who are left out/excluded are removed from the mainstream and secured in the social fringes of society. Morrell (2008) writes that critical literacy is "necessary not only for the critical navigation of hegemonic discourses; it is also essential to the redefining of the self and the transformation of oppressive social structures and relations of production" (p. 5). It is through literacy, Morrell believes, social change can occur and that "no population requires critical literacy more than today's urban youth" (p. 6).

Urban youth are paradoxically targeted and rejected by dominant literacies. The corporate media structure profits from colloquial literacies and language use, but that profit, borrowed from urban youth, is not shared. Urban youth learn both that they are not good enough and that they will not be good enough because they are lacking the necessarily skills to maneuver through the socially dominant terrain. J-Trout and Lucy see Lil Wayne as a kindred spirit, but do not see how Lil Wayne's corporate representation profits from their desire. Lucy will never be rewarded for smoking pot the way Lil Wayne is. Urban youth are literate *enough* to maintain their role in service positions while also knowledgeable that is as far as they are invited. Importantly, it cannot be forgotten that urban youth are less likely to have libraries, bookstores or newsstands in their schools or communities; the presence and use of these institutions inevitably develop invisible literacy skills as part of the fabric of a community. Therefore, dominant literacy rejects urban youth, especially when there is a clear division between terrestrial locations of 'proper' and 'improper' literacy. Delpit (2002) and Kohl (2002) discuss the role of talk within the classroom, a division that punishes students within the very space that should nourish them. Delpit writes, "negative responses to the children's home language on the part of the adults around them insures that they will reject the school's language and everything else the school has to offer" (p. 47). Kohl's discussion of teacher talk, presumably via dominant, proper literacies and language, argues that students listen more closely than believed and therefore learn beyond the specific content of the talk. He writes, "students interpret, reflect, analyze and respond to the nuances of language in the classroom and since most of the permitted language in the classroom is teacher talk, it is to that language that an excessive amount of student emotion and intelligence is committed" (p. 150). Literacy, therefore, is an entry to, a hierarchical organization of, and rejection from, dominant society. Those young people who do not possess dominant literacies are not illiterate, however. The definition and action of literacy must expand.

New London Group: Multiliteracies

In 1994, a collection of 10 scholars met to discuss 'literacy' and all its possible permutations. Naming themselves the New London Group, they worked to re-imagine awareness and knowledge of 'literacy.' The New London Group defined 'multiliteracies' as a pedagogy that "focuses on modes of representation much broader than language alone [that] creates a different kind of pedagogy: one in which language and other modes of meaning are dynamic representational resources, constantly being remade by their users as they work to achieve their various cultural purposes" (Cope & Kalantzis 2000, p. 5). According to the New London Group (2000), successful education leads to "full and equitable social participation" in society and literacy pedagogy "is expected to play a particularly important role in fulfilling this mission" (p. 9). Traditional literacy is wedded to the formal, standard national language. Adherence to the formal, standard national language means that "there are still vast disparities in life chances" because not all students start school with the same (or even similar) skills (p. 10). To change school, the New London Group argues, one must begin by changing the understanding and implementation of literacy.

Their use of literacy pedagogy absolutely and explicitly denies neoliberal impulses; the New London Group call for a democratic education system and a demand to keep the public schools public and work rigorously to improve them for all students. They write, "Access to wealth, power, and symbols must be possible, no matter what identity markers, such as language, dialect, and register, a person happens to have" (p. 15). In part because education is organized by states, not under federal control, states must be strong "as neutral arbiters of difference" and schools and literacy pedagogy must follow as "the basis for a cohesive sociality; a new civility in which differences are the norm" (p. 15). Multiliteracies themselves are not radical; rather, what is radical here is the shift in ways of thinking about literacy to encompass multiliteracies. The New London Group writes, "As lifeworlds become more divergent and their boundaries more blurred, the central fact of language becomes the multiplicity of meanings and their continual intersection. Just as there are multiple layers to everyone's identity, there are multiple discourses of identity and multiple discourses of recognition to be negotiated" (p. 17). The New London Group has had profound influence on understanding and influencing changes from literacy to multiliteracies and their work has influence approaches to critical media literacy. Full embrace of multiliteracies could serve to undo concerns with literacy and power divisions (Delpit 2002; Kohl 2002; Morrell 2008).

Media Education: Critical Media Literacy Revisited

'Literacy' has never been a simple subject or an easy task. The process of learning letters and the process of putting those letters into words, words into sentences, sentences into clear narrative structure–and the corresponding ability to produce such work–is phenomenally complicated. These days, however, there is little room for the luxury of thought that literacy was once 'simple' or the romantic notion that there was one clearly monitored entry to adult knowledge. Literacy encompasses many skills, multiple texts and occurs in a variety of locations, not 'just' in print or 'just' in the classroom. Literacy can also be restrictive; the boundary is clear. Literacy may be one of those subjects whose unfamiliarity is threatening; media education can provide a familiar entry to literacy by respecting students' expertise and guiding them, via their expertise, to formal literacy.

There has been a shift in terminology from media literacy–initially passive and singular–to media education–active and inclusive–and now back to media literacy, respecting the shifting, active and inclusive use of the word 'literacy' (Domaille & Buckingham 2001). The renewed use of 'literacy' is "partly strategic" because it places media, mother tongue/native language and shifting learning needs within a media-saturated world (Domaille & Buckingham p. 14). Contemporary invocations of literacy move beyond the "practical command of the alphabet" to include the "knowledge and skills that render citizens capable of understanding his or her surroundings" (Tornero 2008, p. 7). To 'understand one's surroundings' requires the ability to critically understand written, oral, aural, and visual messages within the broad media landscape. Literacy is not 'simply' a technical skill, but rather "has to do with understanding, critical reading, the ability to analyze and reason, social participation, human relations, and the use of symbolic and cultural codes" (Tornero p. 7).

Multiliteracies and critical media literacy do not disconnect from or dismiss print literacy; indeed, print literacy serves as the foundation of multiliteracies. Multiliteracies and critical media literacy embrace, not reject, multiple ways to maneuver literacy and, in so doing, respect multiple languages as they participate in the process. Included in the study of mother-tongue and formal language are a variety of colloquial, casual and formal languages within the broader project. Mashburn and Weaver (2007) observe that literacy "is not limited to the interpretation of the printed word" because literacy cuts across all subject areas (p. 561). Kellner (2002), Kellner and Share (2007) and Jenkins *et al.* (2006) observe that traditional print literacy is the foundation of understanding new media; without traditional print literacy, new media could not be so infused in society. Kellner (2002) points out that traditional literacy skills are sublimated to new media and multiliteracies wherein "an entirely different sort of test is going to need to be devised in order to register individuals' multiliteracy competencies and to predict success in a new technological and educational environment" (p. 97). Kellner (2002) does not suggest a 'different sort of test,' but rather shows how in a new media and multiliteracy environment, it "becomes increasingly irrational to focus education on producing higher test scores on exams that themselves are becoming obsolete and outdated by the changes in the economy, society and culture" (p. 97). Kellner and Share (2007) observe that in new media and globalization, traditional texts lose ground to visual, aural and mixed media formats. This does not mean that literacy is no longer necessary but rather that it needs to expand to embrace the multiple and complex skills needed to participate in a multi-media, multi-cultural global environment. Print literacy continues to be of utmost significance in a digital, global media environment where citizens confront, and must be critically aware of, significant amounts of data from a variety of sources across media.

Jenkins *et al.* (2006) construct a space where textual literacy is a central skill, one that supports new media and participatory culture. Young people cannot feasibly or competently engage fully with participatory culture without the ability to read and write. Literacy must expand to include new media, not to displace reading and writing. Jenkins *et al.* (2006) write, "Before students can engage with the new participatory culture, they must be able to read and write" (p. 19). They emphasize that new media literacies are social, collaborative and enable ways to interact within communities separated by geography but connected by technology. Multiliteracies and participatory culture chip away at neoliberalism by focusing primarily on the development and sharing of culture and disabling the reliance on standardized tests.

Teacher Training

Trend (1994) writes, "The introduction of media literacy into other courses need not rely on special texts or instructional materials. Like other critical pedagogies, it hinges more on the way a teacher handles existing materials" (p. 238). This is certainly true, but what if the teacher has not had training to 'handle' certain materials?

Absent teacher training, more problems arise than are solved in a media studies classroom. Absent teacher training, teachers interested in incorporating media education concepts do so based on their own colloquial knowledge. This may limit the breadth and depth of media studies inclusion, especially witnessed in the reliance on technology. Absent effective training, teachers grow frustrated with technology, which, in turn, further hindered the educational endeavor (Kellner 2002). Most teachers do not have formal media studies or technology training which has the two fold negative result of leaving teachers unprepared and further hindering the development of media education (Domaille & Buckingham 2001). Teachers may let the technology take over, as was unwittingly expressed by many of the participants in this study, such as when Pyro talks about using computers, or Ivette talks about the Smart Board, or Nino's discussion of watching movies in math class. According to the 2001 UNESCO survey, "the most urgent need identified" by media education scholars was "sustained, in-depth teacher training ... Even in countries where media education is comparatively well-established, there are few opportunities for training, and only a minority of teachers are reached by it" (Domaille & Buckingham 2001, p. 11). While media education is increasing in popularity, inclusion and acceptance, teacher training is still woefully behind. It remains problematic that something deemed important does not have adequate training.

Many educators and media scholars want to organize teacher training. McLaren and Hammer (2007) are focused on "providing conditions for educators to approach the issue of literacy critically," introducing teachers to multiliteracies and their influence on teachers and understandings of the cultural production of teachers (p. 118). Torres and Mercado (2007) focus their discussion on the present "urgency" to include multiliteracies in schools and training for teachers "given the crucial role of media as they touch every aspect of human life" (p. 537). Bringing in teacher training, especially in multiliteracies, can make explicit, for teachers and students, the divisions and hierarchies of dominant literacies (Delpit 2002; Kohl 2002; Morrell 2008).

The 2008 UNESCO conference focused on curricular development and teacher training in media education and observed that teachers need both personal and professional media training. As individuals and citizens living in a global media environment, teachers need critical literacy skills and as educators, they need to learn how to facilitate the learning of that material to their students (Moore 2008). Teacher training is important because teachers should be an active part of curricular development and according to Tornero (2008) there has been insufficient participation for teachers in part "due to a lack of specific training, leading to a culture of reluctance and resistance to the technological innovations and new media" (p. 16; *cf* Goodman 2003). Teacher training is a site where media education needs to leave the high school classroom and enter the university education school classroom.

Skills Assessment and Research

In 1998, Christ and Potter asked, "How is it decided that a student is becoming or has become media literate? Also, what should be assessed? Knowledge? Skills? Behavior? Attitudes? Affect? Values?" (p. 11). In just over 10 years, these questions have not been answered; indeed, they continue to be asked and at greater volume. Media literacy scholars acknowledge the importance of evaluation in any media literacy program. Media literacy scholars and educators agree that evaluation and skill assessment are both necessary and lacking, but what does 'successful completion' of media studies look like? Individual projects involve individual corresponding learning assessments, but there remains no national, state or local standard; 'standards' are project, teacher or class specific. At LSHS, there was no clear rubric of expected skills and generally, if students completed projects in their media literacy or video production classes, this was considered acceptable. There are three obvious and interconnected reasons for this absence of standards of assessment. One, because media education itself has not been embraced, transparent assessment standards cannot be developed. Two, it is possible there is fear woven into the construction of a set of standards of assessment because if the media continue to change and adapt at the current pace, the standards of assessment might quickly be outdated. Three, the development of skills assessment demand confrontation and dismantling of the traditional teacher-student hierarchy when those creating the standards realize their grasp on what counts as successful, competent knowledge might not be 'complete.' The realization that the structure of education needs to be shifted in order to best infuse and assess media education interconnects these three reasons. There remains a certain safety in posing the questions rather than the greater risk in working to answer them.

The fear and risk need not be insurmountable. Teachers might not possess more knowledge about the media than young people, but this does not need to be a threat to their authority as teachers or obstacle to the development of standards of assessment. As Jenkins *et al.* (2006) argue, students deserve a formal inquiry into the study of the media and the teacher's role is to facilitate and guide students to critical analysis, inquiry, research gathering and intellectual production. Students *do* know a lot about the media, possibly more than their teachers, but teachers are trained to guide students through formal inquiry. Scholars developing media education curriculum should simultaneously develop tools of assessment; these assessments need not meet the whim of every change in technology, but rather a more broad measurement of transferable skills, foundational and specialized knowledge.

In addition to the absence of skills of assessment, there is also an absence of research into media education's role in the classroom and school. Media education can play many important roles in the development of critical scholars so there is no one strict answer within research. Research into what media education does may develop a better understanding of what young people know, what they are taught, and what they learn from their formal media studies (Domaille & Buckingham 2001; Scharrer 2002). There is little research documenting the effectiveness of media studies training. Media education does not have a finite knowledge base and because there are so many media outlets, young people experience the media in a variety of locations and because there are multiple, mutual social influences, there can be no 'control' group in research. This text and the data drawn from the participants show media education is *not* happening in any significant way within a school ostensibly focused on the media. However, I am not so cynical to end the text just sharing this absence; if we are committed to media education, we must look for ways to make change and to do so, research must happen concomitantly with work done in media education.

No discussion of research or skills and assessment can operate independent of other pedagogical conversations or contexts of learning. Multiliteracies, teacher training, skills assessment and research are all interconnected and interdependent endeavors. Each needs the other to strengthen the development and inclusion of media studies as part of a radical pedagogical shift. It is difficult to expect teachers and researchers to come up with skills and assessment or engage in research when there is precious little formal knowledge by teachers or researchers themselves. Regarding research into assessment and the development of media knowledge, Scharrer (2002) asks, "How should we expect people who have participated in a media-literacy program to be different from people who have not?" (p. 354). There is no clear answer to this question largely because there is an absence of research into the question. Scharrer writes, "there is a generalized notion" about media literacy outcomes, but no explicitly defined or measured skills (p. 354). What media literacy does do is help "foster critical thinking and discussion of media related issues, including how media messages are created, marketed, and distributed as well as their potential influence (or how they are received)" (pp. 354-355). Participation in media education will not have a singular outcome, so skills, assessment and research must also be flexible. Greater research into media learning will help bolster the need for an implementation of change.

Conclusion

In this chapter and throughout the text I have mentioned many times the belief that change begins in the classroom. I have also stated that the system of education needs radical change. I believe that a formal approach to the study of the media can be the catalyst for change in the classroom and in the system. I do not believe that media education is a panacea nor do I celebrate the inclusion of media education when it is in name and rhetoric only. My experiences at LSHS and what I have learned from the participants has shown me that much more careful, critical work remains.

This chapter has focused on change that can occur in the classroom while making observations and suggestions for larger, more systemic change. I also must adhere to my own challenge and set out on the path to solve problems and answer questions. Media education can and should be infused in classrooms; young people deserve it in order to develop as nuanced, well-trained scholars who will approach higher education and labor with more thorough, interconnected knowledge about the world and their role in it. The last chapter of this text will move outside the classroom to close out this study and stake claims on what need to be done to make structural changes to the system of education.

Chapter 8

Conclusion:

Looking Outside to Understand the Inside

Why do public schools work so well for those already privileged and fail those already oppressed by society? To answer that question, we must move outside the classroom into the larger community. Schools should not operate in isolation from one another or from the larger community in which they are situated. Research that stays within the walls of the classroom may inevitably conclude with baffled disbelief at the absence of success or frustration that success appears only within the classroom walls and cannot be replicated. Teachers care about their students and work to develop innovative curricula and lesson plans in the face of testing, yet are restricted from making significant contributory changes to the larger school system. Students express passionate and emotional concern about their classrooms, teachers and learning environments, yet are not provided the tools to speak formally, or provided the space to have their talk heard. Administrators, caught between the bureaucracy of the system and desire to strengthen their schools engage a constant dance of contradictory, complicated moves. Despite continuous work at formulas for success, the one consistent message is that what works in one school is not necessarily guaranteed to succeed in other schools.

This chapter concludes this text by moving outside the classroom and making the conversation more broad. The majority of this text is grounded within LSHS and within specific classrooms and pedagogical conversations, based on the participants' stories and concerns. I interviewed the students specifically about their school experiences and I situate their words and stories within the environment of their classrooms and school. I discuss what should be done, what students deserve in their classrooms and their knowledge of school, how media education can be integrated, and most importantly, visit a conversation by some of the participants on changes they witness in their communities that portends a challenging, difficult future for their lives and their families' well-being.

The Need to Integrate Media Education

Media education can be integrated and can be successful with teacher training, professional development and research into skills and assessment. This will not happen overnight. Here is what should happen in the meantime.

This text opened with an exploration of the trajectory and current face of media education in the United States. The valuable literature that has developed the field does not speak completely about the difficulties of *actually* including media education into high schools. In the face of bureaucracy, pedagogical expectations, increased disorganization in the urban school system and strict state and local graduation expectations, 'adding in' media education is a luxury at best and making change to the structure of the curriculum is nearly impossible. However, in the spirit of changes made in New York City schools within the miasma of decentralization, it is clear that change can occur. Maybe that change needs to be accidental in order to actually work, but it has been shown to be possible. The participants in this study have shown that they are intuitive individuals who know a great deal about their communities and their understandings of self; they can learn the concepts of media education. Using their talk as evidence via absence, they have not learned the concepts of media education or critical definitions. They equate technology education with media education and cannot construct critical analyses of the media that represents adolescence and education. The participants who cannot speak the language of media education should not be blamed for this absence of knowledge: they are subjects within a larger neo-liberal society that works to keep their bodies in subjugated positions. When able to make interpersonal connections with their teachers, the participants are willing to engage in intellectual risk, an advantage in small schools whose environment is more amenable to these connections.

If students are willing to take intellectual risks because they have solid interpersonal connections with their teachers, it is likely they will take further intellectual risks with unfamiliar or intimidating information if they can enter it via a familiar route. This is where media education can make change in primary and secondary schools: drawing from students' expertise, familiarity and comfort, unfamiliar territory can be broached more confidently. This does not falsely celebrate or unnecessarily reward young people for their colloquial media knowledge, but rather validates that knowledge as a vital part of the learning process. As discussed in Chapter Seven, to promote this, there needs to be a more complex understanding of 'literacy,' embracing multiple forms of literacy, making explicit the boundaries formed around dominant literacies and working to undo arbitrary restrictions or implicit punishments applied to non-dominant literacy use.

A curricular expectation with strict boundaries and clear scaffolding of goals and objectives is required. The goals need not be lofty and the technology need not be fancy, but the expectations and cohesion should be clear. Technology and text inclusion across the curriculum, like watching movies or TV shows, writing reviews of media and using computers, is an exciting and fun part of class, but without complicating the work, with multiple levels of analysis and reflection, learning will not move beyond the superficial. The execution of the lessons in a media-infused class can involve students in a greater capacity than in a traditional or test-prep class. Moore's (1991) discussion of media studies inclusion introduces a variety of ways core courses can draw from media analysis; it does not need to be an 'other' activity. When students begin to see texts and themselves as producers of meaning, they begin to unveil and make ideology material.

Scholarly work in media education needs to focus on teacher training, development of skills and assessment and research into what and how is learned through a media education curriculum. By now, it is well known that students are regularly involved with the media as both audiences, producers and distributors and whether the current face of digital media is a passing trend or a new way to understand the world is less important than teaching and learning how to approach and construct inquiry within this digital environment and how to maneuver through the inevitable changes. Further, irrespective of epistemology, it is well known that media education is a necessary part of any student's education. There is little time to debate the particulars of inclusion. Now there must be a focus on developing courses for teachers to be trained in media education alongside their training in their subject matter. Well-intentioned teachers should not have to cobble together some facsimile of media inclusion, independent of their colleagues and larger administrative focus. Media education lessons need to be turned inside out in order to develop a clear set of skills and ways to measure the material learned by students. Clearly, with a subject as potentially organic as media analysis, there are multiple levels of interpretation and no one, single answer. However, there are levels of inquiry and analysis that can be measured and the process of inquiry needs formalization. Until these things happen, media education in the United States will remain individual, piecemeal and disorganized.

What Change is Needed

Media education can be a catalyst for change; it can serve as the impetus to look more deeply at needed changes in the larger urban school system. Individual subjects cannot bear the brunt of responsibility for the healing needed in the urban public school system. However, individual subjects, such as media education, can illustrate possible steps to take. Just as media education can help make the unfamiliar familiar and the intimidating approachable, larger changes in urban education can make entry into active citizenship actually attainable, not just a topic of discussion. The language of new school reform needs to move beyond rhetoric. If they employ the language of radical change, then schools and their communities need to be open to actual radical change. School systems themselves need solid foundations, not just rhetoric and political catchphrases.

Who controls the school system does not dictate the success or failure of schools, however, history needs to be explored in order to make schools better in the future. The Ocean Hill-Brownsville strikes showed the experiment in decentralization, multiple bureaucracies that further segregate the school system manipulate 'community control,' family involvement and forget those whose geography and skin color did not serve the larger educational mission. The multiple bureaucracies of decentralization meant there was little transparent communication, however, within this, individual schools and administrations were able to make radical, successful changes by capitalizing on the absence of communication to form their own spaces for change. When Mayor Bloomberg took over the school system, he undoubtedly drew inspiration from those individual changes and had the potential to make large-scale radical change. However, mayoral control, with its clear lines of communication, also means that less bad or critical news is released by the controlling faction. Mayor Bloomberg introduced many efforts at change and paved many avenues of change, none of which were thoroughly traversed before moving onward to new change. Schools and their constituents–the teachers, the students–do not operate like businesses and where Bloomberg and Klein met with success in other arenas of their professional lives cannot be replicated in schools. Necessary changes in schools need to work against the private enterprise, free market and individual advancement triangle of neoliberal impulse.

The graduation and course requirements of New York City do not support, in any substantive way, the alternative pedagogies associated with small, theme-based education. This is both structural and financial. Standardized test scores are popular because they are easy to categorize, audit and digest. 'School success' can be encapsulated literally in the black-and-white of the standardized test booklet, and those students who do not succeed are easily categorized in terms of personal inability rather than systemic failure. The necessary financial input to support students in need, to develop critical autonomy, and to successfully participate in the project of new school reform, may be too much for already strained school and city budgets. Within the ethos of neoliberalism, these young people are responsible for their own failures if they cannot follow the stringent expectations of the school system.

If these struggling schools continue to be forgotten and if the rhetoric of new school reform continues to be in spoken and written word only, then individual changes will grow only within individual schools and classrooms. Tenacious, focused individuals with vision and a disregard for politics will work to make change for their students; these will undoubtedly be valuable and important changes. However, would not the largest public school system in the country benefit from this attention to the broader landscape? Would not the largest public school system in the country benefit from being the site of change, where its legend as a powerful, effective and egalitarian model for city schools was true? Urban schools and their unique opportunities deserve critical *positive* attention: right now, there is so much wrong with urban schooling, but this means there is great opportunity to work to make *right* in urban schooling. Ideologically, school is understand to be the place where individuals' social and cultural capital is developed, where individuals learn routes to active citizenship and where individuals learn skills for labor and intellectual pursuit, then urban schools can absolutely be the place where negative stereotypes and labels can be undone.

What Students Deserve

Students deserve their schools to be safe, supportive places where their interests are taken seriously, their questions are answered, their curiosity piqued, their fears allayed and their minds challenged. These qualities should not be geographically or ethnically subdivided: *some* students do not deserve this; *all* students deserve this. Students learn quickly what is expected of them, even if they do not have the critical vocabulary to express those expectations. As the participants in this study have shown, they know they are subjected bodies and have grown, through their own lives and from generations before them, to expect subjugation. However, they do not necessarily possess or speak the critical vocabulary of subjugation.

Even the least motivated students know the 'right' answers: They know what work needs to be done and they know generally what to do to please their teachers. Even the participants who are regularly caught for their negative behavior know exactly what to do to avoid their punishments. Many might choose not to do this, but overall, by high school, most students are familiar with the workings of the school system even if they do not take critical distance to examine their role in the system. This is not an incentive to make beneficial change, but rather, to direct their behavior beyond the confines of school, seeing school (and their school in particular) as a site of oppression. The participants show they are not familiar with the organization or intention of their own school; the work done to adopt alternative pedagogies is not always transparent and students bear the weight of experiments in curricular change. When students are presented with alternative curriculum, freedom of choice and are encouraged to develop and execute work in their own interests, many find this challenging and even overwhelming. From the outside, especially with the factory-like system of school and the emphasis on high-stakes testing, it seems like freedom of choice is a wholly good thing. However, it can be intimidating and what students believe they are learning might not be the case.

Students deserve to know more about their schools and their school systems and to acquire the tools that enable their abilities to understand and speak critically about their environments. This will help make a theme both more valuable and more pertinent to learning. Further, it will help undo the process of replication. Students who are critically aware of their environments, how they are labeled, what is expected of them ideologically as well as pedagogically, might be in a position to contain and ultimately undo forms of oppression. Only when their ideological and neoliberal oppression becomes transparent can these young people make significant change. In the meantime, young people who work within the system are further perpetuating the abuses of the system under the rhetoric of change.

Community Awareness: The "Ghetto Rodeo Drive"

To make significant improvements within schools, the larger environment needs much closer exploration and for that, I return to the participants' words and stories about their communities. The first interview I conducted was with

Genevieve, Alex, Rain and Stacy. These young women introduced me to what was most important in their lives and prepared me for the work that I needed to do to most thoroughly understand the participants' lives, understandings and meaning making. The environment where these young women live is the most complex text of their lives and like any other text, deserves inquiry and analysis.

Their conversation on the changes taking place in their communities proved to me that in order to make change within a school, the larger community needs closer exploration. The very real life of the participants is revealed in their talk about their communities. While the integration of media education and the struggles within the urban school system might be my biggest concern, the entirety of their lives and the changes that are forced upon them by larger economic, consumer and geographic pressures make their lives multidimensional. In the following conversation, Alex, Stacy, Genevieve and Rain reveal knowledge about the changes in their geography and their communities that do not bode well for their future. The struggles of which they speak illustrate that change cannot be made in one location without taking into account the multiple other intersecting variables. The geographic text wherein these young women live is changing: run-down buildings are being renovated, but with corresponding increases in rents, these renovations are not intended for the benefit of the current occupants; new sites of commerce are opening up on their streets, but the brand-name merchandise within these stores price these young women and their families out; commerce and real estate engage in a dance, one continuously upping the expectations of the next, pushing these young women and their families out to make space for those who can afford to move in their places.

In a conversation on changes in housing, the young women speak about the dilapidated quality of apartments available to them but how, even in these apartments, the rents are going up and 'faces that don't belong' are moving into the communities:

> *Alex:* I live in the projects and you have to see how those buildings look. It looks horrible. Like, you have people's names saying 'fuck you' and this and that. I don't like anybody in my building. They're mad retarded.
> *Genevieve:* My building's getting an upgrade and you know what that means. It means the rent is going higher. And soon you will have to leave. And then the elites start coming in here and the colleges, so there'll be students renting or buying the apartments, kicking us out.
> *Stacy:* They just built a brand new brownstone and getting ready to invite people. And

> I'm seeing faces that, no offense, don't belong there.
> *Allison:* What does 'faces that don't belong there' mean?
> *Stacy:* Like, people I've never seen before, of all different races. I've seen an Asian person. And a white person here and there.
> *Alex:* I think it's gonna cause too much drama. Like, if you see white person in like the middle of our projects, they won't live past the night because it won't … it just won't work that way. Someone will purposefully find a reason to get mad and say something to them.

Without using sociological language, the young women speak clearly about gentrification and the inevitable white movement into formerly undesirable neighborhoods, 'undesirable' because of poor housing conditions, poor labor opportunities, absence of consumer opportunities and perceptions of danger. As desirable elements move in and undesirable elements are moved out, the space is prime for gentrification. Genevieve and Alex's contradictions are important to understand further: Alex knows no one will find her public housing project a desirable place to live, not with the graffiti and violence. However, Genevieve's building, undergoing an upgrade, is not for the betterment of the current residents, but for the certain rent increases that will drive out Genevieve and her family but make room for, as Stacy observes, 'faces that don't belong there.' Those faces, clearly, are white individuals and families who desire the perceived convenience and status of a Manhattan address.

Stacy and Rain continue with a lament that the new faces who can afford the upgrades and brownstones do not have an historical connection or awareness of the neighborhood:

> *Stacy:* The sad part is they don't even know the history of our area. Like the areas we lived in, all the immigrants used to live there. They all used to live in our area and they just moved up and out. And they just moved the black people down to that area. That's all that happened. And you just get so used to how things were 'cause it was like that for so long and when they try come back it's like 'what are you doing here?'
> *Rain:* Umm-hmm. And a lot of like stores and stuff are being shut down. And it's a lot of history. Harlem has a lot of history. Especially the blacks, when it started and stuff. And a lot of people they get upset because they saying 'where we gonna go?' And we getting pushed out our homes. 'Cause, basically, honestly, black people and Spanish people, we made Harlem what it was. We were the reason that attracted people down here, now you tryin' to get rid of us, like, what was our time here, like worthless?

Indeed, Harlem was the place where struggling families were pushed *to* when their previous communities were overtaken by increased resident and commercial status. For good and for ill, Harlem and its surrounding communities were ignored for generations. While this made drug, gang and criminal boundaries clear (and therefore easily forgotten), it also made a space for a rich cultural history to develop. Though black and Latino families were sequestered to the area because it was the least desirable part of Manhattan, the families that moved there built vibrant, culturally rich communities. Once those vibrant, culturally rich communities became well known and were perceived convenient and desirable, Harlem and its surrounding areas began to be plucked away by new ventures. Once again, the poor were pushed further to the edges.

Relatively untouched by gentrification are the housing projects of the South Bronx where Alex lives, but the young women know it is just a matter of time before those communities are plucked away from them:

Alex: The Bronx is being left alone for now.
Stacy: For *now*, until they find a place, until they start buying people out.
Alex: I used to live somewhere, where I'm telling you, I would hear sirens every night, but I loved it. I was just so used to it. And they tell everybody to move, they put them in different places and it, just, now they're changing it little by little. It's like the apartments are new and furnished and my grandmother lived there since she was like 30 and she's like 97 now.
Stacy: They're trying to change the face of the area–they're trying to upgrade it so they can get, it's all about money.

'They' is left undefined in Alex's explanation of her grandmother's apartment; 'they' may be a combination of the New York City Housing Authority, real estate developers and venture capitalists, who, in the spirit of neoliberalism, give residents the 'choice' to remain in newly upgraded housing. Stacy introduces the idea of residents being 'bought out' of their homes, which the young women return to, but first they digress to a discussion of new brand-name multinational corporations moving into their neighborhoods. The greater opportunities for commerce and consumption are lost on the current occupants of the neighborhoods, unless they resort to illegal capital acquisition:

Stacy: It's about money now.
Genevieve: Attracting people with money. That's why they're renovating theaters in Harlem now. You have the Apollo Theater, the Magic Johnson Theater. Starbucks. Commerce Bank.
Stacy: They just put in a Bank of America and a New York Sports Club all in one section

> on 125th Street.
> *Rain:* There are so many banks.
> *Genevieve:* 125th Street is like the ghetto Rodeo Drive.
> *Stacy:* It is! And they just put that new Foot Locker Hoops Store. Who is gonna go in there?
> *Genevieve:* No one can afford those sneakers. Or the clothes. They're just setting up false hope and you know getting people to sell drugs and, you know, do stuff on the street, in order to buy those sneakers because they're living in one bedroom apartments, sharing them with rats.
> *Stacy:* Just so they can have them fancy sneakers, I still don't get it. They just don't have enough money.
> *Rain:* I want to make a point about the banks. Like when I used to live in Harlem, like a year ago, my mother said to me, 'Look, you see all these banks that they buildin'?' She said, 'They kickin' us outta here.' She said, 'Now, who have all these different bank accounts?' Like, it was, bank around 116th, at 5th, now it's three different banks. I'm like, on one block! I never heard of these banks! And I'm like, huh, like wow. And they have these apartments that that's so much of money. Like, it's just plain to say: you can't afford it, so leave.

The 'false hope' Genevieve speaks about encourages drug dealing and criminal behavior and invites residents into developing and satisfying immediate desires. That they are not good enough to consume or survive in their own neighborhoods fosters a consistent reminder, a self-loathing and apathy that manifests in acquiescence to subjugated positions. While Genevieve and Stacy argue over the increased quantity of stores, whose products are not affordable to the local members of the community, Rain's astute comment about the banks speaks loudest about the 'ghetto Rodeo Drive': who has all those different bank accounts? The implication is that the members of the community do not possess enough money to fill the quantity of banks being built in the community, so they must be built for assumed future tenants.

The lingering question is which is first or more influential: improvements in housing or increases in commerce? The young women cannot seem to come to consensus on this, but do see the links between commerce and housing and especially links between the development of housing and the absence of concern over who is impacted by the construction:

> *Stacy:* On 110th Street, they're constructing these condos that's gonna cost a million dollars to two million dollars.
> *Genevieve:* I live by there. It used to be rocks, like big rocks and trees. Little by little, they were taking it down, and they would have many trucks taking out the rocks and the soil and everything like that until it was just perfectly structured so they can start build-

ing. So they're building condos, which does disrupt people on the weekends because they do the construction. And I remember, it used to be very loud, like people couldn't even get to sleep because it was so loud. And it's just unnecessary. But it's like you said, it's about the money. And we're slowly being pushed away.

Alex: Yeah, like with me, I live by Target and Marshalls and all those crazy stores. And they're saying how those stores aren't making as much money as they should because of the projects just across the street. And they want to turn those projects into co-ops. And they were offering people money to move out. You know, since a lot of those apartments look like crap, you know they were offering $5000, $10,000, you just leave, or you can take a co-op. And my mom re-did the whole entire apartment because she did not like it. Like, when we first got there, we were scraping off roaches, you could hear them crackling, with a spatula. We're trying to get them out. And we got them out. It looks great. You know, we have our nice TV, but she was like, 'I'm not gonna take that! I'm not gonna take anything less than $20,000.' It's just marble, like the tiles are all new and nice. And they are trying to get everyone out though. Especially by where my grandparents live, they have like Southern Boulevard and it's like a bunch of stores. They have like the train station right there, the 2 is on one side of the Boulevard and the 6 is on the other. So they're making a big, new building right there. I don't know what it's gonna be, but you can already see they're fixing the floors and they're making it all glittery and weird looking.

Stacy: They're trying to have certain areas where all the poor people can be at and have an area for all the rich people to be at. And slowly, inch by inch, they're just gonna buy the poor people out so they can expand the rich people. So it's just, it's all about money. It's not even about like, there are people that have lived in the Bronx and Manhattan for like 50 years, even more, and they're tryin' to buy them out.

Alex: My grandma's almost a century old, she's like, 'Why do I care about money, I'm dyin'.' She looks at them like, 'I'm gonna sleep in my bed till the day I die. You're gonna take my rotting corpse out of it.' And she laughs, 'You're gonna have to pull my dead rotting corpse, and my fingernails off this bed because you know what, I'm too tired to get up.'

Their communities are changing around them and previous obstacles are reframed as conveniences. A neglected space of rocks, trees and rubble is reimagined as high-cost condominiums; the convenience of already-present consumer outlets and multiple subways lines invite renovation of surrounding buildings. The current residents are inconvenient byproducts: the sound of construction that disturbs neighbors is unimportant; that not enough people are shopping does not spark inquiry into what manageable improvements should be made, but rather, inspires high-rent development. That Alex's mother will move out for no less than $20,000 is constructed as a point of pride, but it is certain that she should demand much more if she wants to move her family into a safe environment. When Alex speaks about potential changes in her housing project and her grandmother's private residence, she introduces the probability of gentrification in the South Bronx, a place long ignored with a notorious negative reputation.

Within this space, within this knowledge, these young women attend school. Their school is intimately bound up in the residential and commercial changes in the neighborhoods where they and their classmates reside. When their neighborhoods are forgotten and left asunder, their schools are as well. LSHS has been shown to fail the student body, to perpetuate their subjugated positions and to not adhere to the theme that is supposed to make the school unique and mark it as a rigorous educational opportunity. And while there are clear places of fault and blame that can be pointed to within the walls of the school, the larger, more important conversation points outside the school to the larger community. The larger community is not a collection of individual sites and institutions operating independently, but rather a collection of individual sites and institutions that struggle to operate independently, not realizing that they are mutually dependent and this struggle serves to divide rather than connect them.

Conclusion

There are multiple ways to close this text. I will finish with two tales, one more positive than negative, one more negative than positive, both in possession of their opposite possibilities. Peter worked so diligently his first year in community college he received a scholarship to a private, 4-year liberal arts university outside of New York City and departed in the late summer of 2009. Marlo disappeared, he did not return to school for the fall of 2008 and his location remains unknown. These divergent stories represent the participants' own spectrum: a well-deserved, well-earned opportunity for a solid education and a slipping into obscurity of a bright young man who worked hard to avoid the system and any undo attention placed on him.

Each tale carries its opposite within. Peter will move far away from home to attend a school with social and curricular expectations for which he might not be prepared; he will be farther away from his support systems than he has ever been. He will have to cover some tuition dollars, which might prove difficult for his mother. He very well could fail; he very well could succeed. Inevitably, he will have to work harder than classmates whose invisible social privileges have more fully prepared them for the transition. The positive possibility of Marlo's tale is harder to imagine. He may very well have believed there was a greater shot at success on the street and rejected a third round in the 9th grade. If he stays close to the street, close to his familiar support systems and pays attention to his intelligence, he could avoid trouble, but it seems unlikely. Part of me hopes that he grows weary of the street before the street tires of him and that he returns to and completes school. However, when I think this, I immediately wonder what kind of school he would return *to* and whether there would be *actual* immediate and long-term benefits?

In between these points, the other participants reside: struggling through another school year; dealing with family, economic and community changes; preparing for college or their next year in college; working within or against the system with strong or absent support systems. During his first year in college, Popcorn decided to be a Literature major because he believes it will train him to be both a good reader and a good writer, which, in his estimation, is the basis for any career he chooses. He feels he was intellectually unprepared for college, but upon that realization, spent more time at the library and made sure he worked doubly hard. On a sticky afternoon in August 2009, I met with him for a visit before he returned to university for his sophomore year. He grabbed me in a big bear hug and hollered, "I've got mad books to buy! Mad reading to do! I'm reading Dostoyevksy this fall! He's mad cool!" Absent the emotional void of the text message from the summer prior, I was confident in Popcorn's passion, his positive feelings and the bravery he displayed in undergoing one challenging task after another. Once again, faced with adversity, the system let slide an individual success story in progress and, if the right steps are made, Popcorn, his classmates, and a cautious application of media education can be the catalyst for the necessary systemic, institutional overhaul.

Works Cited

Advancement Project. (March 2005). *Education on lockdown: The schoolhouse to jailhouse track*. Retrieved June 9, 2009, from advancementproject.org.

Advisory & Evaluation Committee on Decentralization. (1969). Niemeyer Report. In M. Berube & M. Gittell (Eds.), *Confrontation at Ocean Hill-Brownsville: The New York school strikes of 1968* (pp. 24-32). New York: Praeger.

Allen, W. R., & Jewell, J. O. (1996). The miseducation of black America: Black education since *An American Dilemma*. In J. Obie Clayton (Ed.), *An American Dilemma revisited: Race relations in a changing world* (pp. 169-190). New York: Russell Sage Foundation.

Alonso, G., Anderson, N. S., Su, C., & Theoharis, J. (2009). *Our schools suck: Students talk back to a segregated nation on the failures of urban education*. New York: New York University Press.

Altman, L. K. (March 12, 2008). Sex infections found in quarter of teenage girls. *The New York Times*. Retrieved March 12, 2008, from nytimes.com.

Alvesson, M., & Skoldberg, K. (2000). *Reflexive methodology: New vistas for qualitative research*. London: Sage.

Anyon, J. (1997). *Ghetto schooling: A political economy of urban education reform*. New York: Teachers College Press.

Aronowitz, S. (February 2004). Against schooling: Education and social class. *Workplace: A Journal for Academic Labor, 6*. Retrieved April 1 2008, from cust.educ.ubc.ca/workplace.

Aufderheide, P. (1993). *Media literacy – A report of the National Leadership Conference on Media Literacy*. Washington, D.C.: The Aspen Institute.

Barbaro, M. (July 17, 2009). Mayor assails senate inaction on school control. *The New York Times*. Retrieved July 20, 2009, from www.nytimes.com.

Barker, M., & Petley, J. (2001). Introduction: From bad research to good - A guide for the perplexed. In M. Barker & J. Petley (Eds.), *Ill effects: The media/violence debate* (2nd ed., pp. 1-26). London: Routledge.

Bazalgette, C. (1992). Key aspects of media education. In M. Alvarado & O. Boyd-Barrett (Eds.), *Media education: An introduction* (pp. 199-219). London: The Open University Press.

Berube, M., & Gittell, M. (Eds.). (1969). *Confrontation at Ocean Hill-Brownsville: The New York school strikes of 1968*. New York: Praeger.

Bourgois, P. (August 1989). Crack in Spanish Harlem: Culture and economy in the inner city. *Anthropology Today, 5*(4), 6-11.

Bragg, S. (2001). Just what the doctors ordered? Media regulation, education and the 'problem' of media violence. In M. Barker & J. Petley (Eds.), *Ill effects: The media/violence debate* (2nd ed., pp. 87-110). London: Routledge.

Brockman, J. (June 22, 2009). 'The clash of ages: How technology divides workers.' All Things Considered. *National Public Radio*.

Brown, J. (1998). Media literacy perspectives. *Journal of Communication, 48*(1), 44-57.

Brown, L. M. (2005). In the bad or good of girlhood: Social class, schooling and white femininities. In L. Weis & M. Fine (Eds.), *Beyond silenced voices: Class, race and gender in United States schools* (pp. 147-161). Albany: State University of New York Press.

Buckingham, D. (1991). Teaching about the media. In D. Lusted (Ed.), *The media studies book: A guide for teachers* (pp. 12-35). London: Routledge.

---. (1993a). *Children talking television: The making of television literacy*. London: The Falmer Press.

---. (1993b). *Reading audiences: Young people and the media*. London: Manchester University Press.

---. (1996). *Moving images: Understanding children's emotional responses to television*. Manchester: Manchester University Press.

---. (2000a). *After the death of childhood: Growing up in the age of electronic Media*. London: Polity Press.
---. (2000b). *The making of citizens: young people, news and politics*. London: Routledge.
---. (2001). Electronic child abuse? Rethinking the media's effects on children. In M. Barker & J. Petley (Eds.), *Ill effects: The media/violence debate* (2nd ed., pp. 63-77). London: Routledge.
---. (2003). *Media education: literacy, learning and contemporary culture*. London: Polity Press.
---. (2007). Media education goes digital: An introduction. *Learning, Media, Technology, 32*(2), 111-119.
---. (2008). Introducing identity. In D. Buckingham (Ed.), *Youth, identity and digital media* (pp. 1-24). Cambridge, MA: MIT Press.
Buckingham, D., Grahame, J., & Sefton-Greene, J. (1995). *Making media: Practical production in media education*. London: English & Media Centre.
Buckingham, D., & Sefton-Green, J. (1994). *Cultural studies goes to school: Reading and teaching popular culture*. London: Taylor & Francis.
---. (2003). Gotta catch 'em all: Structure, agency and pedagogy in children's media culture. *Media, Culture and Society, 25*, 379-399.
Buckley Jr., W. F. (June 24, 2005). A million dollar affair. *Hoover digest: Research and opinion on public policy, 3*. Retrieved May 28, 2009, from hoover.org.
Carlson, D. (February 2004). Leaving children behind: Urban education, class politics, and the machines of transnational capitalism. *Workplace: A Journal for Academic Labor, 6*. Retrieved April 1, 2008, from cust.educ.ubc.ca/workplace.
Cassidy, P. (July 17 2002). Last brick in the kindergulag. *Alternet*. Retrieved May 14, 2009, from alternet.org.
Celis, W. (September 22, 1994). New York receives $100 million gift for 50 new schools. *New York Times*. Retrieved May 21, 2009, from nytimes.com.
Chancellor Levy exits. (August 7, 2002). *New York Times*. Retrieved May 21 2009, from nytimes.com.
Chomsky, N. (May 12, 2000). Assaulting solidarity: Privatizing education. *Z-mag*. Retrieved June 7, 2009, from zmag.org.
Christ, W. G., & Potter, W. J. (1998). Media literacy, media education, and the academy. *Journal of Communication, 48*(1), 5-15.
Coffey, A., & Atkinson, P. (1996). *Making sense of qualitative data: Complementary research strategies*. Thousand Oaks, CA: Sage.
Cope, B., & Kalantzis, M. (2000). Multiliteracies: The beginnings of an idea. In B. Cope & M. Kalantzis (Eds.), *Multiliteracies: Literacy learning and the design of social futures* (pp. 3-8). New York: Taylor & Francis.
Corrigan, P., & Frith, S. (1976). The politics of youth culture. In S. Hall & T. Jefferson (Eds.), *Resistance through rituals* (pp. 231-239). London: Routledge.
Cremin, L. (1988). *American education: The metropolitan experience, 1876-1980*. New York: Harper & Row.
Delpit, L. (2002). No kinda sense. In L. Delpit (Ed.), *The skin that we speak: Thoughts on language and culture in the classroom* (pp. 31-48). New York: The New Press.
Dillon, S. (April 1, 2008). U.S. to require states to use a single school dropout formula. *The New York Times*. Retrieved April 1, 2008, from nytimes.com.
---. (May 22 1995). A school called Vanguard that learned the hard way. *New York Times*. Retrieved May 21, 2009, from nytimes.com.
Domaille, K., & Buckingham, D. (2001). *Youth media education survey*. UNESCO. Retrieved May 14, 2009 from http://portal.unesco.org.
Duncan-Andrade, J., & Morrell, E. (2007). Critical pedagogy and popular culture in an urban secondary English classroom. In P. McLaren & J. L. Kincheloe (Eds.), *Critical pedagogy: Where are we now?* (pp. 183-199). New York: Peter Lang.

Eckholm, E. (March 20, 2006). Plight deepens for black men, studies say. *The New York Times*. Retrieved April 1, 2008, from nytimes.com.

Edin, K. (January 3, 2000). Few good men: Why poor mothers don't marry or remarry. *The American Prospect*, 26-31.

Fertig, B. (July 20, 2009). 'New York City schools in limbo.' All Things Considered. *National Public Radio*.

Fine, G. A., & Sandstrom, K. L. (1988). *Knowing children: Participant observation with minors*. Newbury Park, CA: Sage.

Fine, M. (1998). Working the hyphens: Reinventing self and other in qualitative research. In N. K. Denzin & Y. S. Lincoln (Eds.), *The landscape of qualitative research* (pp. 130-155). Thousand Oaks, CA: Sage.

Fine, M., Bloom, J., & Chajet, L. (Spring 2003). Betrayal: Accountability from the bottom. *VUE: Voices of urban education*, 12-23.

Fisherkeller, J. (2002). *Growing up with television: Everyday learning among young adolescents*. Philadelphia: Temple University Press.

Freire, P. (1970/2000). *Pedagogy of the oppressed*. New York: Continuum Publishing.

Friedman, M. (1955). The role of government in education. *School Choices*. Retrieved May 28, 2009, from schoolchoices.org.

---. (1995). Public schools: Make them private. *Cato*. Retrieved May 28, 2009, from cato.org.

---. (July 2, 2002). The market can transform our schools. *New York Times*. Retrieved May 25, 2009, from nytimes.com.

---. (June 9, 2005). Free to choose. *The Wall Street Journal*. Retrieved May 28, 2009, from opinionjournal.com.

Furness, Z. (2007). Alternative media: The art of rebellion. In D. Macedo & S. Steinberg (Eds.), *Media literacy: A reader* (pp. 187-196). New York: Peter Lang.

Gandy Jr, O. (2002). The real digital divide: Citizens versus consumers. In L. A. Lievrouw & S. Livingstone (Eds.), *Handbook of new media: Social shaping and consequences of ICTs* (pp. 448-460). London: Sage.

Giroux, H. (2003). *The abandoned generation: Democracy beyond the culture of fear*. New York: Palgrave.

---. (February 2004). Class casualties: Disappearing youth in the age of George W. Bush. *Workplace: A Journal for Academic Labor*, 6. Retrieved April 1, 2008, from cust.educ.ubc.ca/workplace.

---. (2007). Drowning democracy: The media, neoliberalism and the politics of Hurricane Katrina. In D. Macedo & S. Steinberg (Eds.), *Media literacy: A reader* (pp. 229-241). New York: Peter Lang.

---. (2008). *Against the terror of neoliberalism: Politics beyond the age of greed*. Boulder, CO: Paradigm Press.

Goldstein, R. (2004). Who are our urban students and what makes them so different? In S. R. Steinberg & J. L. Kincheloe (Eds.), *19 urban questions: Teaching in the city* (pp. 41-51). New York: Peter Lang.

Gonzalez, D. (May 23, 1995). Partnerships help create new schools. *New York Times*. Retrieved May 21, 2009, from nytimes.com.

Goodman, S. (2003). *Teaching youth media: A critical guide to literacy, video production, and social change*. New York: Teachers College Press.

Goodnough, A. (November 16, 2001). Meeting with Bloomberg may signal Levy's future. *New York Times*. Retrieved May 21, 2009, from nytimes.com.

---. (June 7, 2002). Deal would give New York's mayor school authority. *New York Times*. Retrieved May 21, 2009, from nytimes.com.

---. (August 7, 2002). Levy leaving slightly earlier than planned. *New York Times*. Retrieved May 21, 2009, from nytimes.com.

---. (August 11, 2002). Levy packs up with a mix of sadness and euphoria. *New York Times*. Retrieved May 21 2009, from nytimes.com.

---. (February 24, 2003). In picking top schools, Klein trips on urban politics. *The New York Times*. Retrieved April 15, 2008, from nytimes.com.

Gootman, E. (October 14, 2009). Lunch at 9:21, and students are the sardines. *New York Times*. Retrieved May 14, 2009, from nytimes.com.

Gootman, E., & Gebeloff, R. (May 26, 2009). Principals younger and freer, but raise doubts in the schools. *New York Times*. Retrieved May 26, 2009, from nytimes.com.

Gorelick, S. (1996). Contradictions of feminist methodology. In H. Gottfried (Ed.), *Feminism and social changes* (pp. 23-45). Urbana: University of Illinois Press.

Gotbaum, B. (June 17, 2002). Public advocate report advises mayor about steps required for reform in school construction. Retrieved June 9, 2009, from pubadvocate.nyc.gov.

---. (November 21, 2002). Pushing out at-risk students: An analysis of high school discharge figures. Retrieved June 09, 2009, from pubadvocate.nyc.gov.

Grace, M. (March 25, 2009). Date set for Byrd Gang rapper Jim Jones' assault trial in Louis Vuitton store incident. *Daily News*. Retrieved July 20, 2009, from www.dailynews.com.

Grahame, J. (1991). The production process. In D. Lusted (Ed.), *The media studies book: A guide for teachers* (pp. 146-170). London: Routledge.

Grant, G., & Murray, C. E. (1999). *Teaching in America: The slow revolution*. Cambridge, MA: Harvard University Press.

Greene, M. (1988). *The dialectic of freedom*. New York: Teachers College Press.

Grossberg, L. (1994). Introduction: Bringin' it all back home - Pedagogy and cultural studies. In H. Giroux & P. McLaren (Eds.), *Between borders: Pedagogy and the politics of cultural studies* (pp. 1-25). New York: Routledge.

---. (2001). Why does neo-liberalism hate kids? The war on youth and the culture of politics. *The Review of Education, Pedagogy and Cultural Studies, 23*(2), 111-136.

Guba, E. G., & Lincoln, Y. S. (1998). Competing paradigms in qualitative research. In N. K. Denzin & Y. S. Lincoln (Eds.), *The landscape of qualitative research* (pp.195-220). Thousand Oaks, CA: Sage.

Hall, S. (1992). Cultural studies and its theoretical legacies. In L. Grossberg, C. Nelson & P. Treichler (Eds.), *Cultural studies* (pp. 277-286). New York: Routledge.

---. (1996). Introduction: Who needs 'identity'? In S. Hall & P. duGay (Eds.), *Questions of cultural identity* (pp. 1-17). London: Sage.

Hall, S., & Jefferson, T. (Eds.). (1976). *Resistance through rituals*. London: Routledge.

Hall, S., & Whannell, P. (1965). *The popular arts*. New York: Pantheon Books.

Halloran, J. D., & Jones, M. (1992 [orig. 1986]). The inoculation approach. In M. Alvarado & O. Boyd-Barrett (Eds.), *Media education: An introduction* (pp. 10-13). London: The Open University.

Haney, W., Abrams, L., Madaus, G., Wheelock, A., Miao, L., & Gruia, I. M. (2005). The education pipeline in the United States, 1970-2000: Trends in attrition, retention and graduation rates. In L. Weis & M. Fine (Eds.), *Beyond silenced voices: Class, race and gender in United States schools* (pp. 21-45). Albany: State University of New York Press.

Harris, G. (December 6, 2007). Teenage birth rate rises for first time since '91. *The New York Times*. Retrieved December 12, 2007, from nytimes.com.

Hartocollis, A. (June 7, 2002). Consensus on city schools: Growing outrage leads back to centralized leadership. *The New York Times*. Retrieved April 15, 2008, from nytimes.com.

Harvey, D. (2005). *A brief history of neoliberalism*. Oxford: Oxford University Press.

Hebdige, D. (1979). *Subcultures: The meaning of style*. London: Routledge.

Heldke, L. (1998). On being a responsible traitor: A primer. In B. Bar-On & A. Ferguson (Eds.), *Daring to be good: Essays in feminist ethico-politics* (pp. 87-99). London: Routledge.

Hernandez, J. (June 30, 2009). As law expires, Bloomberg moves to keep authority over schools. *New York Times*. Retrieved July 20, 2009, from www.nytimes.com.

Herszenhorn, D. M. (June 30, 2006). Graduation rate improving, schools chancellor says. *New York Times*. Retrieved May 21 2009, from nytimes.com.

Hill, J. (2004). What is urban education in an age of standardization and scripted learning? In S. R. Steinberg & J. L. Kincheloe (Eds.), *19 urban questions: Teaching in the city* (pp. 119-126). New York: Peter Lang.

Hobbs, R. (1998). The seven great debates in the media literacy movement. *Journal of Communication, 48*(1), 16-32.

Hoggart, R. (1959). *The uses of literacy*. London: Chatto & Windus.

Hong, L. K. (1996). *Surviving school reform: A year in the life of one school*. New York: Teachers College Press.

Jenkins, H., Purushotma, R., Clinton, K., Weigel, M., & Robison, A. (2006). *Confronting the challenges of participatory culture: Media education for the 21st century*. Chicago: The MacArthur Foundation. Retrieved May 14, 2009, from digitallearning.macfound.org.

Kalantzis, M., & Cope, B. (2000). Changing the role of schools. In B. Cope & M. Kalantzis (Eds.), *Multiliteracies: Literacy learning and the design of social futures* (pp. 121-148). New York: Taylor & Francis.

Kellner, D. (1995). *Media culture: Cultural studies, identity and politics between the modern and the postmodern*. London: Routledge.

---. (2002). New media and new literacies: Reconstructing education for the new millenium. In L. A. Lievrouw & S. Livingstone (Eds.), *Handbook of new media: Social shaping and consequences of ICTs* (pp. 90-104). London: Sage.

Kellner, D., & Share, J. (2007). Critical media literacy, democracy, and the reconstruction of education. In D. Macedo & S. Steinberg (Eds.), *Media literacy: A reader* (pp. 3-23). New York: Peter Lang.

Kilpatrick, W. (1992). *Why Johnny can't tell right from wrong: And what we can do about it*. New York: Touchstone.

Kincheloe, J. L. (2007). Critical pedagogy in the twenty-first century: Evolution for survival. In P. McLaren & J. L. Kincheloe (Eds.), *Critical pedagogy: Where are we now?* (pp. 9-42). New York: Peter Lang.

King, R. C. (2007). Reading race, reading power. In D. Macedo & S. Steinberg (Eds.), *Media literacy: A reader* (pp. 197-205). New York: Peter Lang.

Kleibard, H. M. (1995). *The struggle for the American curriculum, 1893-1958*. New York: Routledge.

Klein, N. (2007). *The shock doctrine: The rise of disaster capitalism*. New York: Metropolitan Books.

Kohl, H. (2002). Topsy turvies: Teacher talk and student talk. In L. Delpit (Ed.), *The skin that we speak: Thoughts on language and culture in the classroom* (pp. 145-161). New York: The New Press.

Kozol, J. (2000). *Ordinary resurrections: Children in the years of hope*. New York: Harper Perennial.

Kubey, R. (1998). Obstacles to the development of media education in the United States. *Journal of Communication, 48*(1), 58-69.

Ladson-Billings, G. (2002). I ain't writin' nuttin: Permission to fail and demands to succeed in urban classrooms. In L. Delpit (Ed.), *The skin that we speak: Thoughts on language and culture in the classroom.* (pp. 107-120). New York: The New Press.

Leavis, F. R., & Thompson, D. (1933). *Culture and environment: The training of critical awareness*. London: Chatto and Windus.

Leistyna, P. (1999). *Presence of mind: Education and the politics of deception*. Boulder, CO: Westview.

---. (February 2004). Introduction: Youth as a category through which class is lived. *Workplace: A Journal for Academic Labor, 6*. Retrieved April 1, 2008, from cust.educ.ubc.ca/workplace.

---. (2007). Neoliberal non-sense. In P. McLaren & J. L. Kincheloe (Eds.), *Critical pedagogy: Where are we now?* (pp. 97-123). New York: Peter Lang.
Levine, E. (2002). *Upstart startup: Creating and sustaining a public charter school.* New York: Teachers College Press.
Levitt, S. D., & Venkatesh, S. A. (August 2000). An economic analysis of a drug-selling gang's finances. *The Quarterly Journal of Economics*, 755-789.
Lewin, T. (December 9, 2003). Raid at high school leads to racial divide, not drugs. *New York Times.* Retrieved May 14, 2009, from nytimes.com.
---. (March 14, 2008). Report urges changes in teaching math. *The New York Times.* Retrieved March 14, 2008, from nytimes.com.
Lewis, J., & Jhally, S. (1998). The struggle over media literacy. *Journal of Communication, 48*(1), 109-120.
Lindlof, T. R. (1995). *Qualitative communication research methods.* Thousand Oaks, CA: Sage.
Lipsitz, G. (1998). *The possessive investment in whiteness: How white people profit from identity politics.* Chicago: University of Chicago Press.
Liptak, A. (February 28, 2008). 1 in 100 U.S. adults behind bars, new study says. *The New York Times.* Retrieved February 28, 2008, from nytimes.com.
Losen, D. J. (March 20, 2006). Behind the dropout rate. *Gotham Gazette.* Retrieved June 9, 2008, from gothamgazette.com.
Macedo, D. (2000). Introduction. In P. Freire, *Pedagogy of the oppressed* (pp. 11-27). New York: Continuum Press.
Macedo, D., & Steinberg, S. (Eds.). (2007). *Media literacy: A reader.* New York: Peter Lang.
Mashburn, L. B., & Weaver, J. A. (2007). Literacy and learning through digital media: Education or contradiction? In D. Macedo & S. Steinberg (Eds.), *Media literacy: A reader* (pp. 559-566). New York: Peter Lang.
Mayor Bloomberg's public schools. (March 9, 2002). *New York Times.* Retrieved May 21 2009, from nytimes.com.
McCarthy, C., Rodriguez, A., Meecham, S., David, S., Wilson-Brown, C., Godina, H., et al. (2005). Race, suburban resentment, and the representation of the inner city in contemporary film and television. In L. Weiss & M. Fine (Eds.), *Beyond silenced voices: Class, race, and gender in United States schools* (pp. 117-131). Albany: State University of New York Press.
McCoy, R. (1969). The year of the dragon. In M. Berube & M. Gittell (Eds.), *Confrontation at Ocean Hill-Brownsville: The New York school strikes of 1968* (pp. 52-63). New York: Praeger.
McLaren, P. (1999). *Schooling as a ritual performance: Toward a political economy of educational symbols and gestures.* Lanham, MD: Rowman & Littlefield Publishers.
McLaren, P., & Hammer, R. (2007). Media knowledge, warrior citizenry, and postmodern literacies. In D. Macedo & S. Steinberg (Eds.), *Media literacy: A reader* (pp. 116-139). New York: Peter Lang.
McLaren, P., & Kincheloe, J. L. (Eds.). (2007). *Critical pedagogy: Where are we now?* New York: Peter Lang.
McRobbie, A. (1976). Girls and subcultures: An exploration. In S. Hall & T. Jefferson (Eds.), *Resistance through rituals* (pp. 209-222). London: Routledge/Working papers in cultural studies.
---. (1982/1991). The politics of feminist research: Between talk, text and action. In A. McRobbie (Ed.), *Feminism and youth culture* (pp. 118-136). New York: Routledge.
---. (1994). *Postmodernism and popular culture.* London: Routledge.
---. (September 2008). Young women and consumer culture. *Cultural Studies, 22*(5), 531-550.
Meyrowitz, J. (1986). *No sense of place: The impact of electronic media on social behavior.* New York: Oxford University Press.
---. (1998). Multiple media literacies. *Journal of Communication, 48*(1), 96-108.

Miller, J. G. (1996). *Search and destroy: African American males in the criminal justice system*. New York: Cambridge University Press.
Miner, B. (February 2001). Bush's plan is shallow and ignores critical details. *Rethinking schools*. Retrieved May 25 2009, from rethinkingschools.org.
---. (February 2002). Vouchers and the false promise of academic achievement. *Rethinking schools*. Retrieved May 25, 2009, from rethinkingschools.org.
---. (Winter 2003). Vouchers: Special ed students need not apply. *Rethinking schools*. Retrieved May 25, 2009, from rethinkingschools.org.
---. (Fall 2005). Keeping public schools public: Free market education. *Rethinking schools*. Retrieved May 25, 2009, from rethinkingschools.org.
Moore, B. (1991). Media education. In D. Lusted (Ed.), *The media studies book: A guide for teachers* (pp. 171-190). London: Routledge.
Moore, P. (2008). *Teacher training curricula for media and information literacy: Report of the international expert group meeting.* UNESCO. Retrieved May 14, 2009, from http://portal.unesco.org.
Morrell, E. (2008). *Critical literacy and urban youth: Pedagogies of access, dissent and liberation*. New York: Routledge.
Mukherjee, E., & Karpatkin, M. M. (March 2007). *Criminalizing the classroom: The overpolicing of New York City schools.* New York: New York Civil Liberties Union.
Murray, S. (1999). Saving our so-called lives: Girl fandom, adolescent subjectivity and *My So Called Life*. In M. Kinder (Ed.), *Kids' Media Culture* (pp. 221-235). Durham, NC: Duke University Press.
New London Group. (2000). A pedagogy of multiliteracies: Designing social futures. In B. Cope & M. Kalantzis (Eds.), *Multiliteracies: Literacy learning and the design of social futures* (pp. 9-37). New York: Taylor & Francis.
New York City Board of Education. (1969). Board of education policy statement on decentralization. In M. Berube & M. Gittell (Eds.), *Confrontation at Ocean Hill-Brownsville: The New York school strikes of 1968* (pp. 17-18). New York: Praeger.
New York City Department of Education. Getting to know high school. Retrieved November 1, 2009, from schools.nyc.gov.
---. Empowerment schools. Retrieved November 1, 2009, from http://schools.nyc.gov.
---. Choices. Retrieved July 20, 2009, from http://schools.nyc.gov.
---. Other ways to graduate. Retrieved July 20, 2009, from http://schools.nyc.gov.
---. About us. Retrieved July 20, 2009, from http://schools.nyc.gov.
New York Civil Liberties Union. (1969). The burden of the blame: NYCLU report on the Ocean Hill-Brownsville school controversy. In M. Berube & M. Gittell (Eds.), *Confrontation at Ocean Hill-Brownsville: The New York school strikes of 1968* (pp. 104-119). New York: Praeger.
Noguera, P. (2000). Listen first: How student perspectives on violence can be used to create safer schools. In V. Polakow (Ed.), *The public assault on America's children: Poverty, violence and juvenile injustice* (pp. 130-153). New York: Teachers College Press.
---. (October 18, 2003). Going beyond the slogans and rhetoric. *In Motion Magazine*. Retrieved June 11, 2009, from inmotionmagazine.com.
---. (June 2, 2004). Re-thinking school safety. *In Motion Magazine*. Retrieved June 11, 2009, from inmotionmagazine.com.
O'Connor, C., Lewis, R. L., & Mueller, J. (2005). The culture of black femininity and school success. In L. Weis & M. Fine (Eds.), *Beyond silenced voices: Class, race and gender in United States schools* (pp. 163-179). Albany: State University of New York Press.
Orfield, G., & Lee, C. (2005). Segregation 50 years after *Brown*: A metropolitan challenge. In L. Weiss & M. Fine (Eds.), *Beyond silenced voices: Class, race and gender in United States Schools* (pp. 3-20). Albany: State University of New York Press.
Palladino, G. (1996). *Teenagers: An American history*. New York: Basic Books.

Pipher, M. (1994). *Reviving Ophelia: Saving the souls of adolescent girls.* New York: Ballantine Books.
Podair, J. E. (2002). *The strike that changed New York: Blacks, whites and the Ocean Hill-Brownsville crisis.* New Haven, CT: Yale University Press.
Polakow, V. (2000). Savage policies: Systemic violence and the lives of children. In V. Polakow (Ed.), *The public assault on America's children: Poverty, violence and juvenile injustice* (pp. 1-18). New York: Teachers College Press.
Polakow-Suransky, S. (2000). America's least wanted: Zero-tolerance policies and the fate of expelled students. In V. Polakow (Ed.), *The public assault on America's children: Poverty, violence and juvenile injustice* (pp. 101-129). New York: Teachers College Press.
Pollack, W. (1998). *Real boys: Rescuing our sons from the myths of boyhood.* New York: Owl Books.
Postman, N. (1985). *Amusing ourselves to death: Public discourse in the age of show business.* New York: Penguin.
---. (1994). *The disappearance of childhood.* New York: Knopf.
Ravitch, D. (1974/2000). *The great school wars: A history of the New York City public schools.* Baltimore: Johns Hopkins University Press.
---. (1983). *The troubled crusade: American education, 1945-1980.* New York: Basic Books.
Reid, S., & Rodriguez, J. (June 9, 2009). Former Dipset affiliate Max B found guilty of manslaughter. *MTV.* Retrieved July 20, 2009, from mtv.com/news.
Remarks by the President on Education (July 24, 2009). Retrieved November 1, 2009 from whitehouse.gov.
Rimer, S. (January 4, 2004). Unruly students facing arrest, not detention. *New York Times.* Retrieved May 14, 2009, from nytimes.com.
Rivera, A., Huezo, J., Kasica, C., & Muhammad, D. (January 15, 2009). State of the dream 2009: The silent depression. Retrieved June 9, 2009, from ufenet.org.
Robinson, G. (May 17, 2004). New York schools: Fifty years after *Brown. Gotham Gazette.* Retrieved May 21 2009, from gothamgazette.com.
Rolling Stone. (2009). Lil Wayne. *Rolling Stone Magazine.* Retrieved July 20, 2009, from rollingstone.com/biography.
Scharrer, E. (2002). Making a case for media literacy in the curriculum: Outcomes and assessments. *Journal of Adolescent and Adult Literacy, 46*(4), 354-358.
Schwandt, T. A. (1998). Constructivist, interpretivist approaches to human Inquiry. In N. K. Denzin & Y. S. Lincoln (Eds.), *The landscape of qualitative research: Theories and issues* (pp. 221-259). Thousand Oaks, CA: Sage.
Silva, P., & Mackin, R. A. (2002). *Standards of mind and heart: Creating the good high school.* New York: Teachers College Press.
Silverstone, R. (1999). *Why study the media?* London: Sage.
Steele, C. M. (August 1999). Thin ice: "Stereotype threat" and black college students. *The Atlantic Monthly,* 44-54.
Steinberg, S., & Kincheloe, J. (2004a). Introduction: Kinderculture, information saturation, and the socioeducational positioning of childhood. In S. Steinberg & J. Kincheloe (Eds.), *Kinderculture: The corporate construction of childhood* (2nd ed., pp. 1-44). Boulder, CO: Westview Press.
---. (Eds.). (2004b). *19 urban questions: Teaching in the city.* New York: Peter Lang.
Steinhauer, J. (June 13 2002). As Bloomberg takes over schools, Pataki takes center stage. *New York Times.* Retrieved May 21, 2009, from nytimes.com.
---. (July 30 2002). Bloomberg picks a lawyer to run New York schools. *New York Times.* Retrieved May 21, 2009, from nytimes.com.
---. (August 4 2002). Looking at test scores a little less testily; in Mayor's school system, the buck stops here. So does the blame game. *New York Times.* Retrieved May 21, 2009, from nytimes.com.

---. (September 18, 2002). When it comes to school discipline, Bloomberg's motto is safety first. *New York Times*. Retrieved May 21, 2009, from nytimes.com.

Sulzberger, A. (July 19, 2009). Democrats lash out at Mayor over control of public schools. *The New York Times*. Retrieved July 20, 2009, from www.nytimes.com.

Sykes, C. J. (1995). *Dumbing down our kids: Why American children feel good about themselves but can't read, write or add*. New York: St. Martin's Griffin.

Thoman, E., & Jolls, T. (2003). *Literacy for the 21st century: An overview and orientation guide to media literacy education*. Santa Monica, CA: Center for Media Literacy.

Tornero, J. M. P. (2008). *Teacher training curricula for media and information literacy: Background strategy paper*. UNESCO. Retrieved May 14, 2009, from http://portal.unesco.org.

Torres, M. N., & Mercado, M. D. (2007). The need for critical media literacy in teacher education core curricula. In D. Macedo & S. Steinberg (Eds.), *Media literacy: A reader* (pp. 537-558). New York: Peter Lang.

Trend, D. (1994). Nationalities, pedagogies and media. In H. Giroux & P. McLaren (Eds.), *Between borders: Pedagogy and the politics of cultural studies* (pp. 225-241). New York: Routledge.

Tyack, D. (1974). *The one best system: A history of American urban education*. Cambridge, MA: Harvard University Press.

Tyner, K. (1998). *Literacy in a digital world: Teaching and learning in the age of information*. Mahwah, NJ: Lawrence Erlbaum Associates.

Tyner-Mullings, A. R. (July 31, 2008). *Central Park East Secondary School and the alternative school movement in New York City*. Paper presented at the American Sociological Association Annual Meeting. Retrieved May 23, 2009, from allacademic.com.

Venkatesh, S. A., & Levitt, S. D. (2000). 'Are we a family or a business?': History and disjuncture in the urban American street gang. *Theory & Society*, *29*(4) 427-462.

Way, N. (1998). *Everyday courage: The lives and stories of urban teenagers*. New York: New York University Press.

Weinberger, D. (2009). Joho the Blog. Retrieved July 20, 2009, from hyperorg.com/blogger.

Weis, L., & Fine, M. (Eds.). (2005). *Beyond silenced voices: Class, race and gender in United States schools*. Albany: State University of New York Press.

Western, B. (2006). *Punishment and inequality in America*. New York: Russell Sage Foundation.

Williams, R. (1958/1983). *Culture and society, 1780-1950*. New York: Columbia University Press.

---. (1961). *The long revolution*. New York: Columbia University Press.

Willis, P. (1977). *Learning to labour: How working-class kids get working-class jobs*. New York: Columbia University Press.

Winn, M. (1977). *The plug-in drug: Television, computers and family life*. New York: Penguin.

Yonezawa, S., & Wells, A. S. (2005). Reform as redefining the spaces of schools: An examination of detracking by choice. In L. Weiss & M. Fine (Eds.), *Beyond silenced voices: Class, race, and gender in United States schools* (pp. 47-61). Albany: State University of New York.

Zimmerman, J. (2002). *Whose America? Culture wars in the public schools*. Cambridge, MA: Harvard University Press.

Index

A Beautiful Mind 117, 123(n4)
Adolescent identity development 6-7, 135-136, 141-142, 160-168
   Body image 157-158
   Family relationships 111, 112, 115-116, 127-128, 154, 167-168, 169
   Geography 139-142, 154-155, 209-214
   Gender 163-168
   Participant discussion of 160-168
   Race/ethnicity 2, 157-58, 161-62, 165
   Relationships with authority 116, 142-145
   Sexual identification 166-167
Alternative curricula *see* Media literacy *or* Media education
Anyon, Jean 67
Aronowitz, Stanley 52, 67, 71
Aspen Institute *see* National Leadership Conference on Media Literacy
Aufderheide, Patricia 4-5, 33-34
Autonomy Zone *see* Empowerment Zone

Bazalgette, Cary 31, 49 (n3)
Blonsky, Nikki 157-158, 175 (n5)
Bloomberg, Michael (NYC Mayor) 1, 62-64, 67, 178, 206
   New York Times editorials about 63-64
   Takeover of Board of Education 1, 62-64
Brown, James 34-35
Brown vs Board of Education 56, 59, 65
Buckingham, David 5, 25, 26-27, 30-32, 39, 49-50 (n4), 179, 185
   and Julian Sefton Green 27

Central Park East Secondary School 61-62
Citizenship, youth 43
City Schools *see* Urban schools
Civil Rights Act of 1964 56, 59, 65
Community involvement 53, 67
Comprehensive schools 132-133
Computer mediated communication 35-36

Corporate media culture 38-42
   and education 37, 38-41
Criminal behavior, participant experience with 95-96, 128, 170
Critical media literacy 29-30, 36-37, 191, 195-197; *see also* Literacy
Critical pedagogy 7-8
Cultural studies 6-7, 85-87

Decentralization *see* New York City Public Schools
Desegregation *see* New York City Public Schools
Digital divide 39, 179
Digital media 5, 23-24, 26-27, 35-36, 39, 46
Discovery Channel 119, 123 (n6)
Drug use, participant experience with 91-92, 94-95, 95-96, 143-144, 144-145, 156, 160

Education
   Faith in 51, 54
   Of the poor 54, 56, 64-66
   Of young people of color 64-66
   Participant discussion 168-173
   Purpose of 54
Educational policy *see* No Child Left Behind (NCLB), Vouchers
Empowerment Zone 78 (n1)

Feminist methodology 87-89
Feminist researcher responsibility 87-88
Fences 119, 124 (n9)
Fernandez, Joseph 61
Freire, Paolo 7-8, 52, 139
Friedman, Milton 53, 69-70

Gangs, participant affiliation with 95-96, 111, 123 (n2), 162

GED (General Education Development) *see* Graduation
Ghetto communities 208-214
Ghetto families 60
Ghetto ideology 156-157, 208-214
Ghetto schooling 56
Giroux, Henry 10, 45, 52, 67, 72 189
Gotbaum, Betsy (NYC Public Advocate) 75-76
Graduation (New York City)
    Credit requirements 78 (n2)
    Alternative options 169
    GED 64, 75-76, 169
    Participant discussion 170-173
Grossberg, Lawrence 9-10, 191

Hall, Stuart 6, 85
    and Paddy Whannell 6, 30
Harvey, David 9-10, 189
Hobbs, Renee 35
House 119, 123-124 (n10)
Human Trafficking 120, 124 (n10)

Informal learning/education 41-42
Inner city 139-142
    Participant discussion 139-142

Jail *see* prison
Jenkins, Henry 5, 27, 39-40, 42, 44, 46-47, 178, 196-197
Jones, Jim 156-157, 175 (n3)
Journal of Communication (1998) 34-36

Kellner, Douglas 36, 42, 196
    and Jeff Share 28, 29, 36, 46, 182, 196-197
Kincheloe, Joe 8
Klein, Joel 63-64
Klein, Naomi 9-10, 39, 189
Kubey, Ronald 44, 45

Lean on Me 136-138, 150 (n4)
Leistyna, Pepi 51, 52, 65-66, 72
Levy, Harold 63-64
Lewis, Justin and Sut Jhally 35
Lil Wayne 156-157, 175 (n2), 193-194
Lincoln Square High School 1-2, 3, 11-15, 101-108, 178, 186
    Architecture 12-13, 142
    Attendance 12
    Classes:
        Electives 105-106
        English 117, 119-120
        Math 117, 119
        Media literacy 106, 107
        Science 119
        Social Studies 119
        Video production 104, 107, 115-116
    Curricular development 14, 102-108
    Demographics 11, 172-173
    Geography 12
    Media curriculum development 13-14, 101-108
    Safety measures 142, 145-148
Literacy 192-193, 195-197
    Critical literacy 191-194
    Dominant literacy 193
    Multiliteracies 194-197
    Print (traditional) literacy 196-197
    Subordinate literacy 194

Macedo, Donaldo 52, 139
Max B. 156-157, 175 (n4)
Mayor Michael Bloomberg *see* Bloomberg, Michael
McCoy, Rhody 58, 59
McRobbie, Angela 79, 85, 87
Media activism 35
Media arts 28
Media blame 25-26

Index 229

Media education 2-3, 4-5, 134-135, 178-179
    Absence in American schools 5, 42-45
    Celebration *see* media literacy
    Concepts of media education 30-32, 49-50 (n4)
    Definitions 30-37
    In the community 32
    In urban schools 2-3
    Integration across curriculum 187-189
    Integration at LSHS 4, 116-120, 133-135
    Interdisciplinary qualities 183-184
    Key aspects of media education 31, 49 (n3)
    Need to integrate 204-207
    Participant definitions 109-115
    Protection *see* media literacy
    Research needed 199-200
    Self-reflection 183-184
    Skills assessment 198-199
    Teacher training in 13-14, 197-198
    United Kingdom 30-32, 44
    United States 5, 24, 32-37, 38
Media 'effects' 25-26
Media literacy 28, 33, 186-187
    Celebration 26-27
    Changes needed 185-187
    Changing definitions 195-196
    Definitions, United States 33-37
    Interdisciplinary qualities *see* Media education
    Media literacy class at LSHS 13-14, 101, 102-108
    Protectionism 24-26, 32-33
Media production 186-187
    Changes needed 185-187
    Video production class at LSHS 104, 107, 115-116
Media representations 152-160
    Participant discussions of representations of adolescence 153-158
    Participant discussions of representations of school 158-160
Media studies
    at LSHS 115-120
    at university level 2
    in secondary schooling 2
    see also Media education
Meier, Deborah 61-62
Miner, Barbara 70-71
Mo'nique 157-158, 175 (n7)
MTV 123 (n5)
Multiliteracies 194-197 *see also* Literacy
My Super Sweet 16 120, 123 (n5)

National Leadership Conference on Media Literacy 4-5, 33-34
Neoliberalism 8-10, 14, 136
    Education 10, 51-53, 60, 62, 69-71, 71-73
    Friedman, Milton 53, 69-70
    Gandy, Oscar 24
    Giroux, Henry 10, 45, 189
    Grossberg, Lawrence 91-10
    Harvey, David 9-10, 189
    Klein, Naomi 9-10, 39, 189
    Leistyna, Pepi 51-52
    Media education 28-29, 182
    Urban education 51
New London Group 194-195
New school reform 1, 14-15, 67, 126-127
    see also school reform
New York City 1, 208-214
New York City Board of Education 56-60
New York City Department of Education 3, 62-64, 125, 169
New York City Public Schools 3, 10-11, 55-56, 66-69, 74-76, 204
    Attendance 11-12
    Decentralization 57-62, 206
    Desegregation 55

Graduation 64, 75-76, 78 (n2), 169, 170-173
Race/ethnic population 55-56, 57, 75-76
Regents exams 76
Safety measures *see* School safety measures
School strikes *see* Ocean Hill-Brownsville
Segregation 57, 60, 64
Size, overcrowding 75
1960s 55-60
1970-2002 60-62
2002-present 62-64
New York Civil Liberties Union 59
No Child Left Behind (NCLB) 66-67, 71-73
Noguera, Pedro 66, 73-74
Norbit 157-158, 175 (n8)

Obama, Barack 67, 79
Ocean Hill-Brownsville 56-60, 65, 206

Participants 82, 83-85, 86-87, 89-91
   Alex 111-112, 132, 138-139, 140-141, 147, 151, 167-168, 173, 209-214
   Alvin 82, 95-96, 165, 170
   Bruce 113-114, 125, 128-129, 131, 133, 136-138, 141-142, 148-149, 163-164, 172
   CML 127-128, 129, 130-131, 136, 162-163, 164
   Genevieve 111-112, 117, 118, 119-120, 129-130, 132, 134, 138-139, 140-141, 157, 167, 209-214
   Ivette 117, 126, 134, 136, 140, 160-161,
   Joan 82, 93-94, 110-111, 136, 142, 146, 153-154, 155-156, 161, 165
   Jose 109-110, 115-116, 119, 136, 140, 143, 164, 168
   J-Trout 110-111, 140, 146, 156-157, 162, 164, 165, 193-194
   Lucy 82, 94-95, 111, 140, 143-144, 154-155, 156-157, 158-159, 161-162, 166-167, 169, 193-194
   Marlo 82, 91-92, 109-110, 136, 142, 146, 155, 160, 168, 214-215
   Monica 109-110, 126, 136, 140, 143, 158, 160, 165, 168
   Nine 112-113, 117, 118, 134, 136, 155-156, 158-159, 166, 171
   Nino 112-113, 116, 134-135, 136, 140, 153-154, 166, 169-170, 171
   Peter 113-114, 136-138, 214-215
   Popcorn 1, 2, 101, 113-114, 119, 120, 121, 128-129, 131, 136-138, 141-142, 144-145, 159-160, 172-173, 215
   Pyro 115-116, 119, 127, 129, 130-131, 134, 136, 162-163, 164
   Rain 129-130, 138-139, 147, 153-154, 209-214
   Stacy 129-130, 132, 138-139, 147, 209-214
   Tom 109-110, 143, 145, 160, 163, 168
   Ventura 127-128, 129, 130-131, 136, 162-163, 164
Participatory culture *see* Jenkins, Henry
Pedagogy, understandings of 5, 27-28, 191
Pedagogy of the oppressed 7, 52
Planet Earth 119, 123 (n6)
Pokemon 27
Pregnancy, adolescent 11
   Participant experience with 117, 126, 160-161
Prison 11
   Participant experience with 95-96, 165
   Schools like prisons 10, 13, 73

Qualitative methodologies 15-16, 17
   Authority versus friendship 96-98
   Interviews 3-4, 80-82, 83-85, 100 (n1, n2)

Interview Protocol 81-82
Participant observation 16
Researcher responsibility *see* Feminist researcher responsibility
Trust with participants 82, 89-91
Queen Latifah 157-158, 175 (n6)

Race to the Top 67
'Racenicity' 65-66
Rap music, rap artists 155-157
Ravitch, Diane 54-55, 59
Relationships with authority *see* Adolescent identity development

Saved by the Bell 158, 175-176 (n9)
School reform 66-67
School safety measures 73-74
    Impact Schools Initiative 74
    Metal detectors 74
    Participant discussion of 145-148
    Police presence 73-74
    Scanning 74
    School Safety Administrators 74
    Zero Tolerance policies 74
    see also LSHS, school safety measures
School strikes *see* Ocean Hill-Brownsville
Schooling 7, 43-45, 51, 54, 151-153, 158-160, 168-170, 203
Segregation *see* NYC Public Schools
Sexual abuse, participant experience with 112
Silverstone, Roger 33
Skills assessment *see* Media education
Small schools 2, 68-69, 125-130
    Experiments with 61
    Participant discussion 126-130
    see also CPESS, Joseph Fernandez, Deborah Meier
Social media 180-181
Social networking 178

Speak 119, 124 (n8)
Steinberg, Shirley and Joe Kincheloe 36, 40
Suburban schooling 54-55, 158-160
Surveillance in schools *see* School safety measures

Teacher-student hierarchy 36, 182-183
Teacher training *see* media education
Technology 35-36, 179-180, 181-182
    Education 45-47, 118, 134-135, 179
    Fascination with and fears of 23, 45-47
    Inclusion 181-182
Testing 14, 72-73
    Standardized tests 72-73
    see also No Child Left Behind
Theme-based education 2, 3, 68-69, 130-133
    Participant discussion 130-133
Tracking 131-133
Tyner, Kathleen 32-33, 192

Underserved populations 3, 15-139
    Participant discussion 136-139
UNESCO 37-38
    2001 conference 37
    2008 conference 38, 198
    Global survey of media use 37-38, 197-198
Urban schools 2-3, 64-66, 67, 151, 158-160, 207-208
    see LSHS for specific discussion
Urban youth 64-66, 158, 183
    and literacy 193-194
    of color 6-7, 55-56, 57, 71-72, 73, 141-142

Video production *see* Media production
Violence
    In schools 73-74

Participant experience with 156, 161
Vocational education 131-133
Vouchers 69-71
   in Milwaukee, Wisconsin 70-71

White values, privilege 7, 56, 65-66, 151, 158, 183, 210-211
Wire, The 155, 175 (n1)
Workplace: A Journal for Academic Labor (2004) 52-53
World War II and schooling 54-55

Youth
   see Adolescent identity development, citizenship, urban youth

Zero tolerance policies *see* School safety measures

CRITICAL ISSUES
FOR LEARNING AND TEACHING

Shirley R. Steinberg & Pepi Leistyna
General Editors

Minding the Media is a book series specifically designed to address the needs of students and teachers in watching, comprehending, and using media. Books in the series use a wide range of educational settings to raise consciousness about media relations and realities and promote critical, creative alternatives to contemporary mainstream practices. *Minding the Media* seeks theoretical, technical, and practitioner perspectives as they relate to critical pedagogy and public education. Authors are invited to contribute volumes of up to 85,000 words to this series. Possible areas of interest as they connect to learning and teaching include:

- critical media literacy
- popular culture
- video games
- animation
- music
- media activism
- democratizing information systems
- using alternative media
- using the Web/internet
- interactive technologies
- blogs
- multi-media in the classroom
- media representations of race, class, gender, sexuality, disability, etc.
- media/communications studies methodologies
- semiotics
- watchdog journalism/investigative journalism
- visual culture: theater, art, photography
- radio, TV, newspapers, zines, film, documentary film, comic books
- public relations
- globalization and the media
- consumption/consumer culture
- advertising
- censorship
- audience reception

For additional information about this series or for the submission of manuscripts, please contact:
  Shirley R. Steinberg and Pepi Leistyna,
  msgramsci@aol.com | Pepi.Leistyna@umb.edu

To order other books in this series, please contact our Customer Service Department:
  (800) 770-LANG (within the U.S.)
  (212) 647-7706 (outside the U.S.)
  (212) 647-7707 FAX

Or browse online by series:
  www.peterlang.com

www.ingramcontent.com/pod-product-compliance
Ingram Content Group UK Ltd.
Pitfield, Milton Keynes, MK11 3LW, UK
UKHW021839210426
5322IPUK00021B/362